THE LONGEST GENOCIDE – SINCE 29 MAY 1966

Essays

Longest genocide – since 29 May 1966

Herbert Ekwe-Ekwe

AR
African Renaissance

First published in Great Britain and Senegal in 2019 by
African Renaissance
Dakar, Sénégal

African Renaissance
Reading, Berkshire
England

A catalogue record for this book is available from the British Library.

ISBN 0-9552050-3-4
978-0-9552050-3-3

© Herbert Ekwe-Ekwe 2019

All rights reserved. No reproduction, copy or transmission of this publication may be made without written permission from the author.

For
3.1 million Igbo children and women and men murdered during the Igbo genocide, 29 May 1966-12 January 1970 (phases I-III) **and** *the additional tens of thousands of Igbo children and women and men murdered since 13 January 1970-the present day (phase IV)*

"The stink of genocide is everywhere. Certainly, after Hitler's Germany, the world should step in and stop genocide in Biafra. However that becomes impractical when one considers England's investments in Nigeria ... After all, members of the jury, it is only [African] people[s] killing another [African] people."

Leon Uris, QB VII, 1970

CONTENTS

1 Rethinking the state in Africa ... Whose state is it? 1
2 The concatenation of the African role in the 1914-1918 war 15
3 Does *Arrow of God* anticipate the Igbo genocide? 21
4 "Sub-Sahara Africa" is gratuitously racist 30
5 Reminder: What "civil war" isn't 35
6 Britain, Aburi accords, Ghana, Igbo genocide 39
7 Igbo genocide, Britain and the United States 46
8 Okigbo: Africa's most influential poet/epitome of Igbo resistance to genocide 74
9 Baga & Paris – two massacres, contrasting responses and consequences 95
10 Theresa May and Biafra 99
11 BBC: "nationalists" or "secessionists" 105
12 "African American son", US foreign policy and Africa: A statement 110
13 Who wages genocide? Who plans to invade someone else's state? 120
14 Year 50– Biafra before Brexit 129
15 Biafra freedom movement has dinner party dimensions in its dynamics 133
16 Surely, there is no hierarchisation of evil 136
17 Once again, dismissing this gimmick that calls itself "Igbo presidency" 138
18 Britain, Brexit, Igbo genocide, Biafra freedom 142
19 Anti-Biafra columnist acknowledges restoration of Biafra despite themself.144
20 Rights for Scots, Rights for the Igbo 147
21 On that "Handshake-across-the-Niger" summit in Enuugwu, Biafra 154
Index 157

Preface

The Fulani islamist/jihadist-led genocidist Nigeria, *not* Europe, *not* the United States, *not* any extracontinental aggressor state, constitutes, currently, the *principal* retrograde agent of genocide and underdevelopment across Africa:

1. It has murdered more Africans in Biafra, southwestcentral Africa, since 1945 than the total number of Africans murdered in Africa since 1900 by all of Europe's conqueror-powers in Africa: Britain, Belgium, France, Germany, Portugal, Spain – *including* the number of Africans the Germans murdered in the genocide of the Herero, Nama and Berg Damara peoples of southwest Africa (1904-1907).

2. It now rates a not-too-distant second to Belgian King Leopold II's abhorrent position as the lead génocidaire of African peoples since the 19th century in the Leopold II/Belgian state's genocide against Africans in the central regions of the Congo River basin (1878-1908).

It is indeed an extraordinary survival story of history that there is someone who actually walks the face of the earth that goes by the name Obiageli, Nkechi, Chinyere, Ifeoma, Amaechi, Nwakaego, Ngozi, Chinelo, Ada, Uzo, Chibundu, Nkemdilim, Chukwuka, Okwuonicha, Chikwendu, Ogonna, Nwafo, Ikechukwu, Onwuatuegwu, Chukwuemeka, Onyekachi, Nnadozie, Okonkwo, Chido, Okafo, Chibuzo, Nkeiiru, Ifeyinwa, Nkemakolam, Ikenga, Uchendu, Okennwa, Nwaoyiri, Okonta, Ukpabi, Amaka, Ofokaaja, Nnamdi, Mbanefo, Chukwuma, Kanayo, Ndukaeze, Chidi, Kamene, Nneka, Onyeka, Osita, Kalu, Ifekandu, Obioma, Chioma, Ndubuisi... Each and every name just recorded is Igbo ... *survived* the genocide, this programmed sentence of death by Fulani genocidist Nigeria and its suzerain state Britain – beginning on 29 May 1966 and through to 12 January 1970, phases I-III of the genocide. The genocidists murdered the grisly total of 3.1 million Igbo or 25 per cent of this nation's population during the period. They have also murdered tens of thousands of additional Igbo during the course of phase-IV of the genocide, launched on 13 January 1970. The genocide rages on unrelentingly...

None of the lead génocidaires of the slaughter – Harold Wilson, Benjamin Adekunle, Olusegun Obasanjo, Obafemi Awolowo, Murtala Mohammed, Allison Ayida, Ibrahim Haruna, Ibrahim Taiwo, Tony Enaharo, Yakubu Danjuma, Yakubu Gowon, Muhammadu Buhari, Jeremiah Useni, Oluwole Rotimi – reckoned in their dire prognosis of the outcome of the 44 months of Igbo slaughtering that they directed and executed (during phases I-III) that the Igbo stood a chance of surviving. Harold Wilson, then British prime minister who chiefly coordinated the genocide from the comfort of his offices and residence at 10 Downing Street, London, 3000 miles away from Biafra, had notoriously set the pace for his fellows on what he saw as the future of the Igbo when he informed Clyde Ferguson, the United States state department special coordinator for relief to Biafra, that he, *Harold Wilson*, "would accept a half million dead Biafrans if that was what it took"[1] Nigeria to destroy the Igbo resistance to the genocide.

By surviving the genocide, the Igbo have not only dramatically repudiated this vile Wilsonian logic of Igbo mass slaughter, but they are poised today, 17 November 2018, 52 years later, as the Biafra freedom movement has grown inexorably, to resume the interrupted construction of their beloved state of Biafra – the Land of the Rising Sun.

Herbert Ekwe-Ekwe
London, Saturday 17 November 2018

---

[1] Roger Morris, *Uncertain Greatness: Henry Kissinger & American Foreign Policy* (London and New York: Quartet Books, 1977), p. 122.

I Presaging the cataclysm

(**left:** Painting of session of infamous gathering of European leaders in Berlin [15 November 1884-12 February 1885] to formalise the pan-European seizure, planned occupation, and irrepressible exploitation of the gargantuan riches of the African World; **centre-top:** Straight from the horse's mouth! In December 1920, just a few years after Britain's conquest of the constellation of peoples and states in southwestcentral Africa region which it subsequently named "Nigeria" had been formalised, Hugh Clifford [photographed], the British conquest and occupation governor of the territory, couldn't be more candid about the sheer artificiality of this new state created to serve British interests as evident in his contribution to the Lagos Legislative Council debate: "[Nigeria is a] collection of Independent ... States, separated from one another by great distances, by differences of history and traditions and by ... racial ... political, social and religious barrier."; **centre-middle:** face on the youtube video is Ahmadu Bello, sardauna of Sokoto and lead Fulani north Nigeria islamist/jihadist allied to the British conquest and occupation who, in a late 1950s/early 1960s interview on the film clip that has since gone viral, threatened "bloodshed" on the Igbo, a declaration that is devastatingly effectuated on the 29 May 1966 Igbo genocide launch during which the genocidists murder 3.1 million Igbo in 44 months; **centre-base:** Harold Wilson, British prime minister who coordinates the perpetation of the Igbo genocide from his office and residence in London insists at the apogee of the slaughtering, summer 1968: " [I] would accept half a million dead Biafrans if that was what it took" Nigeria to destroy the Igbo resistance to the genocide; **right-top:** map of Nigeria – Africa's most notorious genocidist and kakistocratic state which inaugurated Africa's current "age of pestilence"; **right-base:** cover of novel *Things Fall Apart* (1958), the classic by Chinua Achebe, Father of African Literature, that at once confronts the catastrophe of the European conquest of Africa and sows the seeds for the peoples' quest for the restoration-of-independence.)

(**upper:** Five actors in the stage play "Women's War" [2018, directed by Kenneth Uphopho and produced by Chioma Onyewe, Ranconteur Productions] that commemorates the November-December 1929 *ogu umu nwanyi* Igbo or Igbo women-organised and led resistance against the British conquest and occupation of Biafra – left-right: Deola Gimbiya, Ijeoma Aniebo, Gloria Anozie-Young, Ego Ogbaro, Inna Eriza ... The occupation troops murder 55 women of the freedom movement during the course of the 2-month resistance.)

(**lower:** Miners at the Iva valley colliery [undated], Enuugwu, Biafra, where, on 18 November 1949, 21 coal miners at the Iva Valley colliery, Enuugwu, Biafra, are shot dead by the British occupation police in response to the miners' peaceful, popular protest for a pay increase, improvement in working and safety mine provisions, *and* support for the ongoing restoration-of-independence movement, begun in the 1930s and spearheaded by the Igbo, to terminate 64 years of Britain's conquest of the states and peoples of this southwestcentral region of Africa.)

1 RETHINKING THE STATE IN AFRICA ... WHOSE STATE IS IT?

The most reasonable principles of justice are those everyone would accept and agree to form a fair position – John Rawls

Political instability undermines human and economic development. And the more that economic and human development is undermined, the more disordered the political situation becomes, creating a vicious circle – Ifeanyi Menkiti

In a background paper Professor Menkiti circulated last January on the theme of focus for this conference,[1] from where the quote above is derived, he refers to Kwame Nkrumah's much popularly expressed assertion, "Seek ye first the political kingdom and all other things shall be added unto you",[2] and notes that "Nkrumah, in hindsight, appears to [be] more right than he imagined though not for the reasons he imagined". I couldn't agree more with Professor Menkiti and it is this "though not for the reasons" that Kwame Nkrumah "imagined" that I wish to reflect on in my paper today. I will situate the presentation within the overarching banner of the Rawlsian reference above.

Failed state(s)?

The concept "failed-state" carries an understandable melodramatic import! It refers to the inability or failure of a state to fulfil some of its key roles and responsibilities to its people(s) and others domiciled within its territory and consequently to its neighbour(s) and the wider global community of states. According to the latest Washington-based Fund for Peace think-tank's annual research publication, "The Failed States Index 2013", there are 12 indicators at

---

[1] This chapter is a slightly edited version of a paper I read at a conference in Wellesley College on "Rawls in Africa" in honour of Ifeanyi Menkiti's outstanding career as professor of philosophy at Wellesley for 41 years, Saturday 10 May 2014.
[2] Kwame Nkrumah, "Africa must unite",
https://www.laits.utexas.edu/africa/ads/1519a.html, accessed 18 January 2014.

which state failure materialises and these can be grouped into three broad spheres or categories with respect to the impact on the lives of the people(s): social, political and economic.[3]

African countries, unsurprisingly, fare most poorly at each and across these 12 crucial variables at the centre of the fund's research, but particularly in the following, with the inescapable crushing consequences on the lives and wellbeing of the peoples:

1. legitimacy of the state

2. rise of fractionalised elite

3. chronic and sustained human rights violation

4. uneven economic development

5. poorly, sharp and severe economic decline

6. massive movement of refugees or internally displaced persons

Thus, the highlights for Africa in the fund's current research make for depressing reading and are as follows:[4] 16 out of the world's "worst 20 states"; 20 out of the "worst 30 states"; 34 (well over one-half of all the continent's so-called 54 sovereign states) of the "worst 54 states". It is not inconceivable, given this rate of state failure, that in the next six years, by the time the beginning of the next decade, 2020, "54 out of the worst 54 states" in the world could be in Africa.

For the purposes of this study, the following two key empirical determinants of state failure are keenly explored: (1) the state's inability to provide security and (2) the state's inability to provide essential social services. Let us elaborate on each of them:

1. The state's inability to provide security to its population – This situation may have arisen because the state no longer exercises control across part/parts or all of its territory. Factors such as catastrophic breakdowns in vital internal

---

[3] Fund for Peace, "The Indicators", http://ffp.statesindex.org/indicators, accessed 2 July 2013.
[4] Fund for Peace, "The Failed States Index 2013", http://ffp.statesindex.org/rankings-2013-sortable, accessed 2 July 2013.

sociopolitical and economic relations, intra-regime fractionalism and rivalries, external invasion and occupation of territory, and unmanageable natural disasters would contribute to the failure. It could also be due to the state's violation of the human rights of the people(s) including a deliberate state policy to embark on the destruction of one or more of its constituent nations/peoples/religious groups, etc., etc.

2. The state's inability to provide essential social services (communication infrastructure, health care, education, housing and recreation, development of culture) to its people(s) or the state's deliberate policy to deny or partially offer such services to some of its constituent nations/peoples/religious groups... This failure could be the consequence of a state's dwindling fiscal/material resources or just sheer incompetence in its management capacity. Alternatively, this inability points to the staggering nature of corruption and largely institutionalised norm of non-accountability in the access and control of public-owned finances by state officials and their agents.

Christopher Clapham has argued that the concept "failed-state" is "one of those categories that is named after what it isn't, rather than what it is".[5] This is vital in the discourse to the effect that a *state*, such as Nigeria or Sudan for instance, that embarks on the genocide of its population or does not provide basic services for its people or immanently churns out successive regimes that fleece the collective wealth of the country can hardly merit such a definition in social science. All we need do to highlight the obvious flaw in applying this concept in Africa is to reflect on the fact that crucial state functions such as the provision of security, rule of law, a rationalising but flexible structure of management, accountability and open and unfettered competition, especially with respect to "regime change", have not been in operation in any African state since the conquest and occupation of most of the continent by a constellation of European countries in the 19th century. Tragically, in the 57 years since the concerted African drive towards the restoration of its independence resulted in the supposedly 1956 breakthrough in the Sudan, followed soon in 1957 by Ghana, the situation has not changed significantly in Africa for the realisation of these attributes of the state.

Ultimately, the major limitation of the use of the "failed-state" concept to assess the catastrophic situation in contemporary Africa is that it confers an unjustifiable presumption of rationality to an enterprise in which a spectrum of

---

[5]Christopher Clapham, "Failed States and Non-states in the Modern International Order", paper presented at conference on failed states, Florence, Italy, April 2000, http://www.ippu.purdue.edu/failed_states/2000/papers/clapham.html, accessed 15 June 2013.

outcomes ranging from perhaps "failure" to "outright failure" to "disaster" is predetermined; it is assumed that those who run the state in Africa (Obasanjo, Idi Amin, Taylor, Moi, Habré, Doe, Gowon, Mobutu, Ahidjo, Jonathan, Rawlings, Obote, Babangida, Mengistu, Abacha, Mugabe, Mohammed, Banda, Abubakar, Bokassa, Jammeh, Eyadéma, Buhari, Toure, Museveni, Yar'Adua, Biya, al-Bashier ...) are aware of this test and its evaluative scruples and, like any rational participant, would want to succeed ... If they do not do so well, at some instance, so goes the logic, they will try to improve on their previous score and, hopefully, do better ... Success is always a possibility!

It is on the basis of this possibility that Roland Oliver concludes his own controversial contribution to this debate. If one, for a moment, ignores the gratuitous racism and paternalism embedded in the premise of Oliver's contribution as well as the highly contestable analytical category on which it is hinged, which I will be focussing on shortly, Oliver notes: "With its overriding population problem, Africa can hardly expect to achieve First World standards of economic development within the next century [i.e. 21st century] but with just a little more day-to-day accountability, it could at least recover the confidence to continue the uphill struggle with more success".[6] On the contrary, there is limited indication on the ground that African state operatives currently or indeed in the past 57 years have approached statecraft as a challenge to succeed in *transforming the lives* of their peoples. "Success" is never a goal set along the trajectory of their mission. To that extent, Oliver's conclusion is, ironically, quite optimistic. Furthermore, it should be noted that given the evidently limited concerns on just "measuring" the scoreboard of performance, "failed-states"'s discourses tend to overlook the much more expansive turbulence of underlying history – the kind of project that is being mounted here in this presentation.

So, rather than relations that bring benefits to many of its people, the state in Africa has "evidently been a source of suffering", to quote Clapham,[7] an imagery consistent with Basil Davidson's description of the impact of this state on the African humanity as a "curse".[8] Richard Dowden also uses a health metaphor to capture the failed legacy of the African state when he notes, alluding to its genesis: "[this European]-scissors and paste job [has indeed caused Africa] much blood and

---

[6]Roland Oliver, "The condition of Africa", *Times Literary Supplement*, 20 September 1991, p. 9.
[7]Clapham, "Failed States and Non-states in the Modern International Order".
[8]Basil Davidson, *Black Man's Burden: Africa and the Curse of the Nation-State* (London: James Currey, 1992).

tears".[9] For her own observation, Lynn Innes is in no doubt that the state in Africa has created what she describes as a "deeply diseased [outcome]" on the continent.[10] The health metaphor stretches even to the psychiatric as Thomas Pakenham observes: "One has only to think of the bloody ... wars that followed decolonisation to see the craziness of these lines drawn on maps in Europe by men ignorant of African geography and history".[11] Chester Crocker points to the fundamental problem of the state in Africa. It is "not the absence of nations; it is the absence of states with the legitimacy and authority to manage their affairs ... As such, they have always derived a major, if not dominant, share of their legitimacy from the international system rather than from domestic society".[12] It is this question of *alienability* that is at the crux of this grave crisis.

These references help to underscore the lack of consensus among scholars studying the "failed states" of contemporary Africa on the terms of the evaluative parameters of this enterprise including the crucial constitutive timeframes of assessing and therefore concluding when this or that African state "began to fail" or/and when indeed it "failed". There is a tendency by some experts, including the Fund for Peace, which we referred to earlier, to arbitrarily circumscribe the limit of the focus of interrogation to the so-called African post-conquest epoch (i.e., post-January 1956 – following the presumed restoration of independence in the Sudan from the British conquest and occupation) with the underlying presumption that the state, as formulated and constituted on the eve of the "restoration of independence", has a definitive and enduring internal logic to its being. I would wish to question this presumption in this study by arguing that, to the contrary, quite a number of African states were already "failed states" on the eve of the so-called restoration of independence. Furthermore, there is a surprising "missing link" in these studies. Fund for Peace and others do no interrogate the intrinsic capacity and performance of any of these African states on their *pivotal role* in the global economy all the while, essentially the primary reason for their existence – since their creation. An exploration and a restoration of this "missing link" is very important as we shall realise shortly, and is therefore a major contributing feature in this study. It will enable us answer the question posed in the title of the chapter: *The state in Africa – Whose state is it?*

---

[9]Richard Dowden, "Redrawing the outmoded colonial map of Africa", *Independent*, London, 10 September 1987.
[10]CL Innes, *Chinua Achebe* (Cambridge: Cambridge University, 1990), p. 151.
[11]Thomas Pakenham, "The European share-out of the spoils of Africa", *Financial Times*, London, 15 February 1988.
[12]Chester Crocker, "Engaging Failing States", *Foreign Affairs*, September/October 2003, p. 37.

The longest genocide

Contemporary Africa works!

Africa has uninterruptedly been a net-exporter of capital to the Western World since 1981. The thundering sum of US$400 billion is the total figure that Africa has transferred to the West in this manner to date.[13] These are *legitimate*, accountable transfers, largely covering the ever-increasing interest payments for the "debts" the West claims African regimes owe it, beginning from the 1970s. A 2010 study by Global Financial Integrity, another Washington-based research organisation, shows that Africa may have also transferred the *additional* sum of US$854 billion since the 1970s ("this figure might be more than double, at [US]$1.8 trillion", the study cautions[14] – through *illegitimate* exports by the "leaderships" of corrupt African regimes with Nigeria, a state that I have argued severally failed in 1945 whilst still under British occupation,[15] topping this league at US$89.5 billion[16]). In effect, the state, in Africa, no longer pretends that it exists to serve its peoples.

Additionally, and this might appear paradoxical, trade figures and associated data readily obtainable indicate that these African states of seeming dysfunction have performed their utmost, year in, year out, in that key variable for which their European World creators established them in the first place: *redoubts* for export services of designated mineralogical/agricultural products to the European World/overseas. There are no indications, whatsoever, that any of these countries has found it difficult to fulfil its principal obligations on this accord – not genocidist and kakistocratic Nigeria, no. 16 on the Fund for Peace's current failed states index; not genocidist Democratic Republic of the Congo, no. 2, which has 80 per cent of the world's reserves of **coltan**, refined columbite-tantalite, critical in the manufacture of a range of small electronic equipment including, particularly, laptop computers and mobile phones ;[17] not genocidist Sudan, no. 3; not Chad, no. 5; not even Somalia, the world's no.1 "worst state". This is the context that that seemingly contradictory aphorism, "Africa works", becomes hugely intelligible. Appositely, the *raison d'être* of the "state" in Africa is not really to serve its people(s), *African* peoples; it is, on the contrary, to respond, unfailingly, to the

---

[13]Herbert Ekwe-Ekwe, *Readings from Reading: Essays on African Politics, Genocide, Literature* (Dakar and Reading: African Renaissance, 2011), pp. 41-42, 176-177.
[14]"Illicit financial flows from Africa: Hidden resource for development", http://www.gfintegrity.org/press-release/854-billion-removed-africa-illicit-financial-flows-1970-2008/, accessed 25 April 2013.
[15]Ekwe-Ekwe, *Readings from Reading*, p. 136.
[16]"Illicit financial flows from Africa: Hidden resource for development".
[17]Democratic Republic of the Congo is being currently subjected to a genocidal conflict where 5 million people have been murdered since the 1990s.

objective needs of its creators overseas. And to that extent, Africa, contrary to popular, predictable perception, is a success, is working!

For instance, thanks to the continuing inordinate leverage that Britain and France, the two foremost EuroConqueror league-states of Africa, exercise in these fundamentally anti-African principalities tagged "the state" in Africa, both European countries have a greater *secured* access to Africa's critical resources today than at any time during decades of their formal occupation of the continent. France, right from the post 1939-1945 war leadership of Charles de Gaulle to the current François Hollande's has such glaring contempt for the notion of "sovereignty" in the so-called *francophonie* Africa, ensuring that France has invaded most of these 22 African countries 51 times since 1960.[18] As for Britain, sheer greed and opportunism appear to be the guiding principle to attaining its unenviable position as the leading arms-exporter to Africa, including Africa's leading genocide-states.[19]

Indeed, France and Britain have never had it so good in Africa. This is the background to which the brazenly racist epithet "sub-Sahara Africa" is operationalised currently.[20]

Those crucial African capital exports referred to earlier, legitimate or/and illegitimate, are funds of gargantuan proportions produced by the same humanity that many a commentator or campaign project would be quick to categorise as "poor" and "needy" for "foreign aid". In the past 30 years, these funds could and should easily have provided a comprehensive healthcare programme across Africa, the establishment of schools, colleges and skills' training, the construction of an integrative communication network, the transformation of agriculture to abolish the scourge of malnutrition, hunger and starvation, and, finally, it would have stemmed the emigration of 25 million Africans, including crucial sectors of the continent's middle classes and intellectuals to the Americas, Europe, Asia and elsewhere in the world since the 1980s.

---

[18] For an excellent study on French hegemonic control of the finances/economies of these countries, see Gary Busch, "Africans pay for the bullets the French use to kill them", http://www.afrohistorama.info/article-africans-pay-for-the-bullets-the-french-use-to-kill-them-82337836.html, accessed 15 May 2013.

[19] See, for instance, journalist Charles Onyango-Obbo's candid insight on the subject in a *BBC* interview, "UK arming African countries", http://news.bbc.co.uk/2/hi/uk_news/politics/699255.stm, accessed 12 May 2013.

[20] See chap. 4 here on "sub-Sahara Africa".

Population and food and future

There has often been a "politically correct" rhetoric bandied about incessantly by some in academia, media and elsewhere who discuss this grave crisis of contemporary Africa in the context of population.[21] Africa, it is concluded in these assertions, requires some "decrease" in its population and/or population-growth as an important measure towards achieving a "solution". On the contrary, as we now demonstrate, Africa is, indeed, in no way overpopulated. The population argument is usually advanced on a number of fronts. First, there is a "theory" that the given landmass which presently defines Africa and its various so-called 54 countries cannot sustain the existing populations, but, more critically, the "projected populations" in years to come. We shall examine the degree to which this "theory" is able to stand up to serious scientific scrutiny first by comparing Africa's landmass vis-à-vis its population and those of some of the other countries of the world.

Africa's population is currently 1 billion covering an incredible vast landmass of 30,221,533 sq km or about four times the landmass of Brazil or more than the *combined* landmass of Argentina, the United States, Western Europe, India and China.[22] Ethiopia's landmass is 1,221,892 sq km, five times the size of Britain's at 244,044 sq km. Yet Britain's population of 62 million is three-quarters that of Ethiopia's 83 million. Focusing on these Ethiopia statistics, particularly, the basis and conclusions of naturalist David Attenborough's recent discussion on this subject could not, indeed, have been so comprehensively disingenuous.[23] As for Somalia, it is 2.6 times the size of Britain but has a population of only 9 million. Sudan and South Sudan provide an even more fascinating comparison. Whilst both countries are 10 times the size of Britain, they support a population of 45 million – about 70 per cent the size of Britain. In fact the Sudans have a landmass equal to that of India which is populated by 1.22 billion people – i.e., more than the population of all of Africa! Britain is one-tenth the size of the Democratic Republic of the Congo (DRC) which has a landmass of 2,345,395 sq km,

---

[21] As a useful background to this rhetoric, see, particularly, Roland Oliver, "The condition of Africa", p. 8, already referred to, and to the naturalist David Attenborough below.

[22] All the statistics here on countries' population, landmass and the like are derived from The World Bank, *World Development Report 2012* and United Nations Development Programme, *Human Development Report 2012*).

[23] Hanna Furness, "Sir David Attenborough: If we do not control population, the natural world will", *The Daily Telegraph*, London, 18 September 2013, http://www.telegraph.co.uk/culture/tvandradio/10316271/Sir-David-Attenborough-If-we-do-not-control-population-the-natural-world-will.html, accessed 23 March 2014.

similar to the Sudans and India. In other words, the DRC is about ten times the size of Britain but with a population of 71 million, nine million more than the population of the latter. Even though the DRC's landmass is about twice that of all of Britain, France and Germany (1,275,986 sq km), it has just about one-third of these three west European countries' total population of 208 million. Inevitably, the evidence does beg the question as to where this population really is! Where are these "overpopulated Africans"?! Where are they?

Second, let us examine similarly sized countries. France has a landmass of 547,021 sq km close to Somalia's. However, France's population of 65 million is about seven times the population of Somalia. Similarly, Botswana is slightly larger than France at 660,364 sq km but with a population of 2 million, a minuscule proportion of France's. Uganda's landmass at 236,039 sq km is about the size of Britain's 244,044 sq km. Yet with a population of only 33 million, Uganda is about half that of Britain's. Similarly, Ghana's landmass of 238,535 sq km makes it approximately equal to the size of Britain. Ghana is however populated by only 25 million people, far less than one-half Britain's population.

South World to South World comparisons can also prove useful in exposing the fallacy of either Africa's "large population" or "potential explosive population". Iran's size of 1,647,989 sq km is about two-thirds that of Sudan and South Sudan combined. Yet its population, unlike the Sudans' 45 million, is at least one and one-half times as large at 75 million. Mexico's landmass is 1,943,950 sq km. This is approximately the same size as the Sudans but with a population of 115 million, Mexico is two and one-half times the former. Pakistan's landmass of 803,937 sq km is just about Namibia's 864,284 sq km but Pakistan's population is 174 million while Namibia's is 2 million! Even though Bangladesh's 143,998 sq km-landmass makes it roughly one-eight the size of Angola (1,246,691 sq km) as well as that of South Africa's (1,221,029 sq km), Bangladeshi population at 159 million outstrips Angola's 13 million and South Africa's 50 million. If we were to return to our earlier comparisons, Angola and South Africa are about 4-5 times the size of Britain but with one-fifth and four-fifths respectively of the latter's population. We must ask the two earlier questions yet again: Where are these "overpopulated Africans"?! Where are they?

Crucial reminders: rich Africa

Finally, we should turn to the question of resource, its availability or lack of it, and therefore its ability or inability to support the African population – another component of Africa's "over-population" fallacy. Well over 50 per cent of Uganda's arable land, some of the richest in Africa, remains uncultivated.

Were Uganda to expand its current food production significantly, not only would it be completely self-sufficient, but it would be able to feed all the countries contiguous to its territory without difficulty, and GM free, too! The overall statistics of the African situation are even more revealing as with regards to the continent's long-term possibilities. Just about a quarter of the potential arable land of Africa is being cultivated presently.[24] Even here, an increasingly high proportion of the cultivated area is assigned to so-called cash-crops (cocoa, coffee, tea, groundnut, sisal, floral cultivation, etc.) for exports at a time when there has been a virtual collapse, across the board, of the price of these crops in international commodity markets. In the past 30 years, the average real price of these African products abroad has been about *20 per cent less* than their worth during the 1960s-1970s period which was soon after the "restoration-of-independence". As for the remaining 75 per cent of Africa's uncultivated land, this represents *60 per cent* of the entire world's potential.[25] The world is aware of the array of strategic minerals such as coltan, cobalt, copper, diamonds, gold, industrial diamonds, iron ore, manganese, phosphates, titanium, uranium, and of course petroleum oil found in virtually all regions across the continent.

Africa remains one of the world's most wealthy and potentially one of the world's wealthiest continents. What is not always associated with the profiles of Africa is its vast acreage of rich farmlands with capacity to optimally support the food needs of generations of African peoples indefinitely. In addition, the famous fish industry in Sénégal, Angola, Côte d'Ivoire and Ghana for instance, Botswana's rich cattle farms, west Africa's yam and plantain belts extending from southern Cameroon to southern Sénégal, the continent's rich rice production fields, etc., etc., all highlight the potential Africa has for fully providing for all its food needs. Thus, what the current African socioeconomic situation shows is extraordinarily reassuring, provided the acreage devoted to cultivation is expanded and expressly targeted to address Africa's *own* internal consumption needs. Land-use directed at agriculture for *food output* must become the focus of agricultural policy in the new Africa, as *opposed* to the *calamitous waste* of "cash-crop" production for export and/or the more recently observed "land-grab" – parcelling away of land to foreign governments and organisations – occurring across the continent.[26]

---

[24] FAO and IIED, "What effect will biofuels have on forest land and poor people's access to it?", 2008.
[25] John Endres, "Ready, set, sow", *The Journal of Good Governance Africa*, Issue 6, November 2012, p. 1.
[26] On this, see the excellent work of Emeka Akaezuwa's "Stop Africa Land Grab" movement, http://www.stopafricalandgrab.com/author/emeka-akaezuwa/, accessed 14 May 2013.

It is an inexplicable and inexcusable tragedy that any African child, woman, or man could go without food in the light of the staggering endowment of resources in Africa. Africa constitutes a spacious, rich and arable landmass that can support its population, which is still one of the world's least densely populated and distributed, into the *indefinite* future. There is only one condition, though, for the realisation of this goal – Africa must utilise these immense resources for the benefit of its *own* peoples within newly negotiated, radically decentralised sociopolitical dispensations which must abandon the current murderous "states" or "Berlin-states" as they should be more appropriately categorised.[27] These principalities that dutifully go by the very gibberish names of their creators (Nigeria, Niger, Chad, the Sudan, Central Africa Republic... whatever!) are an agglomeration of inchoate, inorganic and alienating emplacements that have been an asphyxiating trap for swathes of African constituent nations with evidently distinct histories, cultures and aspirations.

John Rawls: "outlaw state" or "rogue state" or genocide state and that expanded focus on interventionism from "liberal people"

We now no longer require any reminders that the primary existence of these principalities is to destroy or disable as many enterprisingly resourceful and resource-based constituent peoples, nations and publics within the polity that are placed in their genocide march and sights. Here, the example of the Igbo people of Biafra, southwestcentral Africa, cannot be overstressed. This is one of the most peaceful and industrious of peoples subjected to the longest-running genocide of the contemporary epoch by the Nigeria state. The Igbo genocide is the foundational genocide of post-(European)conquest Africa. It inaugurated Africa's current *age of pestilence*. During the course of 44 months (29 May 1966-12 January 1970) of indescribable barbarity and carnage not seen in Africa since the German-perpetration of the genocide against the Herero, Nama and Berg Damara peoples of Namibia in the early 1900s, the composite institutions of the Nigeria state, civilian and military, murdered 3.1 million Igbo people or one-quarter of this nation's population. Britain, presumably one of the societies aspiring to the Rawlsian conception of "well ordered societies",[28] and home of "liberal peoples", actively supported the Igbo genocide politically, diplomatically and militarily – right from conceptualisation to execution.[29] Given that genocidist Nigeria state is clearly equivalent to Rawls's characterisation of the "outlaw state" or "rogue

---

[27] Ekwe-Ekwe, *Readings from Reading*, pp. 27, 41, 44, 69, 200.
[28] John Rawls, *A Theory of Liberty* (Cambridge: Harvard University, 1999), pp. 4-5.
[29] See chap. 7 here.

state", a serious crisis indeed arises how a "justifiable war" could be waged against such a state[30] whilst ignoring the expanded focus on a separate kind of state, Britain, *representing* a "liberal people", which itself is simultaneously *actively* involved in the prosecution of *this* genocide.

To understand the multifaceted range of the politics of the Igbo genocide, phases I-III, 29 May 1966-12 January 1970 and phase-IV, 13 January 1970-present day, is to have an invaluable insight into the salient features and constitutive indices of politics across Africa in the past 50 years. Africans elsewhere remained largely silent on the gruesome events in Nigeria but did not foresee the grave consequences of such indifference as subsequent genocides in Rwanda, Darfur, Nuba Mountains, South Kordofan (all three in the Sudan) and Zaïre/Democratic Republic of the Congo, and in other wars in *every geographical region* of Africa during the period have demonstrated catastrophically. Just as the Nigerian operatives of mass murder appeared to have got away without censure from the rest of Africa, other genocidal and brutal African regimes soon followed in Nigeria's footpath, murdering a horrifically additional tally of 12 million people in their countries considered "undesirables" or "opponents". These 12 million murdered in the latter bloodbaths would probably have been saved if Africans and the rest of the world had intervened robustly to stop the initial genocide against the Igbo people.

Post-"Berlin-state" Africa: Freedom – create your own state today, now

It is abundantly clear that the factors which have contributed to determining the very poor quality of life of Africa's population presently have to do with the non use, partial use, or the gross misuse of the continent's resources year in, year out. This is thanks to an asphyxiating "Berlin-state" whose strategic resources are used largely to support the West World and others and an overseer-grouping of local forces which exists solely to police the dire straits of existence that is the lot of the average African.

As a result, the broad sectors of African peoples are yet to lead, centrally, the *entire* process of societal reconstruction and transformation *by themselves*. Surely, an urgently restructured, culturally supportive political framework that enhances the quality of life of Africans is really the pressing subject of focus for Africa.

One immediate move that states across the world, especially Britain, the leading arms exporter to Africa, and the rest of the West, Russia and China and

---

[30]John Rawls, *Law of Peoples* (Cambridge: Harvard University, 2002), pp. 81, 93.

others can make to support the ongoing efforts by peoples across Africa to rid themselves of such frighteningly genocidal and dysfunctional states is to *ban all arms sales* to Africa. This ban must be total and comprehensive. A total and comprehensive arms ban on Africa will radically advance the current quest on the ground by Africans, across the continent, to construct democratic and extensively decentralised new state forms that guarantee and safeguard human rights, equality and freedom for individuals and peoples. Africans have both the vision and the capacity to create alternative states – for them it is an imperative upon which their survival is based.

Forty-seven years and 15 million murders on, Africans finally realise that there cannot be any meaningful advancement without abandoning this post-conquest state, this "Berlin-state", essentially a genocide-state. This state is the bane of African existence and progress. It is in the longer-term interest of the rest of the world, especially in the West, to support African transformations initiated by the peoples rather than the "helmspersons"/"helmsconstituent nations" ostensibly entrenched in the hierarchical architecture that maps the typical continent's genocide-state. Just as in Berlin in 1884-1885 when conquering Europeans formulated their gruesome charter for the occupation of Africa, states are not a gift from the gods but relationships painstakingly formulated and constructed by groups of human beings on planet earth to pursue aspirations and interests *envisioned and articulated* by these same human beings.

Aimé Césaire, the poet, playwright and essayist, once told an interviewer[31] during one of those illuminating discourses of his on history: "History is always dangerous, the world of history is a risky world; but it is up to us at any given moment to establish and readjust the hierarchy of dangers".[32] It is indeed in the very course to disrupt and "readjust" this hierarchy in this age of pestilence in the "cursed" "Berlin-state" in favour of Africa and African peoples that the constituent Africa nation or people (Igbo, Darfuri, Gĩkũyũ, Wolof, Ibibio, Bakongo, Jola, Mongo, Akan, Luba, Ndebele, Mende, Serer, Bamileke, etc., etc) – so long maligned, so long impoverished, so long brutalised, so long humiliated and dehistoricised with often unprintable epithets (t****, n****, n*****, n******, p********, b******, w**, sub-*******, sub-*****, e*****, c***, c******, m*****, d******, h*******, f******-b******, b****, m***, b********,

---

[31]Annick Thebia Melson, "The liberating power of words: An interview with Poet Aimé Césaire", *The Journal of Pan-African Studies*, Vol. 2, No 4, June 2008, http://www.jpanafrican.com/docs/vol2no4/2.4_The_Liberating_Power_of_Words.pdf, accessed 26 February 2014.

[32]Ibid., p. 7.

c*******, b*********...), so long massacred, is recognised, *at last*, as the principal actor and agency of its being and geography.

So, for all African peoples or nations, the message on the unfurled banner for their freedom march couldn't be more confident and focused: "We are because we are free; We are free because we are". Abandon the "Berlin-state" now. Create your own state today, now. Now is the time! This nation, this people, can and should create its own state if it so desires. Freedom. It is its inalienable right.

It does not, therefore, have to explain to anyone else why it has embarked on this track of freedom. It can now decide what precepts, what aspirations, what trajectory, what goals, it has set its new state to embark upon. As Césaire deftly puts it in the interview referred to, the challenges of the times become the "quest to reconquer something, our name (sic), our country ... ourselves".[33]

Thus, the pressing point to reiterate here is that the immediate emergency that threatens the very survival of African peoples is the "Berlin-state" or the EuroConqueror state encased in African existence coupled with the pathetic bunch that masquerades here and there as African leaderships but whose mission is to *oversee* this vassalage, this enthralling edifice. African women and men will sooner, now, rather than later, abandon this fractured, fracturing, conflictive, alienating and terror contraption. Africans must now focus on real transformation – the revitalisation and consolidation of the institutions of Africa's constituent nations and polities. In these institutions and spaces of African civilisation lie the organic framework to ensure transparency, probity, accountability, investment in people, humanised wealth creation, respect for human rights and civil liberties, and a true commitment to radically transform African existence.

***

---

[33]Ibid., p. 2.

2 THE CONCATENATION OF THE AFRICAN ROLE IN THE 1914-1918 WAR

There couldn't be a more appropriate text from which to embark on an on-the-spot reminder to the world of the role of Africa and Africans in the intra-European World war of 1914-1918[1] than *Unbowed: One Woman's Story*,[2] the inimitable memoirs of Wangari Maathai, the award-winning celebrated environmental activist and biologist. In those poignant passages memoralising on uncle Thumbi, conscripted by the British occupation regime in Kenya in 1914 to fight the Germans in neighbouring Italian-occupied Somalia and German-occupied Tanganyika (contemporary Tanzania), Maathai notes:

> In my family there was a missing member, someone I did not find out about until I was well into adulthood. During the First World War, Africans in the colonies were conscripted to fight or serve as porters. In Kenya, if parents had an able-bodied son old enough to go to war, they were ... expected to surrender him to the authorities. My grandparents had such a son, Thumbi. My grandmother did not want her son, who was more than twenty at the time, to join the war. She was in despair. So she advised him to hide in the dense vegetation near a high waterfall in the Tucha River ... [but Thumbi was eventually caught ... and the British] went and seized him ... "He will never come back," my grandmother ... cr[ied]. And he never did. He became one of the more than one hundred thousand Kikuyus who died on the battlefield or from starvation or influenza during the First World War ... My grandmother cried for her son for the rest of her life...[3]

---

[1]An earlier version of this chapter appeared in *Rethinking Africa*, 29 August 2014 and *Pambazuka News: Voice of Freedom and Justice*, 11 September 2014.
[2]Wangari Maathai, *Unbowed: One Woman's Story* (London: Arrow Book, 2008).
[3]Ibid., pp. 27-28.

The longest genocide

Cataclysm

All of Africa lost one million of its peoples[4] fighting in this intra-European Worldwar in battle fronts in East Africa, Cameroon (west Africa) and in Europe Itself– *for* Britain, France, Belgium, Czarist Russia and their allies *against* Germany, Italy, Austro-Hungary, the Ottomans and their allies and *for* Germany, Italy, Austro-Hungary, the Ottomans and their allies *against* Britain, France, Belgium, Czarist Russia and their allies.

Essentially, this was a war, in addition to the follow-up 1939-1945 confrontation, that Africa and African peoples had no business, whatsoever, fighting in. The two principal protagonists in each conflict, Britain and Germany, were lead powers in the pan-European World conqueror-states that had formally occupied Africa since 1885. As we have already indicated, Britain was indeed the foremost conqueror state of Africa from the group, having occupied the continent's prized lands – lands with major population centres and vast and multiple natural resource emplacements in south, central, east and west regions. Such is the importance of this British conqueror and occupying position in Africa history of the epoch that it should be restated here: South Africa, Namibia (proxy control, post-1918 – after the defeat of Germany in 1914-1918 war), Zimbabwe, Botswana, Swaziland, Lesotho, Zambia, Kenya, Uganda, Tanzania (post-1918, after the defeat of Germany in 1914-1918 war), the Sudan, Nigeria, south Cameroons (post-1918, after the defeat of Germany in 1914-1918 war), Ghana, Sierra Leone, Gambia. Britain is also the lead beneficiary of this same pan-European World states' 400 years of enslavement of African peoples, mostly in the Americas, since the 15th century CE.[5] As for Germany, beginning in 1904 and ending in 1911, i.e., prior to the 1914-1918 war, it had carried out the genocide of the Herero, Nama and Berg Damara peoples in its occupied Namibia in southwest Africa with the following catastrophic outcome during the period: wiped out 80 per cent of Herero, 51 per cent of Nama, 30 per cent of Berg Damara.[6] For Belgium, an Anglo-French ally in the 1914-1918 war, indeed the state whose initial attack by Germany triggered this conflict, it, too, entered the intra-European war in 1914 in the wake of committing a 30-year trail (1878-1908) of

---

[4]Joe Harris Lunn, "War Losses (Africa)", *1914-18-online: International Encyclopedia of the First World War*, https://encyclopedia.1914-1918-online.net/article/war_losses_africa, accessed 27 December 2017.
[5]Ekwe-Ekwe, *Readings from Reading*, especially chap. 1.
[6]Herbert Ekwe-Ekwe, *African Literature in Defence of History: An essay on Chinua Achebe* (Dakar and Reading: African Renaissance, 2001), pp. 37-38.

genocide against Africans in the Congo basin in which it annihilated 13 million constituent peoples.[7]

Perverse

It is against this cataclysmic background of history that Africans found themselves conscripted by both sides of the confrontation line in 1914-1918: clearly, the double-jeopardy of conquered and occupied peoples at once fighting wars *for* and *against* ruthless aggressors. In commemorations of a century of this war that have been underway across Europe recently, a recurring theme in the media (and academia) that has been used to articulate African role in the war is "hidden" or "silent", even "unknown".[8] There was indeed an academic who appeared in one of the *BBC* frontline current affairs newsmagazine programmes who used the bizarre phrase "not really well known" in describing "African involvement". "Hidden", "silent", "unknown", "not really well known" – by whom?!

Of course nothing about the role of Africa and Africans in this conflict is "hidden" or "unknown". On the contrary. What has duly been the difficulty that the presumed "gatekeepers" of this history (who have all along been tireless "rationalisers" of the European conquest and occupation of Africa) have had is how to explain the very perverse role of desperately occupied peoples fighting a war of/for their occupiers. I have argued severally[9] that two critical developments of the 20th century – the wars of 1914-1918 and 1939-1945 – shatter the cardinal features of the position of these "rationalisers" irrevocably:

(a) The 1919 treaty of Versailles that ends the 1914-1918 war frees all subjugated European peoples in Russia, Austro-Hungary and the Ottoman whilst African peoples in German-occupied Africa [Namibia, Tanzania, Cameroon, Togo, Rwanda, Burundi] do not have the restoration of their freedom but are, *instead*, occupied by Britain, France and Belgium [ironically, latter two countries hardly withstood the 1914 German juggernaut!]

(b) Africans in mostly British-occupied, French-occupied and Belgian-occupied Africa are again conscripted, beginning in the autumn of 1939, to fight against

---

[7]Isidore Ndaywel è Nziem, *Histoire générale du Congo: De l'héritage ancien à la République Démocratique* (Paris: Duculot, 1998), p. 344.

[8]Cf. Hike Fischer, "Africa and the First World War", *Deutsche Welle*, 16 April 2014, https://www.dw.com/en/africa-and-the-first-world-war/a-17573462, accessed 24 August 2014.

[9]See, for instance, Ekwe-Ekwe, *African Literature in Defence of History*, chap. 1.

The longest genocide

Germany, as the new war erupts, even though Germany had, *since 1918*, ceased to be a conqueror/occupying-state in Africa

(c) Africans in mostly British-occupied and French-occupied Africa are conscripted, beginning in the autumn of 1939, to fight against Japan, in the forests of Myanmar, even though the Japanese were not and have never been conquerors or occupiers of Africa

(d) Belgian king and state which barely resisted the German assault on their territory beyond three weeks in May 1940 had the entire financing of the Belgian war effort [including the entire expenses of the country's exiled royal family and government in London], totalling £40 million,[10] paid for by Belgian-occupied Congo; this is the same Belgian-occupied Congo where the Belgian monarch and state had murdered 13 million Africans in the 30-year old genocide cited earlier

(e) Thousands of Africans perish in the battle fronts of east Africa, Europe and south Asia fighting for Anglo-Franco-Belgian conquerors/occupiers of Africa

(f) Restoration of African independence in the post-war epoch is distinctly rejected by British Prime Minister Winston Churchill in a November 1942 speech in London ["I have not become the King's First Minister in order to preside over the liquidation of the British Empire", he stresses,[11] in his own interpretation of the August 1941 "Atlantic Charter", formulated by him and US President Franklin Roosevelt, which declares unambiguously: "all people had a right to self-determination"[12]

(g) In similar vein, Charles de Gaulle, leader of the "Free French Forces" who had been on exile in England since Germany overran France in 1940, rejects African independence in the post-war era during a 1944 conference of global French occupation-governors in Brazzaville, Congo[13]

---

[10]Walter Rodney, *How Europe Underdeveloped Africa* (London: Bogle-L'Ouverture, 1972), p. 188.
[11]"From our archive: Mr Churchill on our one aim", *The Guardian*, London, 11 November 2009.
[12]Quoted in AN Porter and AA Stockwell, *British Imperial Policy and Decolonisation, 1938-1964, Vol I: 1938-1951* (Basingstoke and London: Macmillan, 1987), p. 103
[13]Hubert Deschamps, "France in Black Africa and Madagascar between 1920 and 1945", in LH Gann and Peter Duiganan, ed., *Colonialism in Africa, 1870-1960. Vol Two: The*

(h) Writing in a 2014 edition of London's *The Mail on Sunday*, George Carey, a former archbishop of Canterbury, recalls: "This year we are reminded by the commemoration of two world wars that the values of our democratic traditions are precious. Our fathers and grandfathers ... fought against totalitarianism for the survival of democratic virtues".[14] Pointedly, Carey's hearty summation does not incorporate the African experience as we have highlighted here. Such has been the asymmetrical character of this history that besides Japan, Czarist Russia/Soviet Union and Austro-Hungary, Africa has been largely under an unparalleled totalitarian straitjacket enforced, since 1885, by each and every dominant state across those two strategic battle lines that map the 1914-1918 and 1939-1945 wars.

Following from (f) and (g) (above), it is in fact no coincidence that Britain would wage two devastating wars against two African nations at the forefront of terminating its occupation of Africa in the immediate post-1939-1945 war era: against the Gĩkũyũ in the east in the 1950s, with the death of tens of thousands of Gĩkũyũ and others and in *co-perpetrating* the Igbo genocide (phases I-III) in southwestcentral Africa with the Fulani/islamist jihadist-led state in Nigeria, 1966-1970, the foundational genocide of post-(European)conquest Africa, with the murder of 3.1 million Igbo or one-quarter of this nation's population. Both the Gĩkũyũ (1950s-1960s) and Igbo (1930s-1960s) had spearheaded the liberation of Kenya and Nigeria respectively from the British occupation.

It should now be evident that on a broader stretch of examination, there can't be any such thing as "hidden" history. Instead, what some practitioners wish to do is obfuscate or, worse, deny. Writing in "On the Concept of History", Walter Benjamin has argued that the "past carries a secret index with it, by which it is referred to its resurrection".[15] He poses two pressing questions: "Are we not touched by the same breath of air which was among that which came before? [I]s there not an echo of those who have been silenced in the voices to which we lend our ears today?".[16] He is uncompromisingly forthright in response:

History and Politics of Colonialism 1914-1960 (Cambridge: Cambridge University, 1970), p. 249.
[14] 16 April 2014.
[15] Walter Benjamin, "On the Concept of History", https://www.marxists.org/reference/archive/benjamin/1940/history.htm, accessed 19 August 2014.
[16] Ibid.

The longest genocide

...The Angel of History must look just so. [Its] face is turned towards the past. Where *we* see the appearance of a chain of events, [*it*] sees one single catastrophe, which unceasingly piles rubble on top of rubble and hurls it before [its] feet ... nothing which has ever happened is to be given as lost to history. Indeed, the past would fully befall only a resurrected humanity. Said another way: only for a resurrected humanity would its past, in each of its moments, be citable. Each of its lived moments becomes a citation *a l'ordre du jour* [order of the day] – whose day is precisely that of the Last Judgement.[17]

At the crux of trying to manufacture this phantom of "lost to history", as far as Africa and Africans are concerned, Chinua Achebe's invaluable insight follows and we will quote him at length:

[The European conquest of Africa] may indeed be a complex affair, but one thing is certain: You do not walk in, seize the land, the person, the history of another, and then sit back and compose hymns of praise in his honour. To do that would amount to calling yourself a bandit; and you won't to do that. So what do you do? You construct very elaborate excuses for your action. You say, for instance, that the man in question is worthless and quite unfit to manage himself or his affairs. If there are valuable things like gold and diamonds which you are carting away from his territory, you proceed to prove that he doesn't own them in the right sense of the word – that he and they had just happened to be lying around the same place when you arrived. Finally if the worse comes to the worse, you may even be prepared to question whether such as he can be, like you, fully human. From denying the presence of a man standing there before you, you end up questioning his very humanity ...[I]n the [European conquest] situation *presence* was the critical question, the crucial word. Its denial was the keynote of [this conquest's] ideology.[18]

In her closing testimony on uncle Thumbi in *Unbowed*, Wangari Maathai writes: "My grandparents ... never received any official word about what had happened to their [son], or any compensation. This is still an open wound. I want to say to the British government 'My uncle went to war and never came back, and nobody ever bothered to come and tell my grandparents what had happened to their son'".[19]

Appropriately, one would wish to modify Wangari Maathai's note to the British government and then *re*-address it, on behalf of African peoples, to all the governments and parliaments of *all states* involved in the confrontation in the wars of 1914-1918 and 1939-1945, bar Japan, Austro-Hungary and Czarist Russia/Soviet Union: "Our conscripted daughters and sons went to war to fight for you and never came back, and nobody ever bothered to come and tell us what had happened to them".

---

[17]Ibid.
[18]Chinua Achebe, "African Literature as Restoration of Celebration", *Kunapipi*, 12, 2, 1990: 4; emphasis added.
[19]Maathai, *Unbowed*, p. 28.

3 DOES *ARROW OF GOD* ANTICIPATE THE IGBO GENOCIDE?[1]

Quite early in 2014, I embarked on a study of the role or involvement of Africa and Africans in the 1914-1918 war. 2014 is the 100th anniversary of the war. This study has been published under the title, "The concatenation of the African role in the 1914-1918 war or World War I".[2] Instructively, my research for the paper had led me to Chinua Achebe's *A Man of the People*, by way of that memorable conversation on African history and future between Cheikh Anta Diop and Carlos Moore, published 20 years ago in the journal *Présence Africaine*. I will return to the Diop-Moore conversation shortly.

2014 is also the year of *Arrow of God*. This is why we are gathered here today, Saturday 4th October 2014, at the University of London's School of Oriental and African Studies. 2014 is the 50th anniversary of the publication of Chinua Achebe's tome. I had to reread it for the jubilee commemoration. And as I had earlier on reread *A Man of the People*, Achebe's fourth novel, for the purposes of my 1914-1918 war study, I suddenly found my follow-up Achebe reread of the season was *Arrow of God*, novel no. 3 – in other words, perhaps not aware of the trend and its consequence or consequences, I had been involved in alternating the sequencing of the epochs of the groundings of the two texts by appearing to reread *Arrow of God* backwards! The result is fascinating, as I will show. The discovery has been quite profound.

---

[1] A shortened version of paper presented at the *Arrow of God* at 50 Symposium, Centre for African Studies, School of Oriental and African Studies, University of London/Igbo Conference (symposium conveners: Dr Kwadwo Osei-Nyame Jnr and Dr Louisa Uchum Egbunike), Saturday 4 October 2014.

[2] See chap. 2 here.

Prophet?

To recall, Chinua Achebe publishes *A Man of the People* in early January 1966. This is a few days before the military coup d'état that overthrows the Abubakar Tafawa Balewa civilian government which the supposedly outgoing British occupation-governor James Robertson had imposed on the country in 1959. This was a follow-up to the fractious election that the British rigged in favour of its north region Fulani islamist-led sociopolitical clients.[3] The latter would, in turn, safeguard those vast expropriatory interests of Britain's in the country subsequently.[4]

A striking feature in the resolution of the grave crisis of this state that Achebe wrestles with in *A Man of the People* is its degeneration into a military coup and rampaging violence ("But the Army obliged us by staging a coup at that point and locking up every member of the Government"[5]), an extraordinary predictive insight, if ever there was one, that confronts the reader, considering the gruesome trajectory of politics in Nigeria, in 1966, the year this same state launches the Igbo genocide, the foundational genocide of post(European)conquest Africa, in which 3.1 million Igbo or one-quarter of this nation's population are murdered during the course of 44 subsequent devastating months. Indeed on the receipt of an advance copy of *A Man of the People*, poet and playwright John Pepper Clarke-Bekederemo observes, "Chinua, I *know* you are a prophet. Everything in this book has happened except a military coup" (emphasis in the original).[6] Ken Post, a British academic working in west Africa at the time, recalls: "Chinua Achebe proved to be a better prophet than any of the political scientists".[7] Once again, "Prophet"! Is Chinua Achebe, the Father of African Literature, also a prophet?

Arrow of God, Achebe's most complex novel, his "richest, most mysterious ... one of the finest works of fiction in English written in this century", according to Robert Wren,[8] remains an inexhaustible farmland for bounty harvests. Fresh readings and

---

[3] Harold Smith, "Harold Smith's Tribute Page", http://haroldsmithmemorial.wordpress.com/harold-smith-fought-our-battle/., accessed 27 September 2014.

[4] Herbert Ekwe-Ekwe, "Elections in Africa – the voter, the court, the outcome", *PENSAR-Revisita de Ciêcias Jurídicas*, Vol. 18, Número 3, 2013, pp. 804-836, , http://www.unifor.br/images/pdfs/Pensar/v18n3_artigo6.pdf, accessed 29 December 2015.

[5] Chinua Achebe, *A Man of the People* (London: Heinemann, 1966), p. 165.

[6] Ezenwa-Ohaeto, *Chinua Achebe: A Bibliography* (Oxford: James Currey Publishers, 1996), p. 109.

[7] Geoff Ferris, "A Man of the People", *Colonial & Postcolonial Literary Dialogues*, https://wmich.edu/dialogues/texts/manofthepeople.htm, accessed 15 October 2018.

[8] Robert Wren, *Achebe's World* (Harlow: Longman, 1990) p. 75.

re-readings of the novel bring forth ever more yields. This also applies to the examination/re-examination of the literature across the spectrum of distinguished critics of the novel. It is striking, right from the outset, that the certainties of Igbo national independence witnessed in the age of *Things Fall Apart* have now clearly dissipated as Ezeulu charts the paths and terms of the consequential relationship between him and Ulu, the god that he serves, and the key centres of bourgeoning European-conquest power in Umuaro and neighbouring Igbo states. Pointedly, Ezeulu instructs son Oduche to attend the Christian mission school as his "eyes and ears"[9] in this power dispensation. But Oduche is much more important here than just a tactical tool in Ezeulu's defence arsenal as shown soon.

Oeuvre

As in the other texts of the Achebean oeuvre, including *A Man of the People*, which has been aptly illustrative, *Arrow of God* presents a highly imaginative and anticipatory power of Achebe's insight to the turbulent trajectory of post-(European)conquest African history and politics. This chapter will explore how this insight anticipates the catastrophe of the Igbo genocide. Thus, the Igbo double jeopardy of foreign conquest and occupation *and* genocide appears to sum up Achebe's mission.

I have chosen Emmanuel Ngara's study of *Arrow of God* in his *Stylistic Criticism and the African Novel* [10] as an important text to employ to discuss Achebe's crucial mission. Ironically, Ngara's clearly stated conclusions in his work couldn't be more appropriate in mapping out the parameters of Achebe's project. Ngara is very unhappy with *Arrow of God*. He writes: "... *Arrow of God* is not a book that fascinates and engages the reader as soon as he picks it up to read". [11] He elaborates in four paragraphs and it is important to quote him at some length:

The narrator is the author himself who tells the story in the third person, giving himself the privilege of entering the characters' minds and recording their innermost thoughts. The narrator is addressing both an African and a western English-speaking audience. He is very successful in his use of African idioms in an English novel – non-Igbo speakers are able to follow the story and to understand the Igbo proverbs and expressions used in the novel. There are, however, some minor shortcomings in the language.

Achebe uses many Igbo terms such as *chi*, *obi*, *ogene*. These are not translated and the reader is expected to understand them in the context in which they are used. In some instances, however,

---

[9] Chinua Achebe, *The African Trilogy* (London: Pan Books, 1988), p. 365.
[10] Emmanuel Ngara, *Stylistic Criticism and the African Novel*. London: Heinemann Educational Books, 1982.
[11] Ibid., p. 79.

> these untranslated terms are somewhat obscure, the reader can only have a vague idea of what they stand for, and this tends to slow down his reading speed as he attempts to puzzle out what they mean ... *Arrow of God* is too culture-bound and sociologically oriented. The emphasis on the multifarious aspects of Igbo society tends to distract the reader and to hamper the smooth flow of events ... Yet another source of difficulty is the novel's complexity of theme and plot and the large number of characters involved. Achebe tries to contain the whole cultural fabric of Igbo society and the various forces threatening it in one volume. This necessitates bringing in too many characters to whom the reader must be introduced before he can clearly see who is playing what role in the conflict. Also, many contradictions are involved...[12]

Spectacularly, Ngara lays out the constituent features of the history and geography that have given rise to the conjunctural crisis, even existential (on this possibility, Ezeulu couldn't be clearer when he refers to the symbolism of the sound of the tolling of the church bell, that overarching ideological signifier of the occupation regime, as the "song of extermination"[13]), which the Igbo are going through and which gives rise to the artist's, the novelist's, Achebe's stated mission – in the first place. One then wonders what problem the critic/scholar has in *their own* response to this pressing endeavour. Isn't the scholar's trade to labour, labour and labour and, at times without much success, try to understand life, and its complexities, society and the universe? When has this task ever been easy or easier? The scholar can't afford to despair over the complexity of the challenge at stake; definitely, he or she mustn't give up; they must continue to labour; they must persist. Even Ezeulu, the half-person, half-spirit, the "Known and at the same time ... Unknowable",[14] attests to the complexities of understanding and responding to the challenges of the times when he beckons his people: "But you cannot know the Thing which beats the drum to which Ezeulu dances ... [W]e have reached the very end of things ... This is what our sages meant when they said that a man who has nowhere else to put his hand for support puts it on his knee".[15]

In the conversation between Cheikh Anta Diop and Carlos Moore that I referred to earlier, Diop asks the pertinent question of the age: "Who can deny that of all peoples, Africans have been the greatest victims of aggression, racism and oppression? The consequences can be seen today in the state of underdevelopment and technical

---

[12]Ibid.
[13]Achebe, *The African Trilogy*, p. 362.
[14]Ibid., p. 455.
[15]Ibid., pp. 455-457

backwardness of African societies".[16] The apogee of this devastation of a heritage for each and every African nation or people, without exception, is what Diop describes, to use his very words, "*loss of national sovereignty*".[17] In *Arrow of God*, Chinua Achebe is examining not only the invasion of Igboland by a European state (this deleterious "loss of national sovereignty") but the multitudinous layers and range of Igbo response to this unprecedented catastrophe which is ongoing, not over by any means. Thus, Ezeulu, the chief priest of Ulu, uses stark epidemiological referencing to describe this grave emergency facing his people: "A disease that has never been seen before cannot be cured with everyday herbs ... [O]ur fathers have told us that it may even happen to an unfortunate generation that they are pushed beyond the end of things, and their back is broken and hung over a fire".[18] Yet in another breadth, the priest's characterisation is bluntly existential as we have just indicated: "extermination".[19]

Abame or genocide or Abame...

Kole Omotoso has argued that, unlike the Yoruba who view the British invasion of their country as a "mere episode, a catalytic episode only",[20] the Igbo see the British invasion of Igboland as a confrontation with a "strange Difference, an Other, a Contradiction, an encounter that can only be negative in terms of the effects on Igbo culture".[21] Umuofia, as we observe in *Things Fall Apart*, surely appreciates the startling implications of this archetypal "clash of civilisations" that Omotoso depicts. The Okonkwo-Obierika studied deliberations on the horrific massacre of the people of Abame by an ever-expanding British invading military force and the impact of the event on Umuofia's national sovereignty is pointedly evident. Indeed, the continuing independence of Umuofia is threatened by this invasion. This gives rise to calls by Okonkwo for a steadfast defence of their homeland by its people, despite the military superiority and the ruthlessness of the enemy it faces as historian Obierika is keen to stress: "Have you not heard how the white man wiped out Abame?"[22] He adds, ominously, "They would go to Umuru and bring the soldiers, and we [Umuofia] would

---

[16]Carlos Moore, "Conversations with Cheikh Anta Diop", *Présence Africaine*, Nos 3/4, 1993, p. 418.
[17]Ibid., p. 381 (emphasis in the original).
[18]Achebe, *The African Trilogy*, pp. 456-457.
[19]Ibid., 362.
[20]Kole Omotoso, *Achebe or Soyinka?* (London: Hans Zell, 1996), p. 17.
[21]Ibid., p. 11.
[22]Achebe, *The African Trilogy*, p. 144.

be like Abame".[23] Obierika and apparently the majority of the leadership of Umuofia want to avoid the *Abameisation* of their own country by the British. Even though he does not state it clearly in his studied philosophical ruminations in *Arrow of God*, it is implicit that one of the reasons, a very important consideration definitely, for Ezeulu's decision to send son Oduche to the conquest mission school is to preempt the Abame débâcle in Umuaro. For Okonkwo, though, the obvious overwhelming military odds against Umuofia notwithstanding, the country must defend its sovereignty resolutely: "We must fight these men and drive them from our land".[24] Okonkwo's forthright response to Obierika's reticence about how to respond to the impending British invasion of Umuofia shows clearly that years of enforced exile in the Mbanta country have not in any way diminished the hero's patriotic instincts and distinctions. Even though Okonkwo subsequently commits suicide after killing the envoy sent by the British to disrupt the crucial Umuofia leadership assembly on the unfolding emergency in addition to his conviction that Umuofia is unwilling to deploy its forces to resist the impending attack on the country, I have argued, elsewhere,[25] that Okonkwo's suicide and its aftermath symbolise the sowing of the regenerative seeds of freedom for the restoration of Igbo national sovereignty.

As a result, this trope of freedom/national sovereignty transmutes to the post-Umuofia-*Arrow of God* epoch, evident, most assuredly if not defiantly, when Ezeulu turns down the occupation's plans to induct him in the operationalising structure of the conquest regime. Again implicitly, perhaps, Ezeulu does not feel that the conquest's mission is complete or definitive. He still hopes that his people's independence would survive. This is why the priest informs occupation administrator Clarke, via the latter's interpreter: "Tell the white man that Ezeulu will not be anybody's chief, except Ulu".[26] Equally, the trope of Abame-murdering/wipe out transmutes to this new epoch. In the Anglo-Igbo confrontation in Umuaro and the contiguous states, the Abame massacre features, most hauntingly, in the narrative. In the wake of the Umuaro-Okperi war which Ezeulu opposes, describing it as an "unjust war",[27] Umuaro reluctantly accepts the terms of the British military intervention because, to quote the narrative voice in *Arrow of God*, "[t]he story of what these [British] soldiers did in Abame was still told with fear, and so Umuaro made no effort to resist but laid down their arms".[28] In fact, Ezeulu himself focuses on Abame broadly

---

[23]Ibid.
[24]Ibid.
[25]Herbert Ekwe-Ekwe, "The Achebean Restoration", *Journal of Asian and African Studies*, Vol. 48, No. 6, 2013, p. 698.
[26]Achebe, *The African Trilogy*, p. 498.
[27]Ibid, p. 334.
[28]Ibid., p. 347.

in a key address to his people in which he reflects on growing African involvement in the murderous forces the conqueror regime is mobilising in these massacres, a principal sphere of this tragedy. He poses three questions which clearly have "pan-Africanist" implications: "Have you not heard that when two brothers fight a stranger reaps the harvest? How many white men went in the party that destroyed Abame? Do you know? Five",[29] clearly an Achebean acknowledgement of that key component of the trajectory of the conquest of Africa and continuing post-conquest violence and murders so dramatically captured by historian Chancellor Williams in his *The Destruction of Black Civilization* (1987: 218):[30]

Now the shadows lengthened. The Europeans had also been busily building up and training strong African armies. Africans trained to hate, kill and conquer Africans. Blood of Africans was to sprinkle and further darken the pages of their history ... Indeed, Africa was conquered for the Europeans by the Africans [themselves], and thereafter kept under [conquest] control by African police and African soldiers. Very little European blood was ever spilled.

So, ages before the Blydens and the Equinaos and the Garveys, and the DuBoises and the Nkrumahs and the Makonnens would begin to theorise and offer progressive, enlightening perspectives on "pan-Africanism", the enemies of Africa had already unleashed "pan-African-'Goodcountry'-assemblages"-of-terror on Africa and Africans to despoil and conquer Africa. In effect, contrary to the usual, quite often understandable romantic presumptions, "pan-Africanism", as a construct, *does not* appear or occur discernibly or intelligibly "ready-made". On the contrary, every feature of this construct for progressive projects or outcomes in the African World has to be worked for actively, painstakingly, and continuously sustained.

Abame to 29 May 1966-present day

To conclude, the Abame massacre and those Umuofia and Umuaro debates and deliberations on its aftermath crucially map the spectrum of milestones that would define the trajectory of the British 100 years of war against Igbo people and the variegated frames of Igbo resistance to it that parallel the very stretch of British occupation of this southwestcentral region of Africa which Britain calls "Nigeria": the 1880s-1914 Ekumeku wars and resistance in Igbo Anioma, west of the Oshimiri River; the 1901-1902 war against the Aru in northeastcentral Igboland; the 1929 *Ogu umu nwanyi Igbo*/Igbo women resistance movement in Aba/Igbo eastcentral region; the 1945 pogrom of Igbo immigrant population in Jos, central Nigeria, organised by Fulani

---

[29]Ibid., p. 455.
[30]Chancellor Williams, *The Destruction of Black Civilization* (Chicago: Third World, 1987), p. 218.

islamists/north region-based clients/allies of the occupation; the 1949 shootings of coal miners in the Enuugwu colliery in northcentral Igboland; the 1953 pogrom of Igbo immigrant population in Kano, north Nigeria, organised by Fulani islamists/north region-based clients/allies of the occupation. The 1945 and 1953 pogroms are indeed the "dress rehearsals" of the Igbo genocide launched on Sunday 29 May 1966 by Britain and its Fulani islamists-led Nigeria allies.[31] Abame, eventually, culminates, catastrophically, in the 29 May 1966-12 January 1970 Igbo genocide, phases I-III, when 3.1 million Igbo, a quarter of the Igbo population, are murdered by Britain and its Fulani islamists-led Nigeria allies. During the course of phase-IV launched by the dual genocidists, beginning on 13 January 1970 and continuing presently, tens of thousands of additional Igbo people have been murdered.

This is the foundational genocide of post-(European)conquest Africa, effectively inaugurating the age of pestilence which, by and large, characterises contemporary Africa. Soon after, the killing fields from Igboland expands almost inexorably across Africa as the following haunting reminders of slaughter, during the age, illustrate: further genocides in Rwanda, the Sudan, and Zaïre/Democratic Republic of Congo, and wars in Republic of Congo, Ethiopia, Somalia, Burundi, Liberia, Sierra Leone, Guinea-Bissau, southern Guinea, Côte d'Ivoire, Mali, Libya. Twelve million were killed in these 13 countries. Added to the 3.1 million Igbo dead, Africa has had a gruesome tally of 15.1 million people murdered by its genocide states and in other conflicts in the past 44 years.

Besides chief priest Ezeulu's often complex philosophical ruminations which also focus, specifically, on the possibilities of Britain unleashing Abame-style, *Things Fall Apart*-era massacres during his very own times, the age of *Arrow of God*, let us end by elaborating more empirically on the contemporary *lived* Igbo Abame age of pestilence of 29 May 1966 to present day because this is precisely the outcome the philosopher-priest has sought to prevent in Umuaro (*Arrow of God*) and what Obierika, hitherto, had saved Umuofia from (*Things Fall Apart*). If we recall those poignant words from Ezeulu to Umuaro, cited earlier, "[O]ur fathers have told us that it may even happen to an unfortunate generation that they are pushed beyond the end of things, and their back is broken and hung over a fire",[32] it suddenly dawns on us that these appear to constitute a pre-dated epitaph for the 3.1 million *and* additional tens of thousands of Igbo murdered in a generation just once or twice removed from the Igbo of Umuaro. As we can see, Chinua Achebe's predictive insights, here in *Arrow of God*, are shatteringly breathtaking... Undoubtedly, the Nigeria genocide state, beginning on 29 May 1966, becomes some savage blood-sucking monster let loose on the Igbo people and Igboland, slaughtering away to effectuate its mission of extirpation...

---

[31]Herbert Ekwe-Ekwe, *Biafra Revisited* (Dakar and Reading: African Renaissance, 2006).
[32]Achebe, *The African Trilogy*, p. 457.

Just in case it isn't quite obvious, Chinua Achebe publishes a sequel to *Arrow of God* 48 years later – in 2012. The sequel is appropriately called, *There was a Country*.

***

4 "SUB-SAHARA AFRICA" IS GRATUITOUSLY RACIST[1]

It appears increasingly fashionable for a number of broadcasters (*BBC*, *CNN*, *France24*, etc., etc), websites (for instance, *CNN*, *France24*, *BBC*), news agencies (*Reuters*, *AP*, *AFP*, etc., etc), newspapers (*The Times*, *Financial Times*, *Washington Post*, *Le Monde*...) and magazines, the United Nations/allied agencies and some governments, writers and academics to use the term "sub-Sahara Africa" to refer to all of Africa (54 countries) except the 5 predominantly Arab states of north Africa (Morocco, Algeria, Tunisia, Libya, Egypt) and the Sudan, a northcentral African country. Even though its territory is *mostly located south of the Sahara Desert*, the Sudan is excluded from the "sub-Sahara Africa" tagging by those who promote the use of the epithet because the regime in power in Khartoum describes the country as "Arab" despite its *African peoples' majority* population.

Which science?

As we now demonstrate, the concept "sub-Sahara Africa" is absurd, misleading, if not a meaningless classificatory schema. Its use defies the science of the fundamentals of geography but prioritises hackneyed, stereotypical, racist labelling. It is not obvious, on the face of it, which of the four possible meanings of the prefix, "sub", its users attach to the "sub-Sahara Africa" labelling. Is it "under" the Sahara Desert or "part of"/"partly" the Sahara Desert? Or, presumably, "partially"/"nearly" the Sahara Desert or is it the application of "in the style of, but inferior to" the Sahara Desert, especially considering that *there is* an Arab people sandwiched between Morocco and Mauritania (northwest Africa) called Saharan?

The example of South Africa is appropriate here. Crucially, this is a reference underlined in the relevant literature of the era especially those emanating from the West, the United Nations (principally UNDP, FAO, WHO, UNCTAD), the World Bank

---

[1]This chapter is a slightly updated version of a paper, Herbert Ekwe-Ekwe, "What is 'sub-Sahara Africa'?", read at the IDeoGRAMS Conference: Contemporary Media, University of Leicester, 14 September 2007.

and IMF, the so-called NGOs/"aid" groups, and some in academia who all are variously responsible for initiating and sustaining the operationalisation of this "sub-Sahara Africa" dogma.

The point is that prior to the formal restoration of African majority government in 1994, South Africa was *never designated* "sub-Sahara Africa" by anyone in this portrait, unlike the rest of the 13 African-led states in southern Africa which were also often referred to, at the time, as the "frontline states" (reference to their strategic support for the historic African liberation movement across their borders in South Africa). South Africa then was either termed "white South Africa" or the "South Africa sub-continent" (as in the "India sub-continent" usage, for instance), meaning "almost"/"partially" a continent – quite clearly a usage of "admiration" or "compliment" employed by its subscribers to essentially project and valorise the perceived geostrategic potentials or capabilities of the erstwhile European-minority population's occupation regime-led country. This occupation regime, we must recall, was a socioeconomic and strategic ally of the West.

But soon after the triumph of the African freedom movement there, South Africa became "sub-Sahara Africa" in the quickly adjusted schema of this representation! What happened suddenly to South Africa's geography to be so differently classified? Is it *African liberation/rule* that renders an African state "sub-Sahara"?[2]

Interestingly, just as in the hitherto South Africa "sub-continent" example, i.e., prior to African restoration-of-independence, the application of the "almost"/"partially" or indeed "part of"/"partly" meaning of prefix "sub-" to "Sahara Africa" focuses unambiguously on the following countries of Africa: Morocco, Algeria, Tunisia, Libya and Egypt, each of which has 25-75 per cent of its territory (especially to the south) covered by the Sahara Desert. It also focuses on Mauritania, Mali, Niger, Chad and the Sudan, which variously have 25-75 per cent of their territories (to the north) covered by the same desert. In effect, these ten states would make up *sub-Sahara Africa*.

Morocco, Algeria, Tunisia, Libya and Egypt, the five Arab north Africa countries, do not, correctly, describe themselves as Africans even though they *unquestionably habituate* African geography, the African continent, since the Arab conquest and occupation of this north one-third of African territory in the 7th century CE. The West governments, press and the transnational bodies we referred to earlier (which are led predominantly by West personnel and interests) have consistently "conceded" to this Arab cultural insistence on racial identity. Presumably, this accounts for the West's non-designation of its "sub-Sahara Africa" dogma to these countries as well as the Sudan, whose successive Arab-minority regimes since January 1956 have claimed, but

---

[2] Roger Tangri, *Politics in Sub-Sahara Africa* (London and Portsmouth, NH: James Currey, 1985), p. ix, *passim*.

incorrectly, that the Sudan "belongs" to the Arab World. On this subject, the West does no doubt know that what it has been engaged in, all along, is blatant sophistry, *not* science. This, however, conveniently suits its current propaganda packaging on Africa, which we shall be elaborating on shortly.

It would appear that we still don't seem to be any closer at establishing, conclusively, what its users mean by "sub-Sahara Africa". Could it, perhaps, just be a benign reference to all the countries "under" the Sahara, whatever their distances from this desert, to interrogate our final, fourth probability? Presently, there are 54 so-called sovereign states in Africa. If the five north Africa Arab states are said to be located "above" the Sahara (even though this is not factually the case as we have just shown above), then 49 are positioned "under". The latter would therefore include all the 5 countries mentioned above whose north frontiers incorporate the southern stretches of the desert (namely, Mauritania, Mali, Niger, Chad and the Sudan), countries in central Africa (the Congos, Rwanda, Burundi, etc., etc), for instance, despite being 2000-2500 miles away, and even the southern African states situated 3000-3500 miles away! In fact, all these 49 countries, *except the Sudan* (alas, not included for the plausible reason already cited), which is clearly "under" the Sahara and situated within the same latitudes as Mali, Niger and Chad (i.e., between 10 and 20 degrees north of the equator), are all categorised by the "sub-Sahara Africa" users as "sub-Sahara Africa".

"Sub-"s of the world?

To replicate this obvious farce of a classification elsewhere in the world, the following random exercise is not such an indistinct scenario for universal, everyday referencing:

1. Australia hence becomes "sub-Great Sandy Australia" after the hot deserts that cover much of west and central Australia

2. East Russia, east of the Urals, becomes "sub-Siberia Asia"

3. China, Japan and Indonesia are reclassified "sub-Gobi Asia"

4. Bhutan, Nepal, Pakistan, India, Sri Lanka, Bangladesh, Myanmar, Thailand, Laos, Cambodia and Vietnam become "sub-Himalaya Asia"

5. All of Europe is "sub-Arctic Europe"

6. Most of England, central and southern counties, is renamed "sub-Pennines Europe"

7. East/southeast France, Italy, Slovenia, Croatia are "sub-Alps Europe"

8. The Americas become "sub-Arctic Americas"

9. All of South America, south of the Amazon, is proclaimed "sub-Amazon South America"; Chile could be "sub-Atacama South America"

10. Most of New Zealand's South Island is renamed "sub-Southern Alps New Zealand"

11. Mexico, Guatemala, Honduras, Nicaragua, Costa Rica and Panama become "sub-Rocky North America"

12. The entire Caribbean becomes "sub-Appalachian Americas"

African peoples-centred scholarship

So, rather than some benign construct, "sub-Sahara Africa" is, in the end, an outlandish nomenclatural code that its users employ to depict an *African-led* "sovereign" state – anywhere in Africa, as distinct from an Arab-led one. It is the very possibility of the unfettered freedom of the peoples of Africa from centuries of European World conquest, subjugation and expropriation that the promoters of this epithet dread. It is the users' non-inclusion of the Sudan in the "sub-Sahara Africa" grouping (despite its majority African population and geographical location) but its inclusion of South Africa only after the latter's 1994 liberation that gives the game away. More seriously to the point, "sub-Sahara Africa" is employed to create the stunning effect of a supposedly shrinking African geographical landmass in the popular imagination, coupled with the continent's supposedly attendant geostrategic global "irrelevance", precisely during an age when Africans are not only *net-exporters* of capital to the West World, but African émigré in the West and elsewhere in the world outside Africa are now the *principal exporters* of capital *back* to Africa – as indeed a 2003 World Bank study clearly shows: in this year, these émigrés transferred the gargantuan sum of US$200 billion to Africa, investing directly in their communities.³ On the crucial subject of Africa's landmass, no amount of racist profiling and propaganda can eradicate the overwhelming scientific data on the ground. Africa's landmass is 30,301,596 sq km. This figure is more than the combined land masses of Western Europe, the United States, Argentina, China and India which amount to 29,843,826 sq km.⁴

"Sub-Sahara Africa" is undoubtedly a *racist geopolitical signature* in which its users aim repeatedly to present the imagery of some ever shrinking landmass, the desolation, aridity, "hopelessness" of a desert environment. This is despite the fact that the overwhelming majority of 1 billion peoples of African do not live anywhere close to the Sahara, nor are their lives so affected by the implied impact of the very loaded meaning that this dogma intends to convey. Except this steadily pervasive use of "sub-Sahara Africa" is robustly challenged by rigorous African-centred scholarship and publicity work, its proponents will succeed, eventually, in substituting the name of the continent "Africa" with "sub-Sahara Africa" and the name of its peoples, Africans, with "sub-Sahara Africans" or, worse still, "sub-Saharans" in the realm of public memory and reckoning.

***

---

³World Bank, "Migrant Labor Remittances in Africa", *Africa Regional Paper Series, No. 64*, Washington, November 2003, p. 12.

⁴"Africa in perspective",
https://www.google.co.uk/search?q=africa+map+compared+to+other+countries&tbm=isch&tbo=u&source=univ&sa=X&ved=2ahUKEwio-7ful_LcAhVkBMAKHS6dAhUQ7Al6BAgGEBs&biw=1517&bih=735#imgrc=DGoUNL5suyscGM, accessed 6 July 2009.

5 REMINDER: WHAT "CIVIL WAR" ISN'T[1]

The oxymoron "civil war" is a strange beast indeed. It neither describes what, by any imagination, is "civil" about it nor does it elucidate on the salient features of the nature or character and range of its being. All that "civil war" connotes is that it is an "internal war" – occurring within a seemingly sovereign state, which, in the Africa case, would be a reference to its "Berlin state(s)". Its opposite, supposedly, is the "inter-state war".

Since the beginning of the presumed restoration-of-African independence epoch in the Sudan in January 1956, "inter-state wars" in Africa are in fact an exception – just a handful, not more than five! Even here, the genesis of, for instance, the Ethiopia-Eritrea War (May 1998-June 2000), one of the five, is located in the "internal" wars of old, imperial Ethiopia. If one were therefore to follow this "internal war"/"external war" dichotomy-characterisation of armed conflicts in Africa during this epoch, the overwhelming majority of the 15 million Africans who have lost their lives, since the 1966-1970 Igbo genocide, the foundational genocide of post-(European)conquest Africa, would be designated as having died in "internal wars".[2]

Recognisable

Scholars and others who promote the "civil war" tag particularly in Africa have often done so merely to privilege the extant "Berlin-state" configuration and its principal or "dominant" protagonist in the conflict ("state", "government", "central government", "federal government", etc., etc.) over oppositional or insurgent protagonists often cast as "regionalists", "secessionists", "rebels" or worse. The trend is to be restricted or trapped in a quaint juridical fidelity of discourse under the overarching, essentially sanitising banner of "civil war" without confronting the much more expansive turbulence of underlying history emplaced.[3]

---

[1]This chapter was a commentary first published in *Rethinking Africa*, 27 July 2015.
[2]Ekwe-Ekwe, *Biafra Revisited*, pp. 1-17.
[3]Ibid.

If most of the 15 million Africans already referred to died in "internal wars", then "civil war" proponents' primary quest to preserve the "Berlin-state" status quo ironically problematises the latter's existence as this "Berlin-state", in Africa, is a *murder-machine*... The salutary lesson from this is obvious: rather than try to obfuscate or sanitise a human-made catastrophe, call it by its instantly, recognisable name!

Besides a reference to a territoriality and its constituent peoples in Africa, there is nothing else *internal* about "internal wars" in Africa. As the Igbo genocide, for example, demonstrates, this crime against humanity would most unlikely have occurred without the central role played by Britain, Nigeria's suzerain state, an *external* power situated 3000 miles away – right from its conceptualisation to execution.[4]

***

---

[4]See chap. 7 in this book.

II Igbo genocide of post-(European) conquest Africa

Flag of Republic of Biafra

The longest genocide

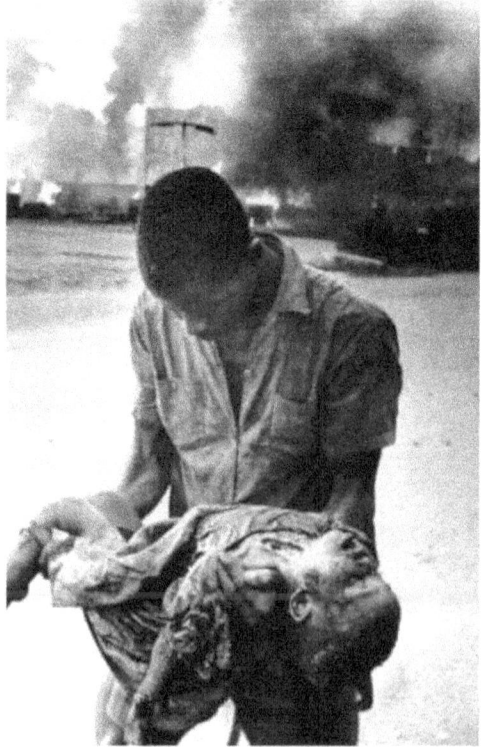

(**First and second level pictures:** cabal of genocidist operatives – left-right from the top: **Benjamin Adekunle** ["We shoot at everything that moves, and when our forces march into the centre of I{g}bo territory, we shoot at everything, even at things that don't move"], **Obafemi Awolowo** [chief genocidist "theorist", "All is fair in war and starvation is one of the weapons of war"] **Olusegun Obasanjo** [commander of genocidist forces in Biafra south panhandle whose forces murder hundreds of thousands of Igbo in towns and villages; on 5 June 1969, Obasanjo orders his air force to shoot down an International Committee of Red Cross plane flying in urgent relief to the encircled and bombarded Igbo and later expresses perverse satisfaction of this crime in his memoirs: "The effect of [this] singular achievement of the Air Force especially on 3 Marine Commando Division {name of the death squad Obasanjo, who subsequently becomes head of Nigeria regime for 11 years, commands} was profound. It raised morale of all service personnel, especially of the Air Force detachment concerned and the troops they supported in {my} 3 Marine Commando Division"], **Muhammadu Buhari** [commander of genocidist forces in northcentral Biafra where his forces murder tens of thousands of Igbo in towns of villages and who, in March 2015, is imposed on Nigeria as head of regime by former US President Obama and former British Prime Minister Cameron] and **Murtala Mohammed** [commander of the genocidist brigade which carried out the programmed slaughter of hundreds of Igbo male, boys and men, in Asaba, west Biafra, 7 October 1967])

Middle (lower level) picture: **Igbo genocide memorial**, Asaba, west Biafra.

Left: **murdered Igbo child as genocide rages**)

6 BRITAIN, ABURI ACCORDS, GHANA, IGBO GENOCIDE

I have argued variously that without the ferociously pursued British military, diplomatic and political support to its client Fulani islamist/jihadist-controlled Nigeria state in southwestcentral Africa, right from the outset, the Igbo genocide, this foundational genocide of post-(European)conquest Africa, would probably not have occurred.[1] Definitely, the Nigerians would not have embarked on this phase-III of the genocide, the direct invasion of Igboland, Biafra, beginning on 6 July 1967, without receiving firm support for the operation from Britain. Robert Scott, who was a British military advisor on the invasion, later broke ranks with his employer, to acknowledge, gravely, that as the Nigerians unleashed their attacks on Biafran towns and villages, they were the "best defoliant agent known".[2] Three million Igbo people were slaughtered during the course of the 30-month stretch of invasion.

Resilience despite catastrophe

Earlier on, 100,000 Igbo had been murdered by the genocidists in waves after waves of meticulously-coordinated savage campaigns across the entire north region of Nigeria as well as in parts of the country's Yoruba/west, Lagos and midwest regions during phases I and II of the slaughter – 29 May 1966-5 July 1967. Two million Igbo survived and escaped from these killing fields and returned to the east. Such a sudden influx of displaced people was a major task that confronted the Chukwuemeka Odumegwu Ojukwu government in Enuugwu. The resources of the east had been stretched extensively between 29 May 1966 and 31 December 1966 after it allocated £3 million in emergency funding for the expansion of housing units, office space, schools, and recreation facilities to cope with the returnees. Thanks to the region's booming economy and the remarkable intervention of its extended-family system in

---

[1]See, for instance, chap. 20 in this book.
[2]*Daily Telegraph*, London, 11 January 1970.

"absorbing" a high proportion of the welfare needs of the returnees, the east was able to avert what was potentially a major humanitarian catastrophe. Unlike the distressful imagery often associated with comparable emergencies in contemporary Africa, there was no *outside aid* involved in this extraordinarily resourceful and successful resettlement programme – not from the Organisation of African Unity, not from the United Nations, and not least from the Yakubu Gowon military junta in Lagos that had itself coordinated the genocide from the end of July 1966. Biafrans and the rest of Africa must be proud of this thrust of resilience.

It was against this background of the brazen brutalisation of Igbo people by fellow compatriots that the head of neighbouring Ghana's military administration, General Joseph Ankrah, invited Ojukwu, Gowon and the rest of the surviving members of Nigeria's pre-Igbo genocide governing military council to Aburi, Ghana, in January 1967 to discuss the Nigerian débâcle. Just prior to the Aburi invitation (the previous month, December 1966), Ojukwu had turned down a British-sponsored "conference of mediation" that would involve all members of the same council on board a British frigate, off the Bight of Biafra, in which the British would chair. The east governor could not accept the presumption of "neutrality" or "even-handedness" inherent in London's invitation to host such a summit, considering Britain's *instrumental* role in the Igbo genocide since the weeks and months leading to the outbreak in May 1966, especially its work with the Yakubu Gowon-Yakubu Danjuma-Murtala Muhammed genocidist cells in the Nigeria military, the north region Fulani islamist/jihadist emirs and, pivotally, with staff and students at the Ahmadu Bello University, the epicentre of the planning and execution of the genocide. Furthermore, Ojukwu, the historian, could not have ignored the lessons of a similar event in the 19th century, 1887. Then, King Jaja of Igwe Nga (Opobo), the Igbo nationalist monarch opposed to British territorial aggression and expansionism along the Atlantic coast of Igboland, was kidnapped by the British navy and exiled to the Caribbean island of St Vincent after accepting, in good faith, a British offer of "peace talks" on board a British vessel berthed off the Igwe Nga shores – Bight of Biafra.

Extraordinary

The Aburi African-led and controlled diplomatic initiative and resultant summit are indeed extraordinary, the likes of which we haven't seen on the African political scene since. After two days of talks, 4-5 January 1967, the delegates achieved an exceptional degree of agreement, in spite of the genocide of the previous seven months. A brief examination of the key points of the agreement underscores our conclusion. Two areas require comment. First, the resolution that focuses on the renouncement of force and the importation of arms: (1) "renounce the use of force as a means of settling the present crisis in Nigeria"³ (2) "agree that there should be no more importation of arms and ammunition until normalcy [is] restored".⁴ Second, the provisions that deal with the ruling military council of which Gowon had declared himself "supreme commander" since he seized power (29 July 1966) during the course of the genocide and the reorganisation of the army. Four articles are relevant here: (1) "military is to be governed by the Supreme Military Council"⁵ (2) "creation of area command corresponding with the existing region and under the charge of an area commander"⁶ (3) "during the period of the military government, military governors will have control over their area commands on matters of internal security"⁷ (4) "agree that any decision affecting the whole country must be determined by the Supreme Military Council and where a meeting is not possible such a matter must be referred to military governors for comment and concurrence".⁸

Peer-review: "cleverest", "compulsive-logic"

In effect, the Aburi decision to transfer the constitutional responsibility of the Nigeria military from the position of the supreme commander to the supreme military council extensively limited the executive (and legislature) powers of the position of "supreme commander and head of state" which Gowon had exercised since the genocide (these powers were originally contained in General Aguyi-Ironsi's January 1966 decree no.1 which had made the occupant of that office, and not the SMC, the principal person in charge of decision making in the country). In future, following the Aburi accord, "any decision affecting the *whole* country must be decided by the Supreme Military Council" (added emphasis) – namely, the eight members that made up the body gathered in Ghana including, pointedly, the military governors of the regions of which Ojukwu, the only member that had refused to recognise genocidist Gowon in that position, was one.

It is of immense significance that this provision on the new powers of the SMC also states that "where a meeting [of the SMC] is not possible such a matter must be referred to military governors for *comment and concurrence*" (added emphasis).⁹ This

---

³*The meeting of the Supreme Military Council – at Aburi, Accra, Ghana, 4-5 January 1967* (Enugu: Government Printer, 1967), http://www.biafraland.com/aburi_minutes.htm, accessed 12 February 2011.
⁴Ibid.
⁵Ibid.
⁶Ibid.
⁷Ibid.
⁸Ibid.
⁹Ibid.

referral procedure was aimed evidently at meeting Ojukwu's contention, repeatedly stated throughout the meeting, that he would not attend any meetings in Nigeria where the Nigerian military, which had played *the* central role in the prosecution of the Igbo genocide, was positioned and operating. Ojukwu had in fact converted the Aburi gathering into a peer-review session, unprecedented in recent African history. Here at Aburi, an African leader bluntly told his colleagues, who only 18 months earlier would have all shared the conviviality of an officers' mess or one of the other's residence to wine and dine, that he had no confidence in them and the troops they commanded because they had been involved in the perpetration of a genocide that claimed the lives of 100,000 Africans within seven months. This was indeed an historic rendezvous. It would take another 40 years for the world at large to increasingly begin to lecture African leaders to openly condemn crimes committed by one of their own.

Back to Aburi (1967), Ojukwu had laid bare, for the crucial reckoning of African history, the apposite moral and juridical dilemma surrounding the status of lead-genocidist leader Yakubu Gowon. Ojukwu had insisted at the talks that Gowon *must neither be seen nor aided by his peers to appropriate the position and the powers* invested in Nigeria's top political and military leadership after his perpetration of the mass murder of tens of thousands of Igbo people and the murder of General Aguyi-Ironsi, the commander-in-chief, under whom Gowon served as chief of army staff. Ojukwu's reply to a question about Gowon's status, posed by Mobalaji Johnson (governor of Lagos), was undoubtedly the turning point at Aburi. It led to the challenge and dramatic reconfiguration of Gowon's acquired position and powers that he had exercised so ruthlessly since 29 July 1966. Astonishingly, this outcome was approved and signed by *all* the eight principal participants at the meeting, including Gowon himself! – Colonel[10] Adebayo, west governor; Colonel Ejoor, midwest governor; Colonel Gowon, head of the genocidist forces in control of Lagos/west/north regions; Major Johnson, Lagos governor; Colonel Katsina, north governor; Colonel Odumegwu-Ojukwu, east governor; Mr Salem, head of the police, and Commodore Wey, head of navy.

Following objections that Ojukwu had earlier made during the proceedings to one of the participants who referred to Gowon as "supreme commander", Johnson had asked: "Is there a government in Nigeria today? Is there a central government in Nigeria today?"[11] Odumegwu-Ojukwu: "That question is such a simple one that anybody who has been listening to what I have been saying would know that I do not

---

[10] All military rank references here to the Aburi conference participants are statuses achieved and recognised prior to the outbreak of the Igbo genocide, 29 May 1966.

[11] "Transcript from tape recording of the Aburi meeting", 5-7 January 1967, https://biafran.org/implementation-of-aburi-agreements/, accessed 30 January 2011.

see a central government in Nigeria today ... [Following the genocide] Nigeria resolved itself into three areas – Lagos, West and North group, the Mid-West, the East".[12]

Ojukwu was in effect highlighting the territorial reach and distribution of the Gowon-controlled genocidist forces across the country – Lagos/west-north regions where they occupied, and the east and midwest regions, which were still free of their presence. In the light of Aburi, Gowon's overall control of the Lagos/west/north regions had in fact come under question. With the newly acquired powers of individual governors on the supreme military council at the expense of those hitherto wielded by Gowon, it followed, for instance, that the governors of Lagos, west and north (where the Gowonist forces were entrenched) would in future be expected to exercise greater powers of control in their respective regions than Gowon.

If an audio audio-recorded transcript of the entire deliberations of the Aburi conference did not exist today[13] as a treasured historic document, it would have been extremely difficult to appreciate Ojukwu's phenomenal success in persuading the rest of the participants to accept an extensively decentralised structural solution to Nigeria's crisis after the devastating first and second phases of genocide, looting, and the displacement of 2 million Igbo people. That Gowon, *himself*, appended his signature to this Ojukwu prepared text at a gathering that had, as a result of these developments, clipped his powers so extensively, was not just because the east governor was the "cleverest ... the only one who understood the real issues",[14] as writer Walter Schwarz has observed, or that the rest of the conferees were "too unserious[ly] minded to meet with Ojukwu's compulsive logic",[15] as Joe Garba, a leading genocidist officer in the Gowonist forces and Nigeria's foreign minister in the 1970s, has noted. On the contrary, Gowon and each of the other Nigerian leaders at Aburi (Adebayo, Ejoor, Johnson, Katsina, Salem, Wey – all of whom, bar Ojukwu, had recognised Gowon as "supreme commander and head of state" since end of July 1966) signed this remarkable document because they were each and collectively in awe of the frankness and rectitude of Ojukwu's strictures of them for executing such a despicable act of genocide against Igbo people during the course of 1966.

---

[12]Ibid.

[13]There are persistent indications that the east conference staff may have additionally filmed the Aburi meetings and their tape(s) are lodged safely in some archives.

[14]Quoted in Olusegun Obasanjo, *My Command* (Ibadan and London: Heinemann, 1980), p. 10.

[15]*ThisWeek*, Lagos, 13 July 1987, p. 23.

Britain, Yoruba, and them all

Overnight, the outcome of the Aburi discourses radically altered the contours of the political landscape of Nigeria. The centralising features of Aguyi-Ironsi's decree no. 34 dispensation of the previous year, since adopted by the Gowon junta despite the irony, had been abandoned. More importantly, though, the powers of the regions vis-à-vis the centre had become more enhanced – much more than at any time in Nigeria's history, even including the epoch of the feverishly-pursued British occupation's "regionalisation drive" of the 1950s. Aburi had in effect inaugurated a *confederal*, extensively decentralised constitutional solution to the Nigerian tragedy, to the consternation of the British, who had followed the talks with nervousness, the north, the military, and the central, essentially Yoruba(now)-run bureaucratic establishment in Lagos. Obafemi Awolowo, the Yoruba leader, would later join the opposition to Aburi when offered the princely position of deputy to Gowon's genocide prosecution-cabinet, effectively regime prime-minister, and head of the powerful finance ministry and "chief theorist" of the genocide campaign.

Britain rejected the Aburi outcome out of hand and began to pressurise Gowon, who for two days during the Ghana conference was out of reach from his British intelligence minders for the first time in almost a year, to renege on it. Britain was therefore pleased when the north and other interest groups in Nigeria joined in the opposition against the accord.

Gowon's ultimate renegation of an accord that he signed, willingly, in Ghana, in the presence of all the other seven members of the Nigerian governing military council, their five secretaries, and General Ankrah, their host, was a reminder, if ever such an evidence was sought, of who, eventually, called the shots at the crucial junctures of the course of the Igbo genocide: Britain. Such was the British disappointment of Gowon's performance in Aburi that they ensured that Gowon would in future no longer be "exposed" to Ojukwu or any of these Igbo with "compulsive logic". Subsequently, the often more "coherent" spokespersons who tried to put across some "form of explanation" of the Anglo/Nigerian position on the Igbo genocide, especially in Britain where there was a groundswell popular opposition to the slaughter, were from a hired pool of consultants of ex-British conquest administrators who had worked in Nigeria.

So, the Aburi critics launched a chorus of fierce opposition on the accord, forcing the Gowon junta to renege on the agreement a few days after returning to Nigeria from Ghana. The groups felt that Gowon and the rest of the non-east delegation at Aburi had capitulated to Ojukwu's uncompromising censure of his former colleagues' involvement in the Igbo genocide. As a consequence, notes the critics, Ojukwu had out-manoeuvred fellow conferees in accepting as *de jure* the increasingly autonomous political direction which the east had embarked upon in the wake of the genocide, in addition to according this same status to the other regions of Nigeria – a move that further eclipsed Gowon's powers as "head of state". But for the east, the implementation of the Aburi agreement was the minimal condition for maintaining further political links with Nigeria: "It was Aburi or a clean break with Nigeria". In a radio broadcast in Enuugwu in February 1967, Ojukwu gave notice that the east would begin to implement the Aburi agreement as from the end of March (1967) even if Gowon and the rest of the accord's signatories did not do so.[16] Gowon responded by threatening to attack the east if it went ahead to implement the agreement. Ironically, Gowon's threat was itself a clear violation of one of the key articles of the accord, which pronounced unambiguously: "renounce[d] the use of force as a means of settling the Nigerian crisis".[17] Ojukwu nonetheless went ahead to implement the Aburi accord after 31 March. This move further enhanced the virtually autonomous position that the east had had in relation to the rest of the country since, especially, and of July 1966. For his part, Gowon imposed a total economic blockade of the east. Effectively, this was the prelude to his forces' invasion, the expansion of the territorial reach of their yearlong genocidal campaign on the Igbo to Igboland, Biafra, itself.

Phase-III

This "final solution" of the "Igbo Question" had become the proffered one sought by the British and their Nigerian genocidist allies since. And they soon unleashed a cataclysmic surge of violence in Biafra in which 3 million Igbo children, women and men or 25 per cent of this nation's population were murdered by 12 January 1970.

***

---

[16]Chukwuemeka Odumegwu Ojukwu, *On Aburi we Stand: A broadcast* (Enugu: Government printer, 1967).
[17]*The meeting of the Supreme Military Council – at Aburi, Accra, Ghana, 4-5 January 1967.*

7 IGBO GENOCIDE, BRITAIN AND THE UNITED STATES

Conqueror's concord

In *Empire: What Ruling the World Did to the British*,[1] Jeremy Paxman allocates just 12 lines of his total 368-page study to British-occupied Nigeria in southwestcentral Africa. But Paxman's pithy commentary undoubtedly speaks volumes of the mindset of the occupation regime on the very eve of its presumed departure from Nigeria in October 1960. This is clearly a regime that is not prepared or willing to abandon the bounty harvest or lucre that is its Nigeria. Instead, it is exploring across a spectrum of strategies to subvert the very goal of the restoration-of-independence movement for the peoples which the Igbo, one of the constituent nations in Nigeria, had led since the 1930s. Using state archival material, Paxman presents the crux of the panoramic conversation on the subject in Lagos (Nigeria's then capital), in January 1960, between James Robertson, the outgoing occupation administrator, and visiting British Prime Minister Harold Macmillan:

MACMILLAN: Are the people fit for self-government?[2]

ROBERTSON: *No, of course not* (added emphasis).[3]

---

[1] Jeremy Paxman, *Empire: What Ruling the World Did to the British* (London: Viking, 2011).
[2] Ibid., p. 272.
[3] Ibid.

According to Paxman, James Robertson reckons that it would take "another 20 or 25 years" for Nigeria to be "*fit* for self-government".⁴ Instructively, this is the same Robertson who had, prior to his Lagos meeting with Macmillan, "concluded" the "terms" of the British "exit" from Nigeria in "negotiations" with the country's restoration-of-independence movement – begun 15 years earlier and had been chaired successively by two previous occupation administrators including sessions scheduled and held in England.⁵ This is the same Robertson who had just rigged the December 1959 countrywide elections in Nigeria (part of the restoration-of-independence "package") in favour of the Fulani north region, as Harold Smith, a member of the occupation regime in Lagos at the time, would recall years later.⁶ Furthermore, this is the same Robertson whose predecessor, in Lagos, had earlier rigged the countrywide census results – again, in favour of Britain's Hausa-Fulani north regional clients,⁷ aimed at ensuring that the latter, with a *fabricated* population majority in the country, has the "electoral clout" to safeguard for the (British)conqueror-state the vast arena of its strategic and economic assets in Nigeria in perpetuity.⁸ As this study will demonstrate, this north region constitutes the core of Britain's local clients in Nigeria, historically opposed vehemently to the restoration-of-African independence – and, therefore, the British exit! Consequently, it would play a key role in the perpetuation of the Igbo genocide which it undertakes *in concert* with Britain. Pointedly, on the broader stretch of the politics of liberation of the South World, during this post 1939-1945 war, the north Nigeria region has the unenviable accolade across this hemisphere of being home to one of the few peoples who wanted the *continuing* occupation of their lands by one of the pan-European powers of global conquest since the 15th century CE.⁹

So, given James Robertson's apparent "unfavourable prognosis" on Nigeria illustrated in *Empire*, Prime Minister Macmillan asks his administrator for advice on the way forward for the British continuing occupation of Nigeria: "What do you recommend me to do?"¹⁰

---

⁴Ibid (added emphasis).
⁵Ekwe-Ekwe, *Biafra Revisited*, pp. 27-43, 121.
⁶Harold Smith, "A squalid end to empire", New Africa, https://www.questia.com/magazine/1G1-189071322/a-squalid-end-to-empire, accessed 14 January 2016 and Ekwe-Ekwe, "Elections in Africa – the voter, the court, the outcome".
⁷Smith, "A squalid end of empire".
⁸Ekwe-Ekwe, *Biafra Revisited*, pp. 8-14 and Ekwe-Ekwe, *Readings from Reading*, pp. 1-6.
⁹Herbert Ekwe-Ekwe, "Léopold Senghor", *The Literary Encyclopedia*, 30 June 2002, https://www.litencyc.com/php/spe ple.php?rec=true&UID=5154, accessed 18 June 2015.
¹⁰Paxman, *Empire*, p. 272.

ROBERTSON: I recommend you give it to them at once.[11]

Really? Why? Doesn't Robertson's suggestion to his boss sound wholly contradictory to the tract that this conclave had trodden so far? Well, no, not really... Both prime minister and administrator have no disagreement, whatsoever, on holding onto British "interests" in Nigeria in perpetuity; they do not believe that they are necessarily bound by the "terms" of the envisaged British "exit" from Nigeria "negotiated" since 1945 even though, ironically, these had largely preserved British "interests", thanks to the *veto-power* that its Fulani north region clients would exercise in the "new" dispensation;[12] most crucially, both men *do not* subscribe to the inalienable rights of Africans to recover their conquered lands.

It is the case, though, that if the British officials were to renege on their "exit" from Nigeria at this 11th hour, they would have to contend with a serious crisis – at least in the short/medium term – right there on the ground in Nigeria: "The alternative [is] that most talented people [read: the Igbo and those others elsewhere in south Nigeria who demanded and supported the drive towards unfettered restoration-of-independence for the African peoples during these past 30 years] would become rebels and the British would spend the next two decades fighting to stave off what [is] inevitable, while incurring the opprobrium of the world".[13]

As the Lagos deliberations end, nine months before the designated British departure date (1 October 1960), both prime minister and administrator needn't agonise, too much, over the future prospects of their country's Nigeria stranglehold. After all, despite the "talented people", Britain is aware that it holds the *trump card* to defend this stranglehold via its Fulani clients. Twice in the previous 15 years (significantly, it should be noted, during those crucial years of British "negotiations" of its "exit" from Nigeria with the "talented people"), the clients organised and unleashed pogroms against Igbo people in the northcentral town of Jos (1945) and north city of Kano (1953). Hundreds of Igbo were murdered during these massacres and tens of thousands of pounds sterling worth of their property looted or destroyed.[14] No perpetrators of these murders were ever apprehended or punished by the occupation regime.

Six and one-half years hence, from Sunday 29 May 1966, these same Fulani north Nigerian British clients, with full British support, would unleash the genocide against the Igbo people. During the course of 44 months, 3.1 million Igbo children, women and men are murdered in this foundational and most gruesome genocide of post-

---

[11] Ibid.
[12] Ekwe-Ekwe, *Biafra Revisited*, pp. 40-43, 121.
[13] Paxman, *Empire*, p. 272.
[14] Ekwe-Ekwe, *Biafra Revisited*, pp. 8, 19-20.

(European)conquest Africa. The Igbo and the world suddenly realise, in retrospect, that those anti-Igbo pogroms, carried out during the years of the Anglo-"talented people"-in-Nigeria doubtful restoration-of-independence negotiations, were indeed "dress rehearsals" for the 29 May 1966-12 January 1970 Igbo genocide.

Britain plays an instrumental role in the perpetration of the genocide – politically, diplomatically and militarily, and its closest international ally, the United States, as we will soon elaborate, is fully aware of its mission. Now, a new Harold-the-prime minister, this time Harold Wilson, beginning in 1964, has no qualms about the "opprobrium of the world" considered by the other Harold during those January 1960 talks with Nigeria conqueror administrator James Robertson. Wilson's reasons are obvious: the architecture of control and execution of mass violence in Nigeria have altered, significantly, since January 1960, and the forces on the ground spearheading the Igbo genocide are the historically trusted Fulani clients in addition to their since locally expanded allies in Yoruba, Itsekiri, Edo and Urhobo west Nigeria – not Britain, directly; precisely, what Macmillan and Robertson had sought to avoid during that Lagos summit! Declassified British state papers indicate the monstrous disposition by the Wilson government, right from the outset, to saturate the Nigerian genocidist armoury on the ground with a wide range of British weapons to ensure that the murder of the Igbo is effected most comprehensively:[15]

In December 1967 ... [British Foreign] Secretary George Thomson said that "[the Nigerians] are most impressed with the Saladins and Ferrets" previously supplied by Britain. As a result Britain supplied six Saladin armoured personnel carriers (APCs), 30 Saracen APCs along with 2,000 machine guns for them, anti-tank guns and 9 million rounds of ammunition. Denis Healey, the Defence Secretary, wrote that he hoped these supplies will encourage the Nigerians "to look to the United Kingdom for their future purchases of defence equipment". By the end of the year [1967] Britain had also approved the export of 1,050 bayonets, 700 grenades, 1,950 rifles with grenade launchers, 15,000 lbs of explosives and two helicopters ... In the first half of the following year, 1968, Britain approved the export of 15 million rounds of ammunition, 21,000 mortar bombs, 42,500 Howitzer rounds, 12 Oerlikon guns, 3 Bofors guns, 500 submachine guns, 12 Saladins with guns and spare parts, 30 Saracens and spare parts, 800 bayonets, 4,000 rifles and two other helicopters. At the same time Wilson was constantly reassuring Gowon of British support for a United Nigeria, saying in April 1968 that "I think we can fairly claim that we have not wavered in this support throughout ...". British arms supplies were stepped up again in November [1968].

---

[15]Mark Curtis, "Nigeria's war over Biafra, 1967-1970", https://markcurtis.wordpress.com/2007/02/13/nigeriabiafra-1967-70/, accessed 23 May 2015.

Foreign Secretary Michael Stewart said the Nigerians could have 5 million more rounds of ammunition, 40,000 more mortar bombs and 2,000 rifles. "You may tell Gowon", Stewart instructed High Commissioner Hunt in Lagos, "that we are certainly ready to consider a further application" to supply similar arms in the future as well. He concluded: "if there is anything else for ground warfare which you... think they need and which would help speed up the end of the fighting, please let us know and we will consider urgently whether we can supply it". Other supplies agreed in November [1968], following meetings with the Nigerians included six Saladins and 20,000 rounds of ammunition for them, and stepped up monthly supplies of ammunition, amounting to a total of 15 million rounds additional to those already agreed. It was recognised by the Defence Minister that "the scale of the UK supply of small arms ammunition to Nigeria in recent months has been and will continue to be on a vast scale". The recent deal meant that Britain was supplying 36 million rounds of ammunition in the last few months alone. Britain's "willingness to supply very large quantities of ammunition", Lord Shepherd [minister of state, foreign office] noted, "meant drawing on the British army's own supplies". By the end of 1968 Britain had sold Nigeria £9 million worth of arms, £6 million of which was spent on small arms ... In March 1969 the government approved the export of 19 million rounds of ammunition, 10,000 grenades and 39,000 mortar bombs ... Two senior British RAF officers secretly visited Nigeria in August 1969 to advise the Nigerians on "how they could better prosecute the air war" ... [I]n December 1969 ... Foreign Secretary Michael Stewart was calling for stepping up military assistance including the supply of more armoured cars. These supplies by Britain, he wrote, "have undoubtedly been the most effective weapons in the ground war and have spear-headed all the major [Nigerian] advances".

So as the slaughter of the Igbo intensifies, particularly in the catastrophic months of 1968-1969, Harold Wilson, is totally unruffled as he informs Clyde Ferguson, the United States state department special coordinator for relief to Biafra, that he, Harold Wilson, "would accept a half million dead Biafrans if that was what it took" Nigeria to destroy the Igbo resistance to the genocide.[16] Such is the grotesquely expressed diminution of African life made by a supposedly leading politician of the world of the 1960s – barely 20 years after the deplorable perpetration of the Jewish genocide in Europe. As the final tally of the murder of the Igbo demonstrates, Harold Wilson probably has the perverted satisfaction of having his Nigerian clients perform far in excess of the prime minister's grim target, a subject coldly stated in Wilson's *own* memoirs where he notes that the Nigerian military, equipped zealously by Britain as we have just highlighted, expends more small arms ammunition in its campaign to achieve its annhilative mission in Biafra than the amount used by the British armed forces *"during the whole"* of the 1939-1945 war.[17] On this feature, Colonel Robert Scott, military advisor in the British diplomatic mission in Nigeria, during the genocide, acknowledges, equally gravely, that as Nigerian

---

[16]Morris, *Uncertain Greatness*, p. 122.
[17]Harold Wilson, *Labour Government, 1964-1970: A Personal Record* (London: Weidenfeld & Nicolson, 1971), p. 630, added emphasis.

genocidist military forces unleash their attacks on Biafran cities, towns and villages, they are the "best defoliant agent known".[18]

Political economy of conquest and occupation – and genocide

The independence of Africa or, more historically correct, the *re-establishment* of African independence after centuries of the European conquest and occupation, was surely to be the turning point in the history of African peoples. It would constitute the beginning of an extensive re-construction process for a continent that had for the greater part of 500 years, starting from the 15th century CE, been the target of a devastating trail of invasions, murders, mass exportations and enslavement of its peoples (chiefly in the Americas and the Caribbean), occupations and subjugations by a constellation of European World states.[19] Ultimately, Britain emerges as the lead conqueror-state-beneficiary of the occupation of Africa, having particularly seized lands with major population centres and vast and multiple natural resource emplacements across the regions of the continent: South Africa, Namibia (proxy control, post-1918 – after the defeat of Germany in 1914-1918), Zimbabwe, Botswana, Swaziland, Lesotho, Zambia, Kenya, Uganda, Tanzania (post-1918, after the defeat of Germany in 1914-1918 war), the Sudan, south Cameroon (post-1918, after the defeat of Germany in 1914-1918 war), Ghana, Sierra Leone, the Gambia, and Nigeria.[20]

Apart from South Africa, Nigeria's is Britain's most "diversified" occupied economy in Africa. This is indeed the British "most-prized land" of west Africa whose fortunes it is prepared to hold onto *with or without* the restoration of African independence. It is indeed to hold onto these fortunes that Britain becomes fully involved in the perpetration of the Igbo genocide – to "punish" the Igbo for daring to spearhead the termination of the British occupation, begun in the 1930s, and further consolidate the envisaged overseeing role of its Fulani north region allies in this evolving dispensation of the age. It is therefore important to highlight the empirical nature and range of this Nigeria "prized land" as these provide an invaluable context within which the catastrophe of the Igbo genocide is executed.

Prior to the outbreak of the 1939-1945 war, the following commodities account for nearly 90 per cent of Nigeria's "diversified" export products: rubber, cocoa, cotton, groundnuts, tin ore and columbite, beniseeds, palm-oil and palm-kernels.[21] This

---

[18]*Daily Telegraph*, London, 11 January 1970.
[19]Ekwe-Ekwe, *African Literature in Defence of History*, pp. 1-54.
[20]Ekwe-Ekwe, *Readings from Reading*, pp. 4-6.
[21]Bade Onimode, *Imperialism and Underdevelopment in Nigeria: The Dialectic of Mass Poverty* (London: Zed Books, 1982), pp. 47-55.

"diversification" occurs as a result of the size of the country, stretching from the south on the Atlantic Ocean shorelines of southwestcentral Africa to the deciduous/savannah vegetation belt of the north hinterland bordering on the Sahel, which ensures that the conquest regime can maximally exploit the varying climatic zones across the territory in its choice of which agricultural products it wishes to grow.

Expectedly, such choices are dictated fundamentally by the imperatives of the British economy *and not* Nigeria's. In this regard, the immediate post-war British reconstruction programme is highly illustrative. The occupied Nigerian economy responds to this emergency, 3500 miles away, by embarking on the intensification of the production of both the country's agricultural and mineralogical commodities listed above. In 1946, the value of Nigerian exports to Britain is £23.7 million.[22] By 1955, it is £129.8 million and in 1960, the year of the supposed restoration of independence, it is £165.5 million.[23] There is a distinct growth in Nigeria's gross domestic product during the period, an annual rate of 4.1 per cent in 1950/51-1957/58.[24] Indeed, not since 1916 had Nigeria enjoyed a favourable net-barter terms of trade with Britain as recorded between 1951-1958, and 1958-1960.[25] Consequently, the huge sum of £276.8 million, the preponderant chunk of the surpluses that accumulated from this unprecedented boom is transferred from Nigeria to Britain between 1947 and 1960.[26] This is not to mention British surpluses enjoyed by the corresponding increases in the value of Nigerian imports from mainly Britain at the time: £19.8 million in 1946, £136.1 million in 1955, and £215.9 million in 1960.[27]

Besides, Britain's more advantageous trade relations with Nigeria is further consolidated in 1955 when Europe slumps into an economic recession. The prices that Europeans are prepared to pay for imports of agricultural and mineral products from abroad fall considerably resulting in an instant blow to the Nigerian economy. Even though its export trade that year increases by 7000 tons in volume, the value falls by £17 million.[28] The result is a further increase in Nigeria's import bills. While a "buoyant" Nigerian economy with its dominant reliance on the British economy for imports is clearly an advantage for Britain, especially at a time of recession at home,

---

[22] R Olufemi Ekundare, *An Economic History of Nigeria: 1860-1960* (London: Methuen, 1973), p. 225.
[23] Ibid.
[24] Onimode, *Imperialism and Underdevelopment in Nigeria*, p. 48.
[25] Ibid.
[26] Ekundare, *An Economic History of Nigeri*a, p. 226.
[27] Ibid.
[28] Okwudiba Nnoli, "A Short History of Nigerian Underdevelopment", in Okwudiba Nnoli, ed., *Path to Nigerian Development* (Dakar: Codesria, 1981) p. 124.

the enormous strain on Nigeria's own accounting is becoming severe. Not only does the country incur deficits in its balance of payments position, it also draws heavily from its external reserves.[29] Such is the situation that Nigeria allocates at least one-fifth of the total investment bill earmarked for the 1955/56-1961/62 development plan to be financed from abroad.[30] While the total investment by leading Western companies (predominately British) in Nigeria stands at about £11.7 million in 1954, the figure for 1959/1960 is £20.5 million.[31]

Twenty years later, on the eve of the Igbo genocide in 1966, the "diversification" character of the Nigerian economy virtually comes to an end. Even though Nigeria had since become "independent", it is acutely significant that the prevailing export product, petroleum, which has now displaced the basket of commodities of economic "diversification" enumerated above, shares an equivalent quota of the country's export trade (90 per cent) as the latter did in the 1940s/early 1950s. As should be expected, the production and marketing of petroleum, this commodity now central in the Nigerian economy, are dictated principally by the needs of the British economy.

Whether as "monocultural" or "dualcultural", formally occupied or nominally "independent", the essential logic and character of this Nigeria economy remains to serve the interests of Britain. Apart from South Africa, Nigeria is now the site of Britain's highest economic and industrial investment in Africa with the total worth of £1.5 billion. The British success story is phenomenal. The British government controls a near-50 per cent shares in Shell-BP (the predominant oil prospecting company in Nigeria) and 60 per cent shares in Amalgamated Tin Mining, a major prospecting tin, cobalt and iron ore mining company.[32] In the non-mining sector of the economy, John Holt, owned by a British family, is one of the two largest in the country with branches located in the principal towns and cities. The United Africa Company (UAC), another British enterprise, accounts for about 40 per cent of Nigeria's entire import and export trade. The UAC is the major African subsidiary of Unilever, the British transnational corporation. It developed from the Royal Niger Company, which, in association with Taubman Goldie, the entrepreneur, and Frederick Lugard, the first British occupation administrator, harnessed the British conquest of the number of states in this southwestcentral territorial stretch of West Africa between 1886 and 1941, and converted them into the amorphous political entity called Nigeria.[33] The UAC, for its

---

[29]Ibid.
[30]Ibid.
[31]Ibid.
[32]William Freund, "Theft and social protest among tin miners in northern Nigeria", Donal Crummey, ed, *Banditry, Rebellion and Social Protest in Africa* (London and Portsmouth, New Hampshire: James Currey/Heinemann, 1986), pp. 49-63.
[33]Ikenna Nzimiro, "The political implications of multinational corporations in Nigeria", Carl Widstrand, ed., *Multi-National Firms in Africa* (Dakar and Uppsala: African Institute for

part, has wholesale and retailing enterprises run in most parts of Nigeria by its numerous subsidiaries, among which the following three are most prominent: Kingsway Chemist, G.B. Ollivant, and African Timber and Plywood.[34] In addition, the UAC has part interest in other well-established companies in the country such as Gulf Oil of Nigeria, Nigerian Prestressed Concrete, Nigerian Breweries, Taylor Woodrow, and Nigelec. Ikenna Nzimiro's often-quoted aphorism, "UAC was Nigeria and Nigeria was UAC", does not therefore exaggerate UAC's effective control of Nigeria's economy at the time.[35] Finally, in the finance sector, Barclays Nigeria (subsidiary of the British Barclays Bank) and Standard Bank Nigeria (owned largely by the British Lloyds Bank and Westminster Bank) control 90 per cent of Nigeria's effective banking system. Once again, these institutions have branches across the country. The 25,000 Britons resident in Nigeria are employed in this extensive network of businesses and related services in the economy.

Igbo, restoration-of-independence, pogrom, genocide

Believing our country is rightfully entitled to liberty and prosperous life ... and determined to work in unity for the realisation of ultimate goal of self-government ... (part of conference communique at the formal launch of Nigeria's lead restoration-of-independence party, the National Council of Nigeria and Cameroons [NCNC], Lagos, 26 August 1944.[36]

Nine months before the end of the 1939-1945 war, as the above declaration shows, the National Council of Nigeria and the Cameroons, the lead restoration-of-independence political party in Nigeria whose principal leaders consisted of notable Igbo intellectuals most of whom were educated in the United States, *not* Britain, had, in an historic move announcing its formation, *forced to the open* the important question of the restoration-of-the-independence of African peoples in Nigeria from the British occupation. This is undoubtedly a momentous development in the peoples' consciousness and aspirations, with its membership drawn across the country including cultural associations of constituent nations, trades' and students' unions, women's organisations, and the youth.

On 22 June 1945, Nigerian workers declare a countrywide strike to back their demands for an increase in wages and improvement in the ever deteriorating conditions of the people made worse by the ongoing war. The strike virtually paralyses

---

Economic Development and Planning/Scandinavia Institute for African Affairs, 1975), pp. 210-243
[34] Ibid., pp. 212-214.
[35] Ibid., p. 217.
[36] James Coleman, *Nigeria* (Berkeley: University of California, 1958), p. 264.

Nigeria's economic life. It goes on for 44 days in the Lagos capital district, but even longer elsewhere in the country – up to 52 days in some places in the regions. The NCNC and the restoration-of-independence press (particularly the vanguard *West African Pilot* and *Daily Comet*, both edited by Nnamdi Azikiwe, then secretary-general of the NCNC) support the strike, underlying the increasingly evident cooperation between the trade unions and the emerging African political leadership in working towards the country's liberation. The strike is the most far-reaching mobilisation of labour in occupied Nigeria and its political implications are not lost on the occupation regime.

It is evident that "Nigerians, when organised", as James Coleman has noted on the impact and significance of the countrywide shutdown, "had great power, that they could defy the white bureaucracy, that they could virtually control strategic centres throughout the country, and that through force or the threat of force they could compel the government to grant concessions".[37] While the regime agrees to enter into negotiations with the workers after the strike is called off, it nonetheless seeks to destroy the huge "political dividend" of liberation consciousness that the shutdown has generated across the country. Earlier on, it had proscribed the circulation of the *West African Pilot* and the *Daily Comet*, and accused editor Nnamdi Azikiwe and Igbo people for engineering the strike.[38] Having exerted its influence on its Fulani north region clients not to participate in the strike, the regime's propaganda on alleged Igbo responsibility for the event becomes an instigator prop to Fulani leaders' organised massacres of Igbo immigrants in Jos and the surrounding tin mining towns and villages in October 1945. Hundreds of Igbo are murdered during the pogrom and tens of thousands of pounds sterling worth of their property looted or destroyed. No perpetrators of these murders are apprehended or punished by the regime. As a result, emboldened Fulani leaders organise yet another pogrom of Igbo immigrants in the north, this time in Kano, in May 1953. In carefully orchestrated attacks that rage uninterruptedly for four days, mobs of Fulani youth attack Igbo population centres across the city. Scores of Igbo people are murdered during the period. Hundreds of thousands of pounds worth of Igbo business enterprises, homes, schools and recreational centres are looted or destroyed. These latest attacks coincide with the heightened debates among Nigerian politicians on the possible date for the formal termination of the British occupation and the restoration of independence. In contrast to the Igbo and other nations in the south who favour the year 1956, the north, with total British connivance, as expected, is vehemently opposed to any such dates. Essentially, the north unleashes the Igbo pogrom in Kano to scuttle these debates –

---

[37]Ibid., p. 259.
[38]Okwudiba Nnoli, *Ethnic Politics in Nigeria* (Enugu: Fourth Dimension Publishers, 1980), pp. 122, 234-235.

which it succeeds in doing, with *evident* British relief and satisfaction. As in Jos, the occupation regime does not apprehend or prosecute anyone for these massacres and destruction. But even more ominous for the future of the Igbo in Nigeria, these Kano attacks are a *portent* of the genocide of the Igbo by Nigeria, beginning in May 1966, in which a total of 3.1 million Igbo are murdered during the course of subsequent 44 months.

In August 1966, the third month into the genocide, Britain is elated with its success in overcoming a potentially strategic rupture with its Fulani clients on the ground on the critical question of the territorial reach or extent of the ongoing murder mission. The Fulani-led Nigeria military and civilian-assisted brigades which had by now murdered tens of thousands of Igbo across north and west Nigeria (during this first phase of the genocide) and forced two million Igbo survivors to take flight to their east region Biafra homeland,[39] were on the verge of formally declaring their Arewa Republic from Nigeria. Genocidist commander Yakubu Gowon had already, correctly, informed the world in a 1 August 1966 radio broadcast that "there was no basis of Nigerian unity".[40] Subsequently, his troops began to fly their Arewa "independence" flag over their headquarters in Lagos as a prelude to evacuating/transferring their military contingent/other residual assets in west Nigeria to their north homeland. These north troops were *nowhere* in the east region or Biafra (300 miles away) at this time and they had no plans, evidently, to extend their killing fields there. From all indications, the genocidists appeared satisfied that they were now on the verge of completing the murder of all Igbo living in their *controlled* Nigeria territory and would have thus reckoned their mission accomplished...

But the British government thinks otherwise... The British government is adamant that the east region, now under *de facto* control by the Igbo "talented people", *should also* be *taken over* by its Fulani north clients as this is the political geography (mapped out above) that ensures that Britain's overarching economic and strategic interests in southwestcentral Africa remain intact. In other words, the British government feels that a Fulani north region "departure" from Nigeria "robs" the conqueror power of its historical potent overseer African-based nurtured force to protect its stranglehold economy that is Nigeria, as we have demonstrated. Britain requires *this* Fulani north region client on the ground to fight to safeguard its interest precisely because it wishes to avoid "incurring the opprobrium of the world"[41] by fighting freedom-quest Africans *more openly and directly* in the mid-1960s. Furthermore, Britain argues that such a "departure" couldn't be beneficial to the long term interests of its genocidist

---

[39] Ekwe-Ekwe, *Readings from Reading*, pp. 75-76.
[40] Obi Ebbe, *Broken Back Axle* (Bloomington: Xlibris, 2010), p. 23.
[41] Paxman, *Empire*, p. 272.

clients either: "Secession would be an economic disaster [for the north]";[42] "Without the Igbo, there is no Nigeria. They [the Igbo] have the skilled manpower that held Nigeria together and they have the resources"[43] Francis Cumming-Bruce, the British chief representative in Nigeria, is charged to communicate his government's view on this subject to the Fulani emirs, that notorious grouping of the north region power bloc responsible for launching the ongoing genocide (and the 1940s/1950s Igbo pogroms). As the following quoted reference attests, Cumming-Bruce's intervention is robustly forthright and it is important to quote him directly at some length:[44]

[I]t wasn't on the face of it easy to get them (the North) to change, but I managed to do it overnight. I drafted letters to the British Prime Minister, to send to Gowon [genocidist commander] ... and for my secretary of state (Michael Stewart) to send letters to each of the Emirs. I wrote an accompanying letter to each of them *because I knew them personally*. I drafted all these and they came back to me duly authorised to push at once. The whole thing was done overnight and it did the trick of stopping them (the North) dividing Nigeria up.

So, by promptly agreeing to British demands to abandon their planned secession from Nigeria in August 1966, the Fulani north region genocidists effectively *became available* to extend their murder campaign to Igboland as a way of securing the country for Britain – i.e., without Britain apparently "incurring the opprobrium of the world".[45] Cumming-Bruce's spirited intervention, contacting key Fulani emir genocidist operatives he "knew ... personally" had indeed done "the trick". Britain would forthwith back this expansive stretch of wholesale murder militarily, politically and diplomatically. Pointedly, Foreign Secretary Michael Stewart, one of the pivotal British officials involved in the Cumming-Bruce deliberations with the north emirs, told the British parliament in one of its numerous debates on the campaign that his government was probably the only country in the world that could not cease its support for the Nigerian mission against the Igbo.[46]

If ever there were any doubts about British intentions on this genocide, since its outbreak in May (1966), it was now clear that the architect of what scholars of the genocide describe as its "phase-III"[47] or the invasion of Igboland or Biafra was essentially none other than Britain. Yet again, on the African scene, as history has shown so catastrophically since the early 1900s, the European conqueror-power on the continent can also double up as a *genocide-power*. In centrally initiating this

---

[42]Michael Gould, *The Biafran War* (London: IB Tauris, 2011), p. 43.
[43]Ebbe, *Broken Back Axle*, p. 23.
[44]Gould, *The Biafran War*, p. 23 (added emphasis).
[45]Paxman, *Empire*, p. 272.
[46]Suzanne Cronje, *The World and Nigeria* (London: Sidgwick and Jackson, 1972), p. 38.
[47]Ekwe-Ekwe, *Readings from Reading*, pp. 86-91.

follow-up phase of the Igbo genocide after August 1966 which would result in the slaughter of 3 million Igbo people, one-quarter of this nation's population, Britain joins Belgium (1878-1908) and Germany (1904-1907) in perpetrating a state-organised genocide against a constituent nation in its occupied African country. In the case of Belgium, during the period, King Leopold II-led Belgian monarchy/state forces organised the genocide of African constituent nations in the Congo basin (central Africa) in which a total of 13 million Africans were murdered.[48] Between 1904 and 1907, Germany carried out the genocide of the Herero, Nama and Berg Damara peoples as it sought to "consolidate" its conquest and occupation of contemporary Namibia. The Germans murdered 65,000 Herero or 80 per cent of the population, 10,000 Nama or 50 per cent of the population, and approximately 30 per cent of Berg Damara people at the time.[49] In April 1994, France, another leading European conqueror power in Africa would join this league of genocide-powers of Africa in the complicity of its military forces based in Rwanda in the genocide against the Tutsi people organised by the country's central government, a close ally of the French government.[50]

Britain is so determined to pursue phase-III of the Igbo genocide, in the wake of the Cumming-Bruce-Fulani emirs north Nigeria accord, that it flagrantly intervenes to scotch a last minute west African regional peace mediatory initiative, led by neighbouring Ghana, to halt any further territorial expansion of the ongoing slaughter. In January 1967, Ghana's head of state invited both the genocidist leadership in Lagos and the Biafran resistance leadership in Igboland to a 2-day closed-door emergency summit in Accra to discuss the tragedy. The outcome of the meeting is extraordinary, the likes of which have not been seen on the African political scene since. After two days of talks, 4-5 January 1967, the delegates achieved an exceptional degree of agreement in spite of the genocide of the previous seven months. They inaugurated a *confederal*, extensively decentralised constitutional framework solution as basis for the future direction of the country.[51] In effect, the regions, including, especially, the east region, acquired more enhanced powers vis-à-vis the centre in Lagos, foreclosing any "legal grounds" for that British plot, hammered out by ambassador Cumming-Bruce, to extend the Igbo killing fields to Igboland. In addition, the delegates unanimously endorsed two areas of agreement that were particularly important to the pressing question of halting the genocide: (1) "renounce the use of force as a means of settling the present crisis in Nigeria" and (2) "agree that there should be no more importation of arms and ammunition until normalcy [is]

---

[48]Isidore Ndaywel è Nziem, *Histoire générale du Congo: De l'héritage ancien à la République Démocratique* (Paris: Duculot, 1998), p. 344.
[49]Horst Drechsler, *"Let Us Die Fighting": The Struggle of the Herero and Nama against German Imperialism, 1884-1915*, (London: Zed, 1980).
[50]Linda Melvern, *Conspiracy to Murder: The Rwandan Genocide* (London: Verso, 2006).
[51]Ekwe-Ekwe, *Readings from Reading*, pp. 79-86.

restored."⁵² All the eight delegates in attendance to these talks, including genocidist commander Yakubu Gowon and Biafra's Chukwuemeka Odumegwu-Ojukwu, signed this historic outcome which was duly witnessed by Ghana's President Joseph Ankrah.

Suddenly, for the first time since 29 May 1966, the agreement reached in the Ghana summit radically altered the contours of the political landscape of Nigeria. But Britain rejected the agreement outright and embarked on pressurising Gowon (and other segments of the north leadership), who for two days, during the Ghana conference, was out of reach from his British intelligence minders for the first time in almost a year, to renege on it. Britain was therefore pleased when Gowon and the north scuttled the agreement just a few days after. Gowon's ultimate renegation of an accord that he signed, willingly, in Ghana, in the presence of all the other seven conferees, their five secretaries, and President Ankrah, their host, was a reminder, if ever such an evidence was sought, of who, eventually, called the shots at the crucial junctures of the course of the Igbo genocide: Britain.

Additionally, Britain must have felt most delighted at this stage of this increasingly deteriorating tragedy that its uncompromisingly steadfast position to safeguard its interests in Nigeria, even at the cost of the *continuing genocide* of the Igbo people, received a decisive boost from one of its closest allies – the United States. Elbert Matthews, the US ambassador in Nigeria, publicly supported the Cummings-Bruce initiative with the Fulani north emirs, indicating, quite bluntly, albeit prosaically, that the conflict was "essentially a Nigerian, African and (British) Commonwealth matter".⁵³ Even though the US would hence claim a position of "neutrality"⁵⁴ as this tragedy intensified, such a disposition ideally suited the British government. But what does US "neutrality" over an ongoing genocide, the first since the Jewish genocide of the 1930s-1940s in Europe and the first since the historic 1948 UN genocide Convention really mean? Some background analysis of the overarching US policy direction towards Africa, especially since the end of the 1939-1945 war, is important to answer this question.

The US: European-occupied Africa, "grand area" planners, genocide

In the early 1940s, as the war raged, two important institutions of the United States government, the Council on Foreign Relations and the War-Peace Study Group, embarked on an extensive study to examine the nature and possibilities of

---

⁵²Ibid., p. 82.
⁵³US Department of State, Confidential State Department Files: Biafra-Nigeria, 1967-1969 – Political Affairs, p. v, http://cisupa.proquest.com/ksc_assets/catalog/101146_CF_Biafra67-69.pdf, accessed 29 April 2015.
⁵⁴Ibid.

exponentially enhancing US interests in the emergent, post-war global political economy. The bodies conceived of "Grand Area" planning[55] within which parts of the world deemed "strategically necessary for [US's] world control" – i.e., "open to investment, the repatriation of profits, access to resources and so on – and dominated by the United States"[56] were mapped out. Crucially, it should be noted, this "Grand Area" envisaged by the Americans included the *entire* Southern World in its geographical spread[57] – in effect, incorporating all countries and peoples that made up the European "empires". Furthermore, the public rhetoric under which US state officials and publicists pursued the implementation of the "new order" was the "right of all peoples to choose the form of government under which they will live",[58] a formulation contained in the "Atlantic Charter" and which had caused too much dissension in Britain soon after the August 1941 Franklin Roosevelt-Winston Churchill summit because it expressed without any ambiguity: "all people had a right to self-determination". Churchill was distinctly outraged by the historic implications of the "Atlantic Charter" for British fortunes across the world. In a speech in London in November 1942, Churchill was adamant: "I have not become the King's First Minister in order to preside over the liquidation of the British Empire".[59] In similar vein, Charles de Gaulle, even though leader of the "Free French Forces" who had been on exile in England since Germany overran France in 1940, rejected African "self-determination" or restoration-of-independence in the post-war era during a 1944 conference of global French occupation-governors in Brazzaville, Congo. De Gaulle was emphatic: "[African] Self-government must be rejected – even in the more distant future".[60]

As it indeed turned out, Britain and France and the other European conqueror-states of Africa needn't get too perturbed about the effect of the US "Grand Area" planning on their occupied African countries. By 1950, thanks largely to the rapidly developing sociopolitical upheavals related to the restoration-of-independence movement in Asia (China, Indo-China, Korea) and the increasingly strident politics of

---

[55] Noam Chomsky, "The United States: From Greece to El Salvador", in Chomsky, et al, *Superpowers in Collision* (Harmondsworth: Penguin, 1982), pp. 20-42.
[56] Ibid., p. 21.
[57] Ibid.
[58] AN Porter and AA Stockwell, *British Imperial Policy and Decolonisation, 1938-1964, Vol I: 1938-51* (Basingstoke and London: Macmillan, 1987), p.103.
[59] "From our archive: Mr Churchill on our one aim", *The Guardian*, London, 11 November 2009.
[60] Hubert Deschamps, "France in Black Africa and Madagascar between 1920 and 1945", in LH Gann and Peter Duiganan, ed., *Colonialism in Africa, 1870-1960. Vol Two: The History and Politics of Colonialism 1914-1960* (Cambridge: Cambridge University, 1970), p. 249.

the evolving Cold War between the US/allies and the Soviet Union and its allies, the US had begun to rethink and readjust the critical features and parameters of the operationalisation of the "Grand Area" concept. Whilst the US was no doubt the most powerful country that had emerged in the West World at the end of the 1939-1945 war, it was soon clear that Washington required the cooperation of these European extant conqueror-states in Africa and elsewhere (Middle East, Asia, the Caribbean especially) to effectively run the "new world order" which was becoming more "complicated" in its evolution. After all Britain, France and the rest represented the prime "survivors" of the leadership of the "old imperialist world order" whose "experience" of "global control" in the past was still likely to be of immense benefit to the United States. Furthermore, Britain, France and the rest had acknowledged, unquestionably, the US's political, military and economic supremacy during the recently concluded war against Germany and its allies.

The latter consideration may have contributed enormously to the US modification of the original conception of the "Grand Area" in the way that this affected the overall character of the "core-states" that made up the leadership of the "new order". Instead of embarking on the task *singularly*, Washington now decided to "broaden" the leadership by assigning important roles to Britain and France, for instance, to play in international relations especially in several supranational organisations which had been formed after the war such as the United Nations, the World Bank, the IMF and the International Court of Justice, not to mention the more exclusive military alliance, the North Atlantic Treaty Organisation. It should also be pointed out that, in constructing a pan-hegemonic concert of states where its supreme leader was accorded full "recognition" by all the "core states", the United States of America succeeded in instilling a vital measure of "stability" among the West's conqueror or imperialist states for the first time since the European World conquest of the world began in the 15th century. It was the absence of this "stability", exacerbated by the "non-recognition" of a clear-cut leader that fuelled the acute intra-imperialist rivalries of the past which ended with two major wars erupting between 1914 and 1939.

Besides the outbreak of the Cold War between the West and the Soviet-led East bloc which would become as frosty as ever in the years ahead, the most important political development of the immediate post 1939-1945 war epoch was of course the struggle for the restoration-of-independence in the South as we highlighted above. The radical nationalism of the movement in Asia (anti-French resistance in Indo-China, Chinese Revolution) had opened up a range of possibilities for the realisation of a *genuine* restoration of independence from European World-control. They emphatically advocated the total control of their societies' resources (human and non-human), the democratisation of the institutions of decision-making and the transformation of the peoples' living standards. But these were precisely the sort of goals of the South restoration-of-independence movement which ran contrary to the critical tenets of the United States's "Grand Area" conceptualisation of the "new world order". Britain and France, among others of the conqueror powers in the South, could not have agreed more with the Americans. Quite clearly, the United States and the principal states of the European pre-1939-1945 war "world order" found much sooner than they would have hoped for after the war that they had no fundamental disagreement over the "containment" nor indeed the blocking of genuine restoration-of-independence initiatives in the South World. On the contrary, it was in their mutual interest as evident in the cooperation and/or solidarity that these powers shared in confronting radical national liberation movements in the South in the subsequent 40 years: China, Vietnam, Cambodia, Tamil Eelam, Kenya, Algeria, Guinea-Bissau, Angola, Mozambique, Eritrea, Namibia, South Africa, Zimbabwe, Cuba, Grenada, Nicaragua, Igboland/Biafra, etc., etc. For the United States, therefore, the restoration of independence in the European-occupied South World after the end of the war in 1945 was at best a version of the South American experience where an entire continent had, in spite of 150-200 years of independence, been "converted" into an American strategic and economic fiefdom, or what some officials in the US government or elsewhere would prefer, more contemptuously, to describe as their "backyard".

Watching anxiously in the early 1950s as the demand for the African restoration-of-independence got intensified, Britain, France, Belgium, Portugal and Spain *did not fail* to learn from this US example. And the US would oblige accordingly: the US would subsequently support the French in its wars in Indo-China, Algeria and elsewhere in Africa and the South World, as well as never ever condemning France for invading most of the countries of the so-called *francophonie* Africa 52 times between 1960 and 2015, in addition to the complicity of the French military, based in Rwanda, in the 1994 Rwanda genocide; the US would support the Belgian military in its involvement in the overthrow and murder of Patrice Lumumba, the democratically elected popular prime minister in the Democratic Republic of the Congo, and the imposition of the notorious dictatorship of Mobutu Sese Seko on the Congo for well over 30 years beginning in 1965; the US would support Portugal in its wars in Angola, Guinea-Bissau, Mozambique against the African restoration-of-independence movements during the timeframe of 1950s-1970s; the US would support the European-minority regimes in Zimbabwe, Namibia and South Africa battling against African restoration-of-independence movements during 1960s-1990s; the US would support Britain in its war against the Gĩkũyũ-led Mau Mau restoration-of-independence movement in Kenya, 1950s-1960s; the US would tacitly support Britain, in league with its Fulani north region clients in Nigeria, in perpetrating the Igbo genocide, the foundational genocide of post-(European)conquest Africa, 29 May 1966-12 January 1970, during which 3.1 million or Igbo or one-quarter of this nation's population were murdered.

Herbert Ekwe-Ekwe

The US, Igbo genocide, contemporary Africa

That August 1966 US support for Britain's plans to expand the territorial reach of the Igbo genocide to Biafra, Igboland, itself, was an invaluable endorsement for the British – coming from their closest ally since the end of the 1939-1945 war. Britain now had such a formidable diplomatic and political backing to wage a murder campaign to "punish" the Igbo which it had sought to engage in the previous 20 years but didn't for reasons we have already reviewed here. One obvious consequence of the US endorsement was the viciousness if not savagery of the campaign. Key spokespersons of the genocidist regime in Lagos publicly stated the genocidal goals of the campaign with scarce inhibition throughout its entire stretch and subsequently. British officials, including Harold Wilson, the prime minister himself, were no more reticent in expressing what their mission goal was. Undoubtedly, the Nigeria genocide state became some haematophagous monster let loose on the Igbo and Igboland, slaughtering away to the hilt ... And just in case anyone doubts the endgame of this mission, three shrilling, chilling proclamations, scripted with unmistakeable Stheno-precepts of obliterating intent from one of the Gorgons stalking the land, punctuate the scene as the following shows:

1. The ghoulish anthem of the genocide, broadcast uninterruptedly on state-owned Kaduna radio (shortwave transmission) and television and with editorial comments on the theme, regularly published in both state-owned *New Nigerian* (daily) newspaper and (Hausa) weekly *Gaskiya Ta fi Kwabo* during the period, has these lyrics in Hausa:
Mu je mu kashe nyamiri
Mu kashe maza su da yan maza su
Mu chi mata su da yan mata su
Mu kwashe kaya su

(English translation: Let's go kill the damned Igbo/Kill off their men and boys/Rape their wives and daughters/Cart off their property)

2. Benjamin Adekunle, one of the most despicable of the genocidist commanders in south Igboland, makes the following statement to the media, including foreign representatives, in an August 1968 press conference: "I want to prevent even one I[g]bo having even one piece to eat before their capitulation. We shoot at everything that moves, and when our forces march into the centre of I[g]bo territory, we shoot at everything, even at things that don't move".[61]

---

[61]*The Economist*, London, 24 August 1968.

The longest genocide

3a. Harold Wilson, prime minister of Britain, the key "centre"-world power that crucially supports the Igbo genocide militarily, diplomatically and politically, right from conceptualisation to actualisation, informs Clyde Ferguson (United States state department special coordinator for relief to Biafra) that he, *Harold Wilson*, "would accept half a million dead Biafrans if that was what it took" the Nigeria genocidists to destroy the Igbo resistance to the genocide.[62] Wilson's statement couldn't have been more audaciously expressed, particularly coming from the prime minister of Britain to an official of his closest ally, the United States. This is indeed extraordinary... For the record, Wilson's "a half a million dead Biafrans" represented 4.2 per cent of the Igbo population then; by the time that that phase of the genocide came to an end, 6-9 months after Wilson's wish-declaration, 25 per cent of this nation's population or 3.1 million Igbo people had been murdered by the genocidists. Harold Wilson's "would accept a half a million dead Biafrans"-wish is not a declaration made by some dictator, some leader of a loony party, a fascist party or anything of that ilk; on the contrary, this is a declaration made by an elected politician, a politician in an advanced West democracy – the leader of the British Labour party, a party that prides itself for having attracted leading thinkers to its ranks in the post 1939-1945 war era. "[W]ould accept a half million dead Biafrans if that was what it took"-wish is made by the prime minister of Britain; not the prime minister of some "peripheral", presumed inconsequential country but the prime minister of a "centre" state and power that was part of the victorious alliance that defeated a fascist global amalgam in a devastating war that ended barely 23 years earlier. This is a prime minister of a "centre" state and power, the sixth to occupy this exalted position since the end of the war, that was one of the key countries that worked on the panel that drafted the historic 1948 United Nations "Convention on the Prevention of the Crime of Genocide" in the wake of the 1930s-1940s deplorable German perpetration of the Jewish genocide in Europe. Six million Jews were murdered then by Germany. It is to ensure that no human beings are ever subjected to what the Jews went through in central Europe and elsewhere that this genocide convention is rated as one of the key international documents of the new age. Britain is a signatory to the convention. Surely, Harold Wilson's "would accept a half million dead Biafrans if that was what it took"-wish cannot fit into the hallowed pages of the 1948 United Nations "Convention on the prevention of the Crime of Genocide". Absolutely not! On the contrary, Wilson's is a mid-1960s declaration *to wage a genocide on a people*, the Igbo people, 3150 miles away in southwestcentral Africa, just 20 years after the Jewish genocide in Europe. In the end, rather than Wilson's 500,000 "dead Biafrans"-wish, there were 3.1 million murdered Biafrans... The world must now know: How many others in Wilson's cabinet identified

---

[62]Morris, *Uncertain Greatness*, p. 122.

with this genocidal position and policy on the Igbo? What was the nature of the debates on this subject? Were there voices of opposition within cabinet? Who were these voices and how did they try to alter both position and policy? An official in the foreign office in London at the time does acknowledge, without ambiguity, the genocidal plank of this administration's policy especially on the issue of the dispatch of urgent relief to the encircled, blockaded and bombarded Igbo: "[my government's position was designed to] show conspicuous zeal in relief while in fact letting the little buggers starve out".[63] How widespread did people in the broader Labour party know of Harold Wilson's genocidal policy on the Igbo? How much of Wilson's Igbo genocide drive did the official British Conservative party opposition aware of?

3b. In May 1969, Olusegun Obasanjo, who had recently taken over the command of the Benjamin Adekunle-death squad, orders his air force to shoot down any Red Cross planes flying in urgently-needed relief supplies to the millions of surviving but encircled, blockaded and bombarded Igbo. Within a week of his infamous order, 5 June 1969, Obasanjo recalls, nostalgically, in his memoirs, aptly titled *My Command*,[64] genocidist air force pilot Gbadomosi King "redeem[s] his promise", as Obasanjo puts it.[65] Gbadomosi King shoots down a clearly marked, incoming relief-bearing International Committee of the Red Cross (ICRC) DC-7 aircraft near Eket, south Biafra, with the loss of its 3-person crew. Obasanjo's perverse satisfaction over the aftermath of this crime is fiendish, grotesquely revolting. He writes: "The effect of [this] singular achievement of the Air Force especially on 3 Marine Commando Division [name of the death squad Obasanjo, who subsequently becomes head of Nigeria regime for 11 years, commands] was profound. It raised morale of all service personnel, especially of the Air Force detachment concerned and the troops they supported in [my] 3 Marine Commando Division".[66] The consequence of this act of terror across the world is, of course, the expression of revulsion. What does Obasanjo do in response? This is hugely revelatory. Olusegun Obasanjo appeals *to* Harold Wilson, the British prime minister, as Obasanjo, himself, scripts in his *My Command*, to "sort out" the raging international outcry generated by the destruction of the ICRC aircraft.[67]

For the Nigerian génocidaires, the fact that, at the end, they have Britain's back is critical in the pursuit of their gruesome campaign. As for Britain, the unrelentingly brazen impunity equally displayed by its officials, including Prime Minister Wilson, is

---

[63]Ibid. See also Michael Leapman, "While the Biafrans starved, the FO moaned about hacks", *The Independent on Sunday*, London, 3 January 1999.
[64]Olusegun Obasanjo, *My Command* (London and Ibadan: Heinemann, 1981).
[65]Ibid., p. 79.
[66]Ibid.
[67]Ibid., p. 165.

anchored on the confidence that they have the United States's government back. It is worth noting that the texture of the vituperative declarations made by either side of the genocidist coalition is pointedly a variation on the central theme of this campaign: to murder Igbo people.

What "neutrality"? What "internal affair"? Whose "internal affair"?

There was an extensive coverage of the Igbo genocide in the international media throughout its duration. In several now declassified US government official papers at the time, expansive references are made to this coverage as well as to reports of variegated initiatives by private, non-governmental and civil society who were monitoring the ever deteriorating features of the genocide especially after members' visits to Biafra or following files dispatched by their representatives on the ground in Igboland. So, an examination of the range of United States government's declassified documents on the genocide, often filed under the captions of "Biafra War", "Biafra-Nigeria War", "Biafra/Nigeria War". or "Nigerian Civil War", underscores the emphasis the US places on the troika concepts of "neutrality", "Nigeria affair" and "British responsibility" which it states characterise its official position on this catastrophe. It often overplays the feature of "British responsibility" but this is barely addressed critically. Britain is portrayed as some lame-duck observer and not an *activist participant* in the genocide. Indeed in a National Security Council Intergovernmental Group "Background Discussion Paper on Nigeria/Biafra" for 19 February 1969, the first sentence on British role, three years into the slaughtering, is astonishingly described as follows: "The British back the FMG [Nigeria] with non-sophisticated arms sales".[68] How the dreadful array of weapons supplied by Britain to Nigerian genocidists, acknowledged, clearly, by British state papers at the time (as shown earlier on in this study), could be classified by anyone as "non-sophisticated" is extraordinary.

Having given its British ally the *carte blanche* to expand the territorial range of the genocide in August 1966, the US, *not* Britain, ironically, is intent on falsifying the very records of the British action on the ground during the 44 months campaign. Contradictorily, perhaps, the papers consistently refer to the ever-increasing death toll in Biafra – especially *death by starvation*, a policy openly advocated by genocidist regime spokespersons and by Prime Minister Wilson in that 1969 conversation with Clyde Ferguson, the United States state department special coordinator for relief to Biafra, that he, Harold Wilson, "would accept a half million

---

[68]US National Security Council Interdepartmental Group, *Background Discussion Paper on Nigeria/Biafra, NSCIG/AF 69-1/REV.A*, February 10, 1969, p. 5., http://2001-2009.state.gov/documents/organization/54579.pdf, accessed 12 April 2014.

dead Biafrans if that was what it took" Nigeria to destroy the Igbo resistance to the genocide.[69] (We should point out that author Roger Morris was at the time a staffer at the National Security Council in Washington.) A state department file states that "between 500,000 and 2 million" had died within 30 months, "most ... died from starvation and disease brought on by the [Nigerian] encirclement" of Biafra.[70] References are made to the widespread responses from the American public on the pictures of the ongoing tragedy on their television screens. On 25 July 1968, citizen Betty Carter from Washington, DC, writes Secretary of State Dean Rusk the following letter:[71]

Yesterday evening while eating dinner and watching the news I was unable to finish eating upon seeing the faces of starving children, babies, men, and women in Biafra. I felt nauseated because of having so much when these people were in obvious pain and in dire need of food. I cannot bear to see anyone in need when I have something to share. Though it is not possible for me to go to Biafra at this time, I felt the least I could do was write to you and express my concern for these people and ask that the U.S. and other concerned governments and the United Nations press for a cease fire. I am sending a check to the World Church Service today to help the starving Biafrans.

Also on 25 July 1968...

U.S. Army Specialist John G. Moss wrote from Vietnam, enclosing a check for $10 "to help these desperate people". Petitions, resolutions, and appeals with dozens (and often hundreds) of signatures came from groups such as the Oregon State Legislature, the Ithaca, New York, Junior Chamber of Commerce, the Washington and Northern Idaho Council of Churches, the Catholic War Veterans of Ohio, the editorial staff of Doubleday publishers in New York, and residents of Ottawa, Kansas, Dayton, Ohio, and Hanover and Lebanon, New Hampshire, and White River Junction, Vermont.[72]

Pressure was now beginning to mount on the outgoing President Johnson administration, especially by mid-1968, to respond to this catastrophe boldly rather than the very unconvincing declarations of "neutrality", "Nigerian internal affair", "British responsibility". Johnson was struck by the outpouring of American public revulsion to the events in Biafra but felt unwilling to engage with an additional "crisis" at a time he was deeply mired at home in the upheaval of the African American

---

[69]Morris, *Uncertain Greatness*, p. 122.
[70]US Department of State, *Confidential State Department Files: Biafra-Nigeria, 1967-1969 – Political Affairs*, p. vi, http://cisupa.proquest.com/ksc_assets/catalog/101146_CF_Biafra67-69.pdf, accessed 29 April 2015.
[71]Ibid.
[72]Ibid.

freedom movement and abroad in war, in Vietnam. Personally "troubled" by the television pictures on the genocide but without much empathy, Johnson reportedly asked the state department to "get those n***** babies off my TV set".[73] The administration nonetheless indicated that it was stepping up "humanitarian relief for the Biafran people"[74] even whilst acknowledging practical difficulties on the ground in distributing relief supplies that would need approval of both Nigeria and the Biafran resistance government.[75]

It should be pointed out, though, that the US reference to "[Nigerian] encirclement" of Biafra[76] was part of the calculated genocidal policy by Nigeria that had been implemented beginning on 31 March 1967, whilst still on phase-II of the slaughtering (a 28 January 1969 Memorandum for the President by Henry Kissinger, presidential advisor on national security, had noted that "30-40,000 I[g]bo [had been] savagely slaughtered at this time"[77]), *four months before* the 6 July 1967 genocidists invaded Biafra, launching phase-III of the genocide.

On that day, 31 March 1967, the genocidist high command had indeed imposed a land, aerial and sea blockade of Igboland, Africa's highest population density landmass outside the Nile Delta, as prelude to the invasion of Biafra. To ensure that the 12 million Igbo people were in fact *bottled-up* in their homeland, the genocidists excised Biafra's southeast peninsular of Bakassi, contiguous to Cameroon, and "awarded" this territory to the regime in Yaoundé, headed by Ahmadou Ahidjo. The conditions on the ground were now in place for chief genocidist "theorist" Obafemi Awolowo, a lawyer, a "senior advocate" of the Nigeria bar, also vice-chair of the genocide-prosecuting junta (prime minister) and head of the finance ministry, to formulate his "starvation"-weapon strategy on Igbo people.[78] This began to have its devastating direct effect and concomitant impact as from mid-1968, precisely the timeframe the US state department files being reviewed attest to. Unlike the experience of tens of thousands of Yoruba people who thronged across the west

---

[73] Terrence Lyons, "Keeping Africa off the Agenda", Warren Cohen and Nancy Bernkopf Tucker, *Lyndon Johnson Confronts the World: American Foreign Policy, 1963-1968* (Cambridge: Cambridge University, 1994), p. 275.

[74] US Department of State, *Confidential State Department Files: Biafra-Nigeria, 1967-1969 – Political Affairs*, p. vi.

[75] US National Security Council Interdepartmental Group, *Background Discussion Paper on Nigeria/Biafra*, NSCIG/AF 69-1/REV.A, p. 10.

[76] US Department of State, *Confidential State Department Files: Biafra-Nigeria, 1967-1969 – Political Affairs*, p. vi.

[77] US Department of State, *Archives, Foreign Relations, 1969-1976, Vol E-5*, "Documents on Africa, Memorandum: Henry Kissinger to the President", 28 January 1969, http://2001-2009.state.gov/r/pa/ho/frus/nixon/e5/55258.htm, accessed 8 March 2015.

[78] Chinua Achebe, *There was a Country* (New York: Penguin, 2012), p. 233.

Nigeria-(Dahomey)/Benin Republic frontiers, seeking refuge in (Dahomey)/Benin and elsewhere in west Africa during the intra-Yoruba conflicts of 1963-1965, Awolowo "reckoned" or "calculated" that the Igbo must be denied similar access to a destination of refuge (outside their homeland) through the only other contiguous land border they have besides Nigeria, namely Cameroon. This restricted space for Igbo domicility to negotiate, in the wake of the planned, soon to be launched invasion of Igboland (phase-III) would guarantee the *optimum range* or outcome of the Igbo slaughter so envisaged in the Awolowoist genocidist projection...

Here lies the apparent difficulties the US government and non-governmental relief agencies and those of the International Committee of the Red Cross and other interested relief organisations across the world encountered, repeatedly, to send humanitarian relief to Biafra during the 44 months campaign. To *starve out* the Igbo was an intrinsic feature in the Nigerian genocidal plan and Nigeria couldn't, therefore, be cooperating with anyone who wanted to send relief to the Igbo whilst this policy was fully operational. Pointedly, this was part of the devastating import of British Prime Minister Wilson's position in his conversation with US Biafra relief coordinator Ferguson (already referred to) and that other vulgar summation on the theme rendered by the official in the British foreign office, already referenced here in the study: "[my government's position was designed to] show conspicuous zeal in relief while in fact letting the little buggers starve out".[79] Surely, the United States was fully aware of this Anglo-Nigerian strategy.

The US, in state paper after state paper, emphasises that all it could do in response to the slaughter was provide "humanitarian assistance" to the Biafrans[80] but that was increasingly a failure[81] because that would have meant challenging, *confronting, a la* April 1948-May 1949 Berlin relief airlift intervention, a deliberate Anglo-Nigerian strategy which predicated on its entrenched position of "neutrality".

Not surprisingly, both Johnson and the subsequent Nixon administration had numerous critics in congress and the rest of the country who wanted a more robust US response. In January 1969, a cross-party resolution involving 59 co-sponsors called on newly-elected President Nixon to "increase significantly the amount of

---

[79]Morris, *Uncertain Greatness*, p. 122.
[80]US Department of State, *Archives, Foreign Relations, 1969-1976, Vol 32*, "African Relations, Outgoing Telegram 016759", US Embassy Lagos, 3 February 1969, p://2001-2009.state.gov/r/pa/ho/frus/nixon/e5/54828.htm, accessed 2 April 2015.
[81]US Department of State, *Archives, Foreign Relations, 1969-1976, Vol E-5*, "Documents on Africa, Telegram 333: US Ambassador in Lagos to US Secretary of State, 14 January 1969", http://2001-2009.state.gov/r/pa/ho/frus/nixon/e5/55257.htm, accessed 8 March 2015; US Department of State, *Archives, Foreign Relations, 1969-1976, Vol 32*, "African Relations, Talking Paper for [presidential] European Trip, TP10, February-March 1969", http://2001-2009.state.gov/r/pa/ho/frus/nixon/e5/54650.htm, accessed 3 June 2015.

surplus food stocks, relief monies, non-combat aircraft, and such other vehicles of transportation as may be necessary for relief purposes".[82] Whilst discussing the resolution, a group of Democratic party senators, including Edward Kennedy (Democratic party, Massachusetts), insisted that the resolution had a "narrow focus on relief". Kennedy argued that "since the conflict already involves the Great Powers, the US has a moral duty, as a world leader, to bring about a resolution".[83]

Rectitude?

Even though he continues to pursue the dubitable US "neutral" position of his predecessor on the Igbo genocide, Richard Nixon appears to wrestle with the moral imperative at stake, raised by Senator Kennedy, over a "world leader" who sta,nds idly by as millions of people are murdered by a close US ally and the latter's client state representatives in southwestcentral Africa, 21 years since the end of the horrors of the Jewish genocide and 18 years after the historic UN Convention on Genocide. Nixon's 12 April 1971 recorded audio tape conversation with Henry Kissinger, his advisor on national security, is indeed highly revelatory.[84] In their conversation, Nixon, who had in 1968, as he campaigned for the presidential election, aptly described the slaughtering in Biafra as "genocide"[85], compares the 1971 genocide in Bangladesh to that of Biafra and the Jews. Nixon then wonders whether it was "immoral" that the US did not support Biafra and alluded to the Biafrans' *African* heritage and their *catholic* faith as, perhaps, factors that accounted for this US inaction.[86]

Surely, what these snippets from this Nixon-Kissinger tape tell the world is that, right at the heart of the US presidency, Richard Nixon, the second president of the republic who oversees the US policy during the Igbo genocide, 29 May 1966-12 January 1970, does not believe a word of his *own* nor the previous government's officially stated position on this catastrophe.

---

[82] US National Security Council Interdepartmental Group, *Background Discussion Paper on Nigeria/Biafra, NSCIG/AF 69-1/REV.A*, p. 1.
[83] Ibid.
[84] Gary Bass, "Looking away from genocide", *The New Yorker*, New York, 19 November 2013, https://www.newyorker.com/news/news-desk/looking-away-from-genocide, accessed 18 March 2015.
[85] Ibid.
[86] Ibid.

Serially catastrophic

Official United States never condemned the Igbo genocide unambiguously despite the comprehensive information at its disposal right from the outset. To describe the US position as "neutral" was in fact part of the tragedy. One couldn't be "neutral" in face of evil. Besides, the US was fully aware that Britain, its closest ally, was spearheading this genocide in Africa just 21 years after the end of the Jewish genocide in Europe. To also categorise the conflict as a "British responsibility",[87] given the US's full knowledge of British involvement in the ongoing crime, amounts to Washington's *tacit support* for the genocide. Finally, for the US to also describe the tragedy as a "Nigerian internal affair" underscores how little the world appears to have learned from the enduring lessons of the Jewish genocide: genocide *cannot* be an internal affair.

The United States *could have stopped* the Igbo genocide; the United States *should have stopped* the Igbo genocide instead of protecting the interests of the Nigeria state, the very perpetrator of the crime, but, more importantly, instead of protecting the socioeconomic and strategic interests of conqueror-state Britain as this study has demonstrated. In the wake of the Jewish genocide of the 1930s-1940s during which 6 million Jews were murdered by Germany, Africa was, with hindsight, most cruelly unlucky to have been the "testing ground" for the presumed global community's resolve to fight genocide subsequently, particularly after the 1948 historic United Nations declaration on this crime against humanity. Only a few would have failed to note that the US's position that this crime was "internal" was staggeringly disingenuous as genocide, as was demonstrated devastatingly 20-30 years earlier on in Europe, would of course occur within some territoriality ("internal") where the perpetrator exercises a permanent or limited or partial or temporary sociopolitical control: cf. Germany and its programme to destroy its Jewish population within Germany itself; Germany and its programme to destroy Jewish populations within those countries in Europe under its occupation from 1939 and 1945. In Africa, between 1966 and 2015, the world would witness genocide carried out against the Igbo, the Tutsi/some Hutu, Darfuri and nations/peoples in Nuba Mountains/South Kordofan and in the east Congo River Basin in "internal" spaces that go by the names Nigeria, Rwanda, the Sudan, and Zaïre/Democratic Republic of the Congo respectively. The contours of the territory where genocide is executed *do not therefore* make the perpetrators less culpable nor the crime permissible as the United Nations's crucial 1948 genocide declaration states most clearly.

---

[87]US Department of State, *Confidential US State Department Files: Biafra-Nigeria, 1967-1969 – Political Affairs*, p. v and Lyons, "Keeping Africa off the Agenda", p. 274.

The very central role played by Britain in support of the Igbo genocide no doubt reinforced the scandalous failure of the United States to exercise robust global leadership to prevent this catastrophe. Britain, a fully-fledged member of the United Nations – indeed a founding member of the organisation who enjoys a permanent seat on its security council and participated in drafting the anti-genocide declaration – supported the Igbo genocide militarily, politically, diplomatically. Without this entrenched British role, there probably would not have been the Igbo genocide. It is extraordinary that, under its watch as one of the superpowers of the post 1939-1945 war epoch, the United States of America, contrary to its often expressed lofty ideals, could have seemed to tolerate the perpetration of this genocide.

To understand the international politics of the Igbo genocide, phases I-III, 29 May 1966-12 January 1970, and the international politics of phase-IV of the genocide, 13 January 1970-present day, is to have an invaluable insight into the salient features and constitutive indices of politics across Africa in the past 50 years. The Fulani-led African-based perpetrators of the Igbo genocide, who have subsequently seized and pillaged the wealthlands of Biafra which could easily have expansively transformed not just these lands of southwestcentral region of Africa but all of Africa with transferable positive impact on other regions of the African World, appear to have got off free from any forms of sanctions from Africa and the world, thanks to a concerted British and, by implication, US diplomatic and political protection for those who, unquestionably, have committed such heinous crimes against humanity. The consequences for the rest of Africa have been serially catastrophic. Several regimes elsewhere on the continent are "convinced" of the conclusions that they have drawn from the escapades of their Nigerian counterpart: "We can murder our peoples at will. There will be no sanctions from Africa – and the world". As a result, the killing fields of this age of pestilence in Africa have stretched almost inexorably beyond Biafra with the murders of 12 million additional Africans, since January 1970, by regimes in further genocide in Rwanda, Darfur/Nuba Mountains/South Kordofan (the Sudan) and Zaïre/Democratic Republic of Congo, and in other armed conflicts in Liberia, Ethiopia, Somalia, Uganda, Sierra Leone, Guinea, Côte d'Ivoire, Central African Republic, Mali, Chad, Libya, Guinea-Bissau, Burundi...

Freedom

Thanks particularly to Harold Wilson, Britain has pursued its genocide against Igbo people under that same overarching ideological rubric of the expressed "diminution-of-African life" chorus of the subjugating anthem of 400 years of pan-European enslavement of the African humanity. It is precisely as a result of this antecedent that the soon to be freed Igbo people have an opportunity to begin to build a new civilisation in Biafra where African life, human life, fundamentally, is *sacrosanct*. This salient feature cannot be overstressed. Britain's Nigeria has been, for the Igbo, a haematophagous quagmire throughout its history as this study has shown.

Igbo will surely free their land. Already, 50 years since the first murders of the genocide were committed in north Nigeria on 29 May 1966, the Igbo have written an extraordinary essay on human survival and fortitude, a beacon of the tenacity of the spirit of human overcoming of the most desperate, unimaginable brutish forces. This long drawn out catastrophe, Britain's Nigeria hotchpotch, is over and truly Africans do stand poised on the eve of a new beginning.

* * *

8 OKIGBO: AFRICA'S MOST INFLUENTIAL POET/EPITOME OF IGBO RESISTANCE TO GENOCIDE[1]

Christopher Ifekandu Okigbo occupied the poetry chair of Africa's post-(European)conquest literary academy in the 1960s with Chinua Achebe the head of the novel institute and Wole Soyinka, head of drama. Since then, Okigbo's poetry has influenced the work of several poets including those of his generation and a stretch of "post"-Igbo genocide generation of poets. Elsewhere, *Heavensgate*, Okigbo's 1962 published work, enriches the concluding thoughts in Jay Wright's poem, "Beginning Again" (from his *The Homecoming Singer* [1971][2]), an exquisite exploratory journey into self-discovery and African-American affirmation across time and space. With immense satisfaction shown by the protagonist as they are about to complete their voyage, Wright quotes four lines from that Okigboan landmark

---

[1] The first version of this chapter, entitled "Christopher Okigbo", was published in the *Literary Encyclopedia*,
http://www.litencyc.com/php/speople.php?rec=true&UID=3403, 26 July 2004 (accessed 13 August 2010) and a second version, "Okigbo, the Africa state, genocide and the peoples", was read at the Christopher Okigbo International Conference, Harvard University, Cambridge, Mass., United States, 24 September 2007, convened by Chukwuma Azuonye, the distinguished Okigbo scholar. A third version was presented in a lecture to faculty, students and the public at the Universidade Federal de Pernambuco, Recife, Brazil (17 July 2009) and Universidade Federal do Rio de Janeiro, Rio de Janeiro, Brazil (27 July 2010). A fourth version is published as a contributing chapter to my *Reading from Reading: Essays on African Politics, Genocide, Literature* (Dakar and Reading: African Renaissance, 2011), pp. 72-92.
[2] Jay Wright, *Transfigurations: Collected Poems* (Baton Rouge: Louisiana State University, 2000).

signature inscribed in the opening cycle of poems in *Heavensgate* ("Before you, mother Idoto,/naked I stand.../a prodigal.../lost in your legend..."³) that has been the focus of intense scholarship and debates in the past 43 years:

> And now my ancient rhythm calls me,
> out of ashes and fraternal death,
> "Before you, mother Idoto,
> naked I stand...
> a prodigal...
> lost in your legend..."
> An aching prodigal,
> who would make miracles
> to understand the simple given.⁴

Okigbo was born in Ojoto, Biafra, on 16 August 1930.⁵ He was the fourth child of James Okoye Okigbo, a schoolmaster in the local catholic primary school, and Anna Onugwalobi Okigbo, his most beloved mother who would impact so powerfully on his writing throughout his career. The work and memory of Okigbo's maternal grandfather who was a priest of the local river goddess, Idoto, would have a profound impact on the artistic development of the future poet. Like his siblings, including the renowned economist Pius Okigbo, Christopher Okigbo studied at the local primary school where his father worked. In 1945, he was admitted to the prestigious Umuahia Government College where he distinguished himself both academically and in sports, especially cricket. Umuahia holds the impressive record of having produced several other leading African artistic and literary figures such as sculptor and painter Ben Enwonwu, novelists Chinua Achebe, Chukwuemeka Ike, Chike Momah, Ken Saro-Wiwa, Elechi Amadi, I.N.C. Aniebo, and the novelist and poet Gabriel Okara.

In 1950 Okigbo was admitted to the University of London College, Ibadan, that would within a few years play an historic role in the transformation of African literature in the 20th century. As was the case two years earlier for schoolmate and close friend Chinua Achebe, Okigbo enrolled initially at Ibadan to study medicine but subsequently changed his course to the humanities, graduating in western classics in 1956. Okigbo soon joined the impressive circle of bourgeoning writers, artists and

---

³Christopher Okigbo, *Labyrinths with Path of Thunder* (New York and Ibadan: Africana Publishing & Mbari Publications, 1971), p. 3.
⁴Wright, *Transfigurations*, p. 89.
⁵With appreciation to Inyom Victoria Okuzu, Okigbo's younger sister, who gave her brother's correct date of birth (instead of the mistaken 16 August 1932 date that the world had had until then) in an address at the September 2007 Christopher Okigbo International Conference at Harvard University, United States.

scholars on the university student body, which included Achebe, Amadi, Ike, Momah, Soyinka, Flora Nwapa, John Munonye, Nkem Nwankwo, Obiajunwa Wali and John Pepper Clark-Bekederemo. Later, Okigbo became a member of the Mbari Club of writers and artists, also based in Ibadan. Other members of the club included Achebe, Soyinka and Clark-Bekederemo, as well as Ulli Beier (writer and critic), Janheinz Jahn (historian), Ezekiel Mphahlele (novelist, critic and academic), D.O. Fagunwa (novelist), Amos Tutuola (novelist), Demas Nwoko (sculptor and painter) and Uche Okeke (painter and poet).

Okigbo edited the university publication, *University Weekly*, where he often translated Latin and Greek poetry into English. He also contributed his own poetry to the literary and cultural journals *Horn* (which was then edited by Clark-Bekedermo), *Black Orpheus*,[6] and *Transition*.[7] In 1962, Okigbo published *Heavensgate*,[8] which received extensive critical acclaim. The work is organised in five sections that map out the protagonist's spiritual awakening and life's quest: "The Passage", "Initiations", "Watermaid", "Lustra" and "Newcomer". Four years earlier, shortly after his 28th birthday, Okigbo had come to the definitive conclusion of what he felt his life's mission was, as he recalled later:

[T]here was a stage when I found that I couldn't be anything else. And I think that the turning point came in December 1958, when I knew that I couldn't be anything else than a poet. It's just like somebody who receives a call in the middle of the night to religious service, in order to become a priest ... and I didn't have any choice in the matter. I just obeyed.[9]

Yet besides his poetic engagement, Okigbo found time for other tasks and these are incredibly eclectic by any standard. Between 1956 and 1967, Okigbo had been a civil servant, a high school teacher, a literary journal editor, West African representative of the Cambridge University Press, business associate in an industrial enterprise, university librarian, co-founder (with Chinua Achebe) of a book publishing company, and a major in the Biafran resistance army. But it was his poetic work that preoccupied him.

As the opening lines of "The Passage" demonstrate, Okigbo had indeed completed the necessary labour required, since his "call", to embark on his exalted mission. The poet-protagonist would now await his initiation for service as he stands before the shrine of his people's river goddess – the goddess, Okigbo reminds his readers, who is at once "the earth mother and ... the mother of the whole family":

---

[6]Published by the Mbari Club.
[7]Publication then based at Makarere University, Kampala, Uganda.
[8]Okigbo, *Labyrinths with Path of Thunder*, pp. 3-19.
[9]Marjory Whitelaw, "Interview with Christopher Okigbo, 1965", *The Journal of Commonwealth Literature*, July 1970, no. 9, p. 35.

BEFORE YOU, mother Idoto
naked I stand;
before your watery presence,
a prodigal

leaning on an oilbean,
lost in legend.

Under your power wait I
on barefoot,
watchman for the watchword
at *Heavensgate*;

out of the depths my cry:
give ear and hearken ...[10]

"Earth mother" or the *ani* goddess is arguably the most revered deity in the Igbo pantheon as she is the guardian of society's moral order. Okigbo's maternal grandfather, as was indicated earlier, was the priest at the shrine where *ani* or Idoto is worshipped. Okigbo was perceived by his family at birth as the reincarnation of his grandfather and was therefore expected to "carry on" with the grandfather's "duties";[11] hence, the very intensive and extensive scholarship of the spiritual and religious heritage within which Okigbo's formidable poetic enterprise is cast. As the poet himself recalls, "in 1958, when I started taking poetry very seriously, it was as though I had felt a sudden call to begin performing my full functions as the priest of Idoto".[12]

Nzegwu, in *Love, Motherhood and the African Heritage*, her path-breaking study on African literature, has discussed the seminal contributions of Chinua Achebe and Flora Nwapa to the development of contemporary African literature, following decades of the European conquest and occupation of the continent. Beginning with *Things Fall Apart* (1958), Achebe focuses on what Nzegwu describes as the "high drama of state politics, international politics and racism",[13] discourses that have raged variously on invasions, seizures, expropriation, alienation, liberation and restoration. Nwapa, on the other hand, launches a "new theatre" of discourse focusing on women centrally

---

[10]Okigbo, *Labyrinths with Path of Thunder*, p. 3.
[11]Whitelaw, "Interview with Christopher Okigbo, 1965", p. 36.
[12]Ibid.
[13]Nzegwu, *Love, Motherhood and the African Heritage*, p. 96.

in her publication of *Efuru* – to interrogate the African "home or domestic life environment" in the wake of the occupation.[14] Okigbo's own contribution to this historic mapping of the tenets of African-renaissance scholarship is his focus on redeeming the occupation's assault on the African spiritual embodiment. He must have wrestled intensely with that crucial question posed by the Umuofia interlocutor in *Things Fall Apart* when the Africans engaged a representative of the European occupation regime on the pressing existential subject of the day: "'If we leave our gods and follow your god,' asked another man, 'who will protect us from the anger of our neglected gods and ancestors?'"[15] Okigbo surely considered the answer to this question a momentous task that required a rigorous scholarship and expansive contemplation. He reflects upon these meditatively in *Limits*:

> AND the gods lie instate
> And the gods lie in state
> Without the long-drum.
> And the gods lie unsung
> Veiled only with mould,
> Behind the shrinehouse.
> Gods grow out,
> Abandoned;
> And so do they ...[16]

The outcome of his scholarship would incorporate syncretic excursions across the world's faiths and traditions, its discourse presenting at times daunting challenges to the reader. These features of Okigbo's work have attracted criticism from some,[17] a reaction that barely bothered the poet. Chinua Achebe has rightly observed that Okigbo "relished challenges and the more unusual or difficult the better it made him feel".[18] Okigbo would have equally felt unperturbed by those critics who, particularly after his death in 1967, indicated their "preference" for his last poem cycle (contained in *Path of Thunder*) over his earlier works on the grounds that the later work is "less obscure".[19] Okigbo had insisted that all his published poetry is, "in fact, organically

---

[14]Ibid., especially pp. 96-130.
[15]Achebe, *The African Trilogy*, p. 121.
[16]Okigbo, *Labyrinths with Path of Thunder*, p. 34
[17]See, for instance, Chinweizu, Onwuchekwa Jemie and Ihechukwu Madubuike, *Toward the Decolonization of African Literature, Vol. 1* (Enugu: Fourth Dimension Publishers, 1980), especially chs. 2 and 3.
[18]Achebe, *Hopes and Impediments*, p. 79.
[19]Chinweizu, Jemie and Madubuike, *Toward the Decolonization of African Literature, Vol. 1*, pp. 193-194.

related".[20] Whilst *Path of Thunder* was first published posthumously in 1968, there is no compelling evidence here to suggest that this is not also *related organically* to the ensemble of the Okigboan poetics that emerged in 1962. The robust poetic voice that had spoken so eloquently on his people's fate since the overrun of their lands by European imperial forces was equally ready to pronounce vigorously on the catastrophic genocide perpetrated by Nigeria on this same people, beginning on 29 May 1966. The poet himself was killed defending his people's homeland during the genocide.

In "Initiations", the second segment of *Heavensgate*, the poet articulates the salient features of the ideological façade of the European occupation regime that is of utmost importance to its long-term project:

so comes John the Baptist
with bowl of salt water
preaching the gambit:
life without sin, without

life; which accepted,
way leads downward
down orthocenter
avoiding decisions.

Or forms fourth angle –
duty, obligation:

square yields the moron,
fanatics and priests and popes,
organizing secretaries and
party managers; better still,

the rhombus – brothers and deacons,
liberal politicians,
selfish selfseekers – all who are good
doing nothing at all;

the quadrangle, the rest, me and you ...[21]

---

[20] Okigbo, *Labyrinths with Path of Thunder*, p. xi.
[21] Ibid., pp. 6-7.

For Okigbo, the spiritual is a crucial sphere of resistance and restoration of sovereignty. This is precisely because the eventual goal of the occupation's assault is aimed at burrowing a cataclastic fault-line in the soul of the people to pre-empt or complicate their determined process of recovery on the morrow of the triumph of freedom. Such is the urgency felt that towards the end of the haunting meditations in "Newcomer" (final sequence in *Heavensgate*), Okigbo evokes his saintly mother's memory, the poet's organic link to his ministering duties at Idoto, to come to his aid: "*Anna of the panel oblongs,/protect me/from them fucking angels;/protect me/my sandhouse and bones*" (itals. in original). Okigbo responds to the emergency with a multi-layered, panoramic and often-complex architecture of ideas, which meditates on the variegated spiritual universe of the people. Okigbo's worldview does not tolerate any excuses for either the perpetration or perpetuation of any forms of tyranny and subjugation of peoples. It is against this background that the astute critic Emmanuel Obiechina describes Okigbo as "poet of destiny".[22]

Okigbo's poetry is constructed through an intensely pursued labour of exposition. It is studious, insightful, if not prophetic; it is vividly picturesque; intimate, interactive, meditatory or intercessional; it broadcasts, turns dialogical, then monological, haunting, incantatory, improvisational, lyrical. Okigbo sings, sings and sings. He is town crier, *griot*, diarist. He chronicles the people's everyday life-experiences – the individual, at home with the family, during meditations, at school, on the farm, at the market place, their joys and celebrations, their aspirations, their fears, their disappointments, at the community, and the debates on society's course of direction. Everything, everything, seems to be a subject for intense scrutiny and record. This explains the improvisational nature of Okigbo's artistry with the numerous ellipses found in his poetry and sentences finishing off with three dots: "out of the depths my cry:/give ear and hearken ...";[23] "SILENT FACES at crossroads:/festivity in black ...";[24] "where all roads meet:/festivity in black...";[25] "listening to the wind leaning over/its loveliest fragment ...".[26] On occasions there is evidence that an update has occurred to an item in the chronicle and this is final ("& the cancelling out is complete."[27]) or that an entry is still provisional ("& this poem will be finished"[28]). This tendency to revise also explains the repetition of lines ("in

---

[22]Emmanuel Obiechina, *Language and Theme* (Washington, D.C.: Howard University, 1990), p. 207.
[23]Okigbo, *Labyrinths with Path of Thunder*, p. 3.
[24]Ibid., p. 5.
[25]Ibid.
[26]Ibid.
[27]Ibid., p. 35.
[28]Ibid., p. 27.

palm grove",[29] "& the mortar is not yet dry ...",[30] "I was the sole witness to my homecoming ..."[31]), words and phrases in a number of his poem-sequences: words often repeated include "mother",[32] "drums" ("AND THE DRUMS", "lament of the drums", "the drums of curfew", "Long-drums", "The drums' lament"),[33] "thunder" ("thunder among the clouds", "thunder of tanks", "This day belongs to a miracle of thunder", "Hurrah for thunder", "How does one say NO in thunder"),[34] "prodigal" ("eyes open, of the prodigal", "I have visited, the prodigal", "let me be the prodigal"),[35] "elephants"[36] and condolences.[37]

Okigbo's scholarship and influences are extensive and varied: Igbo history, mythology, art and philosophy, ancient world religious and spiritual heritage encompassing Kemet ("ancient Egypt"), Nri, Babylon, Judaism, Hinduism, Buddhism, Christianity, Greece and Roman as well as the poetry of Ovid, Virgil, Dante, Milton, Yeats, Mallarmé, Eliot, Pound, Tagore, Lorca, Hopkins. Equally, Okigbo's aesthetic appreciation is varied and virtuosic. As he wrote *Heavensgate*, Okigbo, who played the clarinet in jazz bands and whose favourite jazz composers included Ellington, Parker, Monk and Mingus, recalled that he was also "working under the spell of the impressionist composers Debussy, César Franck, Ravel ..."[38] In his emotionally charged "Lament of the Lavender Mist" (from "Four Canzones"[39]), the pain of disenchanted love in a couple's relationship in the final lines is brilliantly caught in a poem whose techniques resemble those of the Imagistes who were contemporaries of Debussy:

The moon has ascended between us-
Between two pines
That bow to each other;

---

[29]Ibid., p. 15, p. 16, p. 23.
[30]Ibid., p. 25, p. 26.
[31]Ibid., p. 53, p. 60.
[32]Ibid., p. 3, p. 4, p.71.
[33]Ibid., p. 15, p. 16, p. 34, p. 45, p. 46, p. 49, p. 60, p. 63, p. 66, p. 68, Christopher Okigbo, "Lament of the Masks", 1965, *Web Concordance to the Poetry of Christopher Okigbo*, at http://echeruo.syr.edu/okigbo/19Okigbopeopms.htm (accessed 3 September 2010).
[34]Ibid., p. 39, p. 43, p. 45, p. 65, p. 66, p. 70, p. 71.
[35]Ibid., p. 10, p. 16, p. 72.
[36]Ibid., p. 46, p. 63, p. 69, p. 70.
[37]Ibid., p. 68, p. 69, p. 70.
[38]Angus Calder, review of Christopher Okigbo, *Labyrinth*, in New Statesman (London), 28 April 1972, at http://www.complete-review.com/reviews/nigeria/okigbo1.htm (accessed 10 May 2003).
[39]"Poems Okigbo wrote between 1957-61", published in Christopher Okigbo, *Collected Poems* (Oxford: William Heinemann, 1986).

Love with the moon has ascended,
Has fed on our solitary stems;
And we are now shadows
That cling to each other
But kiss the air only.[40]

Was Okigbo listening to that insistent and captivating two-way dialogue on "What Love" between Charles Mingus (bass) and Eric Dolphy (bass clarinet) in the *Charles Mingus Presents Charles Mingus* album[41] as he worked on "Lament of the Lavender Mist"? If indeed he was, it is tempting to speculate that Mingus's very humorous composition (on the same album) entitled "All The Things You Could Be By Now If Sigmund Freud's Wife Was Your Mother" provided the creative musical background mood as Okigbo wrote his lines on Kepkanly, the 1930s primary school teacher in occupied Igboland.[42] This is an exhilarating parody of the seeming confidence and exacting arrogance of the occupation regime, which the poet compares with Kepkanly's mathematical preoccupation:

Elemental, united in vision
of present and future,
the pure line, whose innocence
denies inhibitions.

At confluences, of planes, the angle:
man loses man, loses vision;[43]

Yet just as Kepkanly's experience later shows (the teacher dies of "excess of joy" after receiving salary arrears awarded by a salary-review commission appointed by the regime[44]), the occupation's apparent confidence – and therefore long-term stability – is at best tenuous; it does not have the organic stranglehold on society that it often portrays.[45]

---

[40]Christopher Okigbo, "Lament of the Lavender List", 1961, Web Concordance to the Poetry of Christopher Okigbo, at http://echeruo.syr.edu/okigbo/19Okigbopeopms.htm (accessed 3 September 2010).
[41]Charles Mingus, *Charles Mingus Presents Charles Mingus*, Candid CCD 79021 (personnel: Mingus, bass; Ted Curson, trumpet; Eric Dolphy, alto saxophone, bass clarinet; Dannie Richmond, drums), New York, October 1960.
[42] Okigbo, *Labyrinths with Path of Thunder*, p. 6.
[43]Ibid.
[44]Ibid., p. 7.
[45]Unlike Elaine Savory Fido's, this is a more historical reading of the significance of this subject. See Fido, "Okigbo's *Labyrinths* and the Context of Igbo Attitudes to the Female

In 1964, Okigbo published *Limits* and *Distances*. Both continue to focus on the poet's concerns in *Heavensgate*, namely the state of Igbo religion and culture in the aftermath of the European invasion. The poet's syncretic strides across the globe's ancient cultures continue apace. *Distances* is an intrusive sequence of reminiscences as the protagonist embarks on their journey to accept the call of destiny. We are reminded time and time again that "I was the sole witness to my homecoming ..."[46] The journey is long and enduring with the vividly mixed fortunes that such an enterprise would entail. These include coming across sites of promising and profound beauty ("Serene lights on the other balcony:/redolent fountains bristling with signs-"[47]) to encountering some danger and challenges ("DEATH LAY in ambush that evening in that island;/voice sought its echo that evening in that island"[48]), to yet more danger and challenges in the form of some Ku Klux Klan-like procession (with "an immense crucifix/of phosphorescent mantles:"[49])[50] but arriving safely at last to an ecstatic welcome: "*Come into my cavern,/Shake the mildew from your hair;/Let your ear listen:/My mouth calls from a cavern ...*" (itals. in the original).[51] The journey of initiation now over, the protagonist only knows that this signals the beginning of yet another phase of their mission, but the outcome of the one just completed is a resounding success as the traveller, now a town-crier, proclaims: "I have fed out of the drum/I have drunk out of the cymbal".[52]

Limits brings together two poems, "Siren Limits" and "Fragments out of Deluge",[53] which Okigbo had published in 1964 in the *Transition* journal. *Limits* is a lush environment with rich and lively flora of palm grove, bamboo towers, poplars, oil bean and the like. Rivers abound and it is populated by many types of birds – sunbird, weaverbird, eagle – and a variety of other fauna, including elephants, lions, and tortoise and python – "the twin-gods of the forest".[54] Significantly, the tortoise, the python, and the oil bean constitute the *totems* for the worship of the river goddess, Idoto.[55] This evergreen lush of life is indeed the reverential and regenerative shrine for the priest of the goddess, engaged in his spiritual task of rebirth and service for

---

Principle", in Carole Boyce Davies and Anne Adams Graves, *Ngambika: Studies of Women in African Literature* (Trenton: African World, 1986), pp. 232-233.
[46]Okigbo, *Labyrinths with Path of Thunder*, p. 53.
[47]Ibid.
[48]Ibid., p. 54.
[49]Ibid., p. 57.
[50]Cf. Fido, "Okigbo's *Labyrinths* and the Context of Igbo Attitudes to the Female Principle", p. 233.
[51]Okigbo, *Labyrinths with Path of Thunder*, p. 59.
[52]Ibid., p. 60.
[53]Ibid., pp. 21-35.
[54]Ibid., p. 33.
[55]Ibid., p. 3.

the people. The poem is suffused with a range of symbolisms that underscore the solemnity of worship in progress: the "moonlit" sweep of night (very much associated with time for worship as well as the crucial *egwu onwa* story-telling sessions that children love – highlighted, in this context, with the presence of *mbekwu nwa anuga*, the wily tortoise, eggs ("I hang my egg-shells"[56]), *manya nkwu*, palm wine ("Hang, dripping with yesterupwine"[57]), a tiger mask and a spear. As is the case with Okigbo's symbolic interplays, they vary from the very subtle to the distinctly diverse and expansive. Here, he continues to pursue his interest in the image of the lioness ("Oblong-headed lioness–/No shield is proof against her–"[58]) which he had begun in *Heavensgate* ("BRIGHT/with the armpit-dazzle of a lioness,/she answers,/wearing white light about her;/and the waves escort her,/my lioness,/crowned with moonlight"[59]). Okigbo wishes to stress the element of *continuity* in some features of Igbo religion with those of Kemet, as he identifies with the "Kemet Thesis" of Igbo migratory origins. The line "with the armpit-dazzle of a lioness" refers to the popular Igbo story of the monkey and the lioness in this multilayered imagery in which the former is so "dazzled by the armpit" of the latter that it destroys itself.[60] The revered, powerful and dependable Idoto obviously protects her own. Idoto is linked to Isis, the Kemet goddess, who has the grand title of the "lioness of the sacred assembly",[61] among others. Moonlight, eggs, pythons, wine, rivers, lush vegetation are associated with the worship of Isis as is Idoto. Just as the worship of Isis and the feminine order in the ancient world was violently suppressed by an ascending patriarchy, so is the assault on Igboland by a rampaging European occupation regime, via its ideology of clearly anti-feminine/people religion:

Past the village orchard where
Flannagan
Preached the Pope's message,
To where drowning nuns suspired,
Asking the key-word from stone;
& he said:

To sow the fireseed among the grasses,

---

[56]Ibid., p. 23.
[57]Ibid.
[58]Ibid., p. 27.
[59]Ibid., p. 11.
[60]Fido, "Okigbo's *Labyrinths* and the Context of Igbo Attitudes to the Female Principle", p. 229
[61]Ibid.

& lo, to keep it till it burns out ...[62]

It is to uproot these fireseeds of conquest that Okigbo focuses on increasingly in his subsequent poetic enterprise. This begins in 1965 with the poet's "Lament of the Masks" which is his contribution to a book commemorating the life of W. B. Yeats.[63] Okigbo has until now referred to "the white elephant" or "the big white elephant" in a number of his poem sequences without much elaboration. This is now the opportunity to work through the theme which, in this poem, refers to Britain but could also be used in describing brutal African regimes as he certainly does in *Path of Thunder*. As usual, Okigbo picks up a "common thread" in his cyclical reading of history and juxtaposes seemingly disparate events along the course within a controlled time frame to enable us focus our mind more intensely on pressing issues of human concern. The "common thread" here is twin-track: aggression and universal human quest for justice. "Lament of the Masks" focuses simultaneously on Yeats on Britain in Ireland, that first outpost of the march of British imperialism, and on the challenges that those far-flung events have had, and would have on artists, like him, responding to the subsequent British outrage in Igboland/Africa. In that case, "Lament of the Masks" can also be read as a commentary by Okigbo on Britain in Igboland/Africa or Okigbo on Britain/the Nigeria genocide state-in-the-making of the first half of the 1960s. For the latter, it is important to note that Okigbo's contribution on the Yeats study would have been written sometime between 1964-65; just 1-2 years later, Britain would emerge as the principal country that champions the devastating Nigeria state genocide on the Igbo people which costs 3.1 million lives. The resplendent musicality of the lines on the resistance to the "white elephant" is vintage Okigbo:

> THEY THOUGHT you would stop pursing the white elephant
> They thought you would stop pursing the white elephant
> But you pursued the white elephant without turning back—
> You who chained the white elephant with your magic flute
> You who trapped the white elephant like a common rabbit
> You who sent the white elephant trembling into your net—
> And stripped him of his horns, and made them your own
> You who fashioned his horns into ivory trumpets—
> They put you into the eaves thatch
> You split the thatch
> They poured you into an iron mould;

---

[62]*Labyrinths with Path of Thunder*, p. 30.
[63]D.E. Maxwell and S.B. Bushrui, eds., *W.B. Yeats 1865-1965: Centenary Essays* (Ibadan: Ibadan University, 1965).

For like the dog's mouth you were never at rest,
Who, fighting a battle in front,
Mapped out, with dust-of-combat ahead of you,
The next battle field at the rear

That generations unborn
Might never taste steel –

Who converted a jungle into marble palaces
Who watered a dry valley and weeded its banks
...

Who transformed a desert into green pasture
Who commanded highways to pass thro the forest –
And will remain a mountain
Even in your sleep ...

BUT WILL a flutist never stop to wipe his nose?
Two arms can never encircle a giant iroko.

Night breezes drum on the plantain leaf:
Let the plantain leaf take over the dance ...[64]

Before 1965 is over, Okigbo publishes *Silences*.[65] He also planned to re-issue all his poems to date under the title *Labyrinths*. In his 4-page introduction to this new edition, Okigbo notes that "although these poems were written and published separately, they are, in fact, organically related".[66] *Labyrinths*, for him, is a "fable of [a person's] perennial quest for fulfilment ... [A] poet-protagonist is assumed throughout ... a personage for whom the progression through 'Heavensgate' through 'Limits' through 'Distances' is like telling the beads of a rosary; except that the beads are neither stone nor agate but globules of anguish strung together in memory".[67] *Labyrinths* is not published until 1971, four years after the poet's death. By the time it comes out, *Path*

---

[64]Christopher Okigbo, "Lament of the Masks", 1965, *Web Concordance to the Poetry of Christopher Okigbo*, at http://echeruo.syr.edu/okigbo/19Okigbopeopms.htm (accessed 3 September 2010).
[65]Okigbo, *Labyrinths with Path of Thunder*, pp. 37-50.
[66]Ibid., p. xi.
[67]Ibid., p. xiv.

of Thunder (his last poetic output published posthumously in 1968) and *Silences* are added to the volume.

Silences is Okigbo's last publication before his death in 1967. *Silences* contains two poems – "Lament of the Silent Sisters",[68] which is a variation on a number of themes on culture, love and spirituality that he had earlier dealt with in his works and "Lament of the Drums".[69] The latter is a poem of support for two influential African politicians, Patrice Lumumba and Obafemi Awolowo. Lumumba was the leader of the Congolese liberation movement and prime minister of the new republic of the Congo, formally occupied by Belgium until 1960.. He was overthrown in a coup d'état shortly after the country's "restoration of independence" by the then Colonel Mobutu, the army commander, with the complicity of a Belgian military garrison in the country. Mobutu would later transform himself to a dictator and embark on a 30-year old terrorisation of his population and the exploitation of the country that would rival that of Belgian King Leopold II the previous century. Awolowo was the Nigerian opposition leader who had been jailed for 10 years by the pro-British Nigeria central government for apparently plotting a coup in 1962. Okigbo is sceptical of the fairness of Awolowo's trial and incarceration. He agrees with the popular opinion in the country that the government that had imprisoned Awolowo and rigged the general elections of 1964 still planned to impose its illegal rule on the people: "The robbers will strip us of our tendons!";[70] "The robbers will strip us of our thunder ..."[71]

Awolowo was later released from prison after a coup in 1966. But in a quirk in the course of history that would have been a fascinating challenge for Okigbo himself at his keyboard, if he had survived the genocide, Awolowo failed, utterly, to reciprocate Okigbo's immense gesture of solidarity against state injustice and arbitrariness. Awolowo supported the Nigeria genocide against the Igbo. In return, he was appointed deputy chair of the genocidist prosecution cabinet and minister of finance. He formulated the infamous strategy of "starvation as weapon/quick kill" during the genocide which, three years on, accounted for 80 per cent of all 3.1 million Igbo murdered. Subsequently, Awolowo continued with his virulent anti-Igbo project by enunciating the "financial/economic strangulation" of Igbo assets across Nigeria. All pre-war Igbo savings and other banking accounts were seized, which amounted to a ready income of £5 million in 1970 for Nigeria. Finally, the Awolowo directive restricted any meaningful development activity in occupied Igboland including the reconstruction of damaged transport, telecommunication, and power station facilities, a policy that all successive governments in Nigeria have strictly adhered to since 1970.

---

[68]First published in *Transition*, No. 8, 1963.
[69]First published in 1965 by Mbari.
[70]Okigbo, *Labyrinths with Path of Thunder*, p. 46.
[71]Ibid., p. 49.

Whilst still on the Igbo genocide, we should recall that the most outlandish criticism of Christopher Okigbo's own involvement in the defence of the Igbo during the slaughter is found in *The Trial of Christopher Okigbo* by Ali Mazrui. The text is less of a discourse of Okigbo's celebrated poetry but an attack on the poet's *active* role in the Igbo resistance in which he lost his life. In its imaginary trial of Okigbo after his death by some "after-life" tribunal, the novel criticises the poet for "putting society before art in his scale of values".[72] Furthermore, it alleges that "[n]o great artist has a right to carry patriotism to the extent of destroying his creative potential".[73] This is indeed a bewildering criticism from Mazrui, himself an historian and political scientist who is surely aware that hundreds of Igbo artists and intellectuals and hundreds of thousands of potential ones were murdered during the genocide. Igbo artists and intellectuals were not immune from the bullet or cudgel of the genocidist horde. Okigbo himself and the great Chinua Achebe, for instance, barely escaped with their lives from Lagos to Igboland after being trailed and hunted for days by the horde. Achebe's cousin, Lieutenant Achebe, was not so fortunate. He was murdered by the genocidists. Artists and intellectuals, over the ages, have supported the defence of the existential rights of their people. This defence has ranged from those artists and intellectuals who have focused actively on the subject in their creative activity to those who have *physically* defended their people, their homeland, from whatever is perceived as a danger to these rights. African humanity has been no exception to this trend. Alioune Diop, the critic and founding publisher of the respected *Présence Africaine* has noted that "[w]e live in an epoch where artists [and other intellectuals] carry testaments, where they all more or less are committed. One has to take sides ..."[74] Presumably, the author of *The Trial of Christopher Okigbo* would agree with Diop, but the world knows which side he took, whose testament he projected! Mazrui took the side of the genocidists; Mazrui projected the testament of the Nigerian genocidists who murdered 3.1 million Igbo people...

Not only does Mazrui condemn the right of the Igbo to defend themselves from the genocide (natural law, rights to life and property guaranteed by the relevant articles in the Nigerian constitution at the time, United Nations declaration of human rights to which the Nigerian state was – and still remains – a signatory), he also derides their very act of defence through his *The Trial of Christopher Okigbo*.

Mazrui has written expansively in the past 50 years, valorising every conceivable islamist cause or project in Hausa-Fulani north Nigeria as well as other parts of west Africa, the rest of Africa, the Middle East, and elsewhere in the world. As a result,

---

[72]Ali Mazrui, *The Trial of Christopher Okigbo*, at http://www.completereview.com/reviews/nigeria/okigbo2.htm,, accessed 30 January 2004.
[73]Ibid.
[74]Quoted in Madubuike, *The Senegalese Novel*, p. 63.

Mazrui has never condemned the Igbo genocide unambiguously nor its Hausa-Fulani/north perpetrators, who, in addition, have carried out other series of pogroms against the Igbo since 1945 under the ideological rubric of islam, nor their British government accomplices. On the contrary, to the shock of all human sensibility and decency, Mazrui exonerates the perpetrators of this heinous crime, this crime against humanity. On the morrow of its publication in 1971, soon after the January 1970 presumed end of the Igbo genocide, *The Trial of Christopher Okigbo* becomes a manual that *rationalises* genocide on the African scene, some oracular edict to any would-be genocidist operative in a Uganda, Central African Empire/Republic, Liberia, Sierra Leone, the Congos, the-return-slaughters-in-Nigeria, Rwanda, Darfur, wherever!, to murder as many millions of African children, women and men as they deem fit, without any fears of sanctions from Africa and the rest of the world, similar to the Nigerian foundational genocidists who had carried out their own crime so brazenly between 1966-1970.[75] If *The Trial of Christopher Okigbo* had unequivocally condemned the Igbo genocide and called for the apprehension and the trial of its leading perpetrators, perhaps Africa would have been spared the slaughter of the additional 12 million of its people murdered across the continent (west, east, northcentral, central) since the Igbo holocaust.

In sharp contrast to Mazrui's choice, several African World artists and other intellectuals over the ages have taken sides with the oppressed in the African humanity and have carried and projected such "testaments" of commitment for the defence/liberation of threatened or subjugated African interests in history. These heroic Africans include Eze Nri, Olaudah Equiano, Chukwuemeka Odumegwu-Ojukwu, Nelson Mandela, Malcolm X, Martin Luther King, Chinua Achebe, Mary Seacole, Pius Okigbo, Cheikh Anta Diop, Onwuka Dike, Christopher Okigbo, Sojourner Truth, Angulu Onwuejiogwu, Zora Neale Hurston, James Africanus Beale Horton, Edward Wilmot Blyden, Adiele Afigbo, George Washington Carver, Eni Njoku, John Coltrane, Molefi Kete Asante, Morgan Freeman, Donatus Nwoga, J.E.K. Aggrey, George Russell, Nina Simone, Amiri Baraka, Ella Fitzgerald, Oscar Pettiford, Walter Rodney, Sun Ra, Nnamdi Azikiwe, Charles Mingus, Frederick Douglass, Clark Terry, Danny Richmond, Flora Nwapa, Thelonious Monk, James Brown, Harriet Tubman, Joe Henderson, Woody Shaw, Elvin Jones, Chike Obi, Frantz Fanon, Uche Okeke, Horace Silver, James Baldwin, King Jaja of Opobo, McCoy Tyner, J.B. Danquah, George Duvivier, Ray Charles, Toni

---

[75]Forty-one years on, Ali Mazrui fails to utilise the opportunity presented at the September 2007 historic Okigbo international conference at Harvard University to denounce the perpetration of the Igbo genocide. On this, see particularly Femi Nzegwu's poignant review: "Reflections on the Christopher Okigbo Conference", http://www.sentinelpoetry.org.uk/1207/reviews_femi_nzegwu.htm, accessed 18 January 2008.

Morrison, Andrew Hill, Léopold Sédar Senghor, Louis Armstrong, Ben Enwonwu, Charlie Parker, Okot p'Bitek, Duke Ellington, Mbonu Ojike, Jackie McLean, Theophilus Enwezor Nzegwu, George James, Jimmy Garrison, Ousmanne Sembene, Aretha Franklin, Patrice Lumumba, Wynton Marsalis, Maurice Bishop, Michael Echeruo, Eric Dolphy, Agostinho Neto, Emmanuel Obiechina, Billie Holiday, Bud Powell, Efua Sutherland, Ossie Davis, Ruby Dee, Aimé Césaire, Clifford Jordan, Martin Delaney, Pharoah Sanders, Nicolás Guillén, Sam Rivers, Amilcar Cabral, Mahaila Jackson, Ladipo Solanke, Booker Little, Jacob Carruthers, Steve Coleman, Steve Biko, Sunny Murray, Marcus Garvey, Albert Ayler, Casely Hayford, Alice Coltrane, Dizzy Gillespie, Funmilayo Ransome-Kuti, James Earl Jones, Richard Davis, Spike Lee, Ron Carter, Marcus Roberts, Countee Cullen, Cecil Taylor, David Diop, David Murray, Kofi Awoonor, Peter Tosh, Ivan Van Sertima, Danny Glover, Tony Williams, Claude MacKay, Herbie Nichols, Don Ohadike, Lee Morgan, Gani Fawehinmi, Art Tatum, Oprah Winfrey, Don Cherry, John Henrik Clarke, Fela Anikulapo-Kuti, Jay Wright, Edward Kamau Brathwaite, Art Farmer, Miles Davis, Louis Mbanefo, Théophile Obenga, George Lamming, Max Roach, Chancellor Williams, Jimmy Cobb, Billy Higgins, Julius Nyerere, Ornette Coleman, Maulana Karenga, Roy Haynes, Ama Ata Aidoo, Archie Shepp, Denzel Washington, Ngũgĩ wa Thiong'o, Jaki Byard, Kofi Anyidoho, Léon-Gontran Damas, Wynton Kelly, Mariama Bâ, Bob Marley, Sydney Poitier, E. Franklin Frazier, Stevie Wonder, C.L.R. James, Johnny Coles, Langston Hughes, Sonny Rollins, Mariamba Ani, W.E.B. Du Bois, George Coleman, Wayne Shorter, Herbie Hancock, Billy Strayhorn, Ed Blackwell, James Clay and Alioune Diop.

It is not different in the history of the Igbo people, especially in defending themselves against the rampaging forces of genocide when it began in north Nigeria on 29 May 1966. Igbo resistance to the genocide began right from the outset in the north Nigerian city, town or village where they were being attacked. The objective of the resistance was to save one's life, the lives of family, relatives, friends, from the marauding hordes dispatched to kill, rape, maim, burn, waste ... Every Igbo caught up in this unfolding tragedy – whether they were a mother, a father, medical doctor, a school teacher, a hotelier, a pilot, a shopkeeper, a judge, a carpenter, a builder, a university professor, an artisan, a student, an engineer, a writer, a painter, a musician, etc., etc., was involved in the desperate effort to save a threatened life (or lives), beginning with theirs. No Igbo person was immune from instant death if caught by the mob ranged against them and theirs. No professions were spared. The horde's target was defined unproblematically: "nyamiri", "the damned Igbo". The defence of life, the defence for life, was therefore organised and coordinated by the Igbo in the collective spirit of a shared threat and shared desire to survive. The phrase that captures the Igbo resistance here and indeed in the subsequent phases of this genocide throughout its 42 months' duration is "quest for survival". Indeed, following the 12 January 1970 "truce" that Nigeria proclaimed on its campaign, the Igbo prefaced their exchange of greetings with each other for quite a while with the exaltation, "Happy Survival!": "Happy Survival! *Nne*", "Happy Survival! *Nna*", "Happy Survival! *Nwannem*", "Happy Survival! *Nwanna*", "Happy Survival! *Nwunyem*", "Happy Survival! *Oriaku*", "Happy Survival! *Dim*", "Happy Survival! *Kedu*?", "Happy Survival! *Ndeewo*", "Happy Survival! *Ke Kwanu*?", "Happy Survival! *Odogwu*", "Happy Survival! *Okee Mmadu*", "Happy Survival! *Dianyi*", "Happy Survival! *Umu* Igbo", "Happy Survival Ndiigbo".

So, contrary to Ali Mazrui's assertion, no effort could have been nobler by any Igbo person, *including* artists and intellectuals, than to offer their support for such defence or resistance against genocide. It was at once a resistance for the personal as well as for the Igbo community/nation. There was therefore a concerted "testament" of commitment by several artists and other intellectuals in support of the defence of the Igbo at each phase of the genocide as the following examples show: Flora Nwapa, Louis Mbanefo, Michael Echeruo, Ifeagwu Eke, S.J. Cookey, Sam Mbakwe, Janet Mokelu, Obiora Udechukwu, Uche Chukwumerije, Kalu Ezera, Philip Efiong, Ignatius Kogbara, Alvan Ikoku, Celestine Okwu, Benedict Obumselu, Donatus Nwoga, N.U. Akpan, Adiele Afigbo, Michael Okpara, Akanu Ibiam, C.C. Mojekwu, Okoko Ndem, Agwu Okpanku, Tim Onwuatuegwu, Chudi Sokei, Pol Ndu, Ben Gbulie, Dennis Osadebe, Osita Osadebe, Chuba Okadigbo, Chukwuemeka Odumegwu-Ojukwu, Okechukwu Ikejiani, Anthony Modebe, Alex Nwokedi, Chukwuedo Nwokolo, Pius Okigbo, Godian Ezekwe, Felix Oragwu, Ogbogu Kalu, Kevin Echeruo, Emmanuel Obiechina, Uche Okeke, Chukwuma Azuonye, Onuora Nzekwu, Chukuemeka Ike, Cyprian Ekwensi, Nkem Nwankwo, John Munonye, Gabriel Okara, Chinua Achebe, Onwuka Dike, Eni Njoku, Okechukwu Mezu, William Achukwu and of course Christopher Ifekandu Okigbo.

In the end, Mazrui's choice of focusing on Christopher Okigbo as a means of attacking the Igbo people's *right to defend themselves* from the genocide, was more calculated than it might otherwise appear. This is not just the case of a non-literary scholar trying their hands on some form of literary criticism or work of fiction as some studies have suggested.[76] Much more than that, *The Trial of Christopher Okigbo* is an ideopolitical statement by Mazrui, indicating, quite clearly, that in this worst act of genocide in Africa of the 20th century, his sympathies definitely did not lie with the besieged and bombarded Igbo humanity that supposedly habituate the *dar el harb* (abode of war) enclosures of islamic formulations.[77] For Mazrui, the extraordinary Igbo defence of their lives and property in these enclosures under attack, whether in

---

[76]Cf. Benedict Obumselu, literary critic and historian and very close friend of Okigbo's, in an interview with James Eze, entitled "Ali Mazrui's submission is rubbish", *Daily Sun* Lagos, 21 August 2005.

[77]For an insight into this islamic view of the world, see, for instance, Ali Mazrui, "The Reincarnation of the African State", *Présence Africaine*, 3rd and 4th Quaterlies, Nos. 127/128, p. 116.

north Nigeria or in the Igbo homeland of Biafra, was an affront to the seemingly hallowed diktat of this example of extra-African continental ideoreligious dogma – the proselytisation of which has been the hallmark of Mazrui's writings throughout his career. Extra-continental ideoreligious dogmas and sensibilities, which have in the main been *anti*-African – both in their propagation and their ready-use for the rationalisation of the millennium-long, dual Arab/islamist and European World conquests and occupations of Africa –[78] are precisely part of the compendium of ideas and themes which Okigbo's formidable African-centred poetry wrestled with in the aftermath of the so-called "restoration" of African independence. There was no comparable intellectual working on Africa between 1960 and 1967 who pursued with rigour and perspicacity a wide-ranging stretch of subjects from history to the arts, politics and spirituality/religion as Christopher Ifekandu Okigbo. Okigbo posits the primacy of African spirituality and religiocultural system in the quest for the African renaissance, in the wake of the Arab/European World conquest and occupation of Africa and the contemporary realities of genocidist African regimes. Okigbo's is undoubtedly a clash of ideas, a "clash of civilisation" with Mazrui's so-called African-triple heritage construct.[79]

It is with the advantage of hindsight that the world is now able to evaluate the foresight evident in Okigbo's last poem cycle, *Path of Thunder*, which he worked on before the outbreak of the Igbo genocide. Okigbo had intensely studied the unfolding of Nigerian politics between 1962-66 and produced his last "testament" in which he "prophesised" mass slaughter as an outcome of the crisis and ended with a foreboding of his own death:

AND THE HORN may now paw the air howling goodbye ...

For the Eagles are now in sight:
Shadows in the horizon –

THE ROBBERS are here in black sudden steps of showers, of
caterpillar –

THE EAGLES have come again,

---

[78]Ekwe-Ekwe, *Readings from Reading*, pp. 61-64.
[79]Mazrui, "The Reincarnation of the African State", pp. 114-127 and Mazrui, *The Africans: A Triple Heritage* (London: BBC Publications, 1986). For a critique of the principal features of this bizarre imagery, see Herbert Ekwe-Ekwe, "The antimonies of Ali Mazui's worldview", *West Africa*, London, 11 May 1987, pp. 919-920.

Herbert Ekwe-Ekwe

The eagles rain down on us –

POLITICIANS are back in giant hidden steps of howitzers, of detonators –
THE EAGLES descend on us,
Bayonets and cannons –

THE ROBBERS descend on us to strip us of our laughter, of our thunder–

THE EAGLES have chosen their game,
    ...

POLITICIANS are here in this iron dance of mortars,
of generators –

THE EAGLES are suddenly there,
New stars of iron dawn;

So let the horn paw the air howling goodbye ...

O mother mother Earth, unbind me, let this be
My last testament; let this be
The ram's hidden wish to the sword the sword's
    secret prayer to the scabbard –

THE ROBBERS are back in black hidden steps of detonators –
...

BEYOND the iron path careering along the same beaten track –

THE GLIMPSE of a dream lies smouldering in a cave,
together with the mortally wounded birds.
Earth, unbind me; let me be the prodigal; let this be
the ram's ultimate prayer to the tether ...

AN OLD STAR departs, leaves us here on the shore
Gazing heavenward for a new star approaching;
The new star appears, foreshadows its going

The longest genocide

Before a going and coming that goes on forever ...[80]

Christopher Okigbo's contribution to the development of 20th century African literature is extraordinary given the slim volume of his "collected works" of poetry. Kevin Echeruo, the 22-year old poet and painter whose work was very much influenced by Okigbo and who was also killed (1969) defending the Biafran homeland during the genocide, had dedicated the following poem, "Lament of an Artist", to the memory of Okigbo soon after the older poet fell near the university town of Nsukka on the 20th September 1967:

SHE will weep for me,
now the priest has left
the palm grove,
left the palm groves
the masks dance
in blood ...

Am I Christ for sacrifice?

Lord hear our prayers,
give the faithful departed
his pen and deep ink-pot
and Idoto shall rejoice
when *ögbanje* and his bangles
shall return,
never to leave
The Palm Grove for the Theatre.[81]

The *ögbanje* has indeed since returned and on this occasion, thankfully, he does not seem to be in a hurry to depart soon.

* * *

---

[80]Okigbo, *Labyrinths with Path of Thunder*, pp. 71-72.
[81]Kevin Echeruo, "Lament of an Artist", 1967, first published in *Nsukka Harvest: Poetry fron Nsukka*, 1972, available at http://echeruo.syr.edu/okigbo/kevin%20on%20okigbo.htm, accessed 7 February 2004.

9 BAGA & PARIS – TWO MASSACRES, CONTRASTING RESPONSES AND CONSEQUENCES

As the world witnessed in this first week of New Year 2015,[1] rarely have there been two dreadful massacres carried out almost simultaneously in two separate continents by two organisations surely operating autonomously but belonging to the same overarching religiopolitical agency. Boko Haram, the islamist insurgent group based in north Nigeria, massacred 2000 people in Baga[2] during the course of two days. In Paris, France, over a 2-day stretch, during the same week, a French-based cell affiliated to some islamist caliphate brigade in the Mid East massacred 17 people including cartoonists of the satirical journal, *Charlie Hebdo*, and staff and shoppers at a Jewish supermarket.[3]

Boko Haram is ideologically allied to the global islamist causes and projects of the Mid East amalgam including al-Qaeda in the Arabian peninsula and the Islamic State (controls vast swathes of territory in Iraq and Syria), as well as the Taleban in Afghanistan and al-Qaeda in the Islamic Maghreb in west/northwest Africa and al-Shabaab in Somalia. Boko Haram leader Abubakar Shekau never tires to extend solidarity messages to these fellow organisations in his regular video releases that

---

[1] Week beginning Sunday 4 January 2015. An earlier version of this chapter was published in *Rethinking Africa*, 16 January 2015 and *Pambazuka: Voices for Freedom and Justice*, 22 January 2015.
[2] *The Guardian*, London, 10 January 2015.
[3] *France24*, "Charlie Hebdo attack", http://webdoc.france24.com/france-paris-charlie-kosher-terrorism/, accessed 14 January 2015.

update the strategic objectives and expectations of the ongoing transnational insurgency.⁴

The responses of Nigeria and France to these tragedies couldn't be so trenchantly different though. Right from the outset, the French state robustly came out in defence of its population. It mobilised the entire range of its security forces to hunt down the murderous cell, stepped up security for its citizens whilst continually reassuring them, attended to the dead, the dying and the wounded, and organised a solidarity march in honour of the 17 and their families and for the reaffirmation of the crucial tenets and ethos that underpin the existence of the French republic. 3.7 million French people turned out in Paris on Sunday 11th January for this historic gathering.⁵ The heads of state or government of most countries of the European World and beyond attended the march in support of France. The global media covered this story of a week comprehensively.

Morbid silence

In Nigeria, in contrast, the country's regime-leadership and its expanded establishment exercised a morbid silence over the outrage in Baga – not a word on Baga from the then head-of-regime nor from any of the seven ex-heads of regime (Buhari, Obasanjo, Shonekan, Shagari, Babangida, Gowon, Abubakar). None of the eight was moved to act in defence of Baga from its ruthless assailants, not even in the wake of that haunting, graphic account of the tragedy of his town rendered soon after by Baga district head survivor Baba Abba Hassan who told reporters that "…most victims are children, women and elderly people who could not run fast enough when insurgents drove in … firing rocket-propelled grenades and assault rifles on town residents".⁶

Silence, punishing silence, utter silence: such was the staggering indifference displayed by the Nigeria state to this massacre, within its frontier, that an observer would be forgiven if they thought that the slaughter that *occurred* in Baga never happened or that Baga were somewhere else on the planet or, perhaps, that Baga didn't really exist… In effect, this state no longer pretends that it exists to serve its peoples.⁷ If anyone is still unsure of this crucial characteristic, a reminder of the final segment of Nigeria's response to these massacres of a week might be of help: despite the silence on Baga, the state's head of regime found the time and purpose to send a

---

⁴"Boko Haram releases new video on captured towns, Shekau seen preaching to locals", *Sahara Reporters*, New York, 9 November 2014.
⁵*France24*, "Charlie Hebdo attack".
⁶*The Guardian*, London, 10 January 2015.
⁷As chap. 1 above demonstrates.

message of condolence to the French head of state on the murder in Paris; equally silent on Baga, another senior regime official found the time and purpose to tweet a message of condolence to the people of France on the murder in Paris. It shouldn't be found surprising to add that no one marched in Nigeria on behalf of the 2000 murdered in Baga nor for their families nor indeed for any exhortative values of a doubtful state. As for the world's media, the lenses of their camera, during the week, were of course focussed 2600 miles away from Baga – Paris.

It is to this focus of the world media and some of its wider consequences that led Simon Allison of the *Daily Maverick* to observe: "It may be the 21st century, but African lives are still deemed less newsworthy – and, by implication, less valuable – than western lives".[8] Allison is undoubtedly alluding to the catastrophic diminution of the African humanity by the pan-European World during 400 years of the latter's enslavement of African peoples and its conquest and occupation of Africa. But as we now show, the perceived "less valuable" status of African life in the contemporary epoch has not just been a teleological transposition from a somewhat distant past. On the contrary, it is a thoroughly, consciously mapped-out package and practice designed and formally launched much more recently, in the mid-1960s, by a not-too-unfamiliar global power *central* in this visceral African subjugated history/international politics.

Diarchy

Finally, let us return to Nigeria's deafening silence on Baga. Given Nigeria's past and recurring history, does one *realistically* expect this state to defend Baga from Boko Haram, comment or mourn the murder of the 2000 from Baga – almost 49 years to the day after it embarked on the murder of 3.1 million of its Igbo people's population in a studiously-organised genocide that is still ongoing? Each of the seven of Nigeria's ex-heads of regime, referred to earlier, particularly Buhari, Obasanjo, Babangida, Gowon, Abubakar, is a structural participant in this foundational genocide of post-(European)conquest Africa. The latter constitute a *génocidaire quintet*. The Igbo genocide at once shapes the architecture of the present Nigeria establishment as the world knows it. Therefore, no one from any spheres or levers of this state assemblage could have had anything intelligible or/and credible to say on Baga. Part of the reason of Nigeria's silence on Baga is that given the country's genocide antecedent, few would have believed any word declared on this massacre by any officials of its state.

---

[8]Simon Allison, "I am Charlie, but I am Baga too: On Nigeria's forgotten massacre", *Daily Marverick*, https://www.dailymaverick.co.za/article/2015-01-12-i-am-charlie-but-i-am-baga-too-on-nigerias-forgotten-massacre/#.VLON32SsVc4, accessed 13 January 2015.

The longest genocide

Britain, the ex-conqueror but still quasi-occupying state in Nigeria supported the Igbo genocide from conceptualisation to execution. In supporting the genocide, Britain sought to "punish" the Igbo for being in the *vanguard*, since the 1930s, to terminate the British occupation of Nigeria – one of the very prized lands of the British conquest of Africa. During the course of the 1968/1969 gruesomely devastating apogee of the genocide, Harold Wilson, the British prime minister, informed C. Clyde Ferguson, the US state department special coordinator for relief to Biafra, that *he*, Harold Wilson, "would accept a half million dead Biafrans if that was what it took" Nigeria to destroy the Igbo resistance to the genocide.[9] For the record, Wilson's "a half a million dead Biafrans"-wish represented 4.2 per cent of the Igbo population then; by the time that that phase of the genocide came to an end (phase III, 6 July 1967-12 January 1970), 6-9 months after Wilson's wish-declaration, 25 per cent of this nation's population or 3.1 million Igbo people had been murdered by the genocidists.

Undoubtedly, the Nigerians had handsomely obliged Harold Wilson's wish. Those hauntingly punching words of historian Chancellor Williams's were at once vindicated, most dramatically: "... The Europeans had also been busily building up and training strong African armies. Africans trained to hate, kill and conquer Africans...".[10]

Thus, in the construction of the template of international relations that would embody the post-1939-1945 war era, the British-Nigerian genocide diarchy had elevated the "dispensability of African life in national and international politics" to the highest calibrated level possible.

* * *

---

[9]Morris, *Uncertain Greatness*, p. 122.
[10]Williams, *The Destruction of Black Civilization*, p. 218.

10 THERESA MAY AND BIAFRA

In January 2017, British Prime Minister Theresa May made a major declaration on the future of her country's policy on foreign military intervention.[1] May had told a US Republican party assembly in Philadelphia (29 January 2017) that Britain would henceforth abandon foreign invasions which she categorised as "failed policies of the past". May couldn't be more insistent: "the days of Britain and America intervening in sovereign countries in an attempt to remake the world in our own image are over".[2]

May's declaration is indeed extraordinary – not, though, for her stated reasons of "failed policies of the past" (possible references to British-allied invasions of Afghanistan, Iraq, Libya, quasi-intervention in Syria, complicit support for the April 2011 French invasion of Côte d'Ivoire and the latter's invasions of a cluster of other so-called *francophonie* states of Africa particularly in the past two decades), important as these may be, but from a snap examination of a more expanded excursion into history.

Gargantuan wealth

It should be stressed that Britain added the prefix "great" to its name configuration to demonstrate its seemingly daunting triumph at expansive global conquest and occupation. Britain, the first truly effective West global power, employed the gargantuan wealth it acquired during the course of its late 17th century/early 18th century pre-eminent role in the enslavement and mass exportation of millions of African peoples from Africa to the Americas to consolidate its conquest of the Americas (especially the north/the Caribbean basin), embark on its conquest of India and other regions of Asia, embark on the subsequent pan-European (Britain, France, Portugal, Belgium, Spain, Germany and Italy) conquest and occupation of a (subsequently) weakened Africa, and lastly, but surely not least in importance, finance its 19th

---

[1] An earlier version of this chapter was published in *Rethinking Africa*, 14 February 2017 and *Pambazuka News: Voices of Freedom and Justice*, 16 February 2017.
[2] *The Independent*, London, 29 January 2017.

century industrial revolution which is the turning point in the development of West capitalism.

Britain's success on this score cannot be exaggerated.³ This was a country which, prior to the mid-17th century, was still a "cultural and scientific backwater", to quote the graphic description made by Christopher Hill, the eminent British historian who is an authority on this period of British history.⁴ By the beginning of the 18th century, Britain had established virtual world monopoly in the seizure and transportation of millions of Africans from their homelands to the Americas after displacing the hitherto lead-roles therein by the Iberian states of Portugal and Spain. Britain used the enormous resources that accrued to it as a result to finance its burgeoning scientific and technological enterprises.⁵ Soon, as Hill further notes, Britain became the "centre of world science".⁶

Yet in that egregious overdrive by those in successive generations of British writers and scholars who proclaimed outright denial or sought to provide the requisite "intellectual" rationalisation for this crime against African peoples, Britain, in effect, emerged from this exercise with the unenviable position as the creator, cardinal codifier, and central publicist of European World racism as an ideology.⁷

Tony Blair's "ethical foreign policy"

In December 2006, in apparent response to this sordid history of Britain to the peoples of Africa, Tony Blair, then British prime minister, observed in an article in the *New Nation* (the London-based weekly newspaper that appeals to a wide African peoples' readership), that he felt "deep sorrow" for Britain's central role in the European World's enslavement of African peoples.⁸ This pronouncement was surely not good enough as Britain is the leading beneficiary of this crime. Blair should have apologised unreservedly to African peoples across the world for Britain's role in a catastrophe that remains humanity's most gruesome, most expansive, and most enduring. Blair should also have announced a comprehensive package of reparations paid to all surviving Africans in Africa, Europe, the Americas and elsewhere in the world for the crime.

---

³Ekwe-Ekwe, *Readings from Reading*, pp. 1-6.
⁴Christopher Hill, "Lies about crimes", *The Guardian*, London, 29 May 1989.
⁵Ekwe-Ekwe, *Readings from Reading*, pp. 1-3.
⁶Hill, "Lies about crimes".
⁷Ekwe-Ekwe, *African Literature in Defence of History*, especially pp. 1-54.
⁸*The Telegraph*, London, 27 November 2006.

Despite Blair's feeble response to this scourge of history or precisely because of it, this prime minister pursued a policy on Africa, throughout his 11 years in office (1997-2007), that were largely variations on those definitive themes of 400 years of Britain's appalling history towards the peoples of Africa. Blair advanced an aggressive programme of British arms sales to Africa which, by 2004, yielded phenomenal dividend to Britain's treasury as it became the world's premier arms exporter to Africa: in 1999 alone, Britain sold £65 million worth of arms to Africa; in 2000, the total was £150 million[9] and, by 2004, these sales had crossed the £1 billion threshold.[10] Blair's exports' targets included Africa's notorious genocide-states, especially Nigeria, the Sudan, and the Democratic Republic of Congo (DRC). Furthermore, Britain sold arms to 10 out of 13 conflict-stricken countries on the continent during the epoch including states in east/central Africa then involved in the so-called Great Lakes's War where London in fact sold arms to both sides of the principal protagonists (DRC, Rwanda, Namibia, Zimbabwe, Burundi, Uganda) which led Charles Onyango-Obbo, the east African journalist, to reflect, at the time, that "Britain is supporting both sides [in the war] – it just robs them of any moral authority and a lot of people rightly do despise the British government on this affair".[11]

That Blair actually categorised this foreign policy to Africa (and elsewhere in the South) as "ethical foreign policy" (despite his arms sales record), underscored the staggering depth of contempt that his administration had for the peoples of this part of the world.

Back to Biafra

For Blair on Biafra, southwestcentral Africa, as should be expected from the bold strokes of his "ethical foreign policy" thrust to the rest of Africa, it was indeed business as usual... The Igbo genocide was now in its 30th year with phase-IV, begun on 13 January 1970, entering its 27th year. Britain had in league with its client state of Nigeria, beginning on 29 May 1966, launched the Igbo genocide, the foundational genocide of post-(European)conquest Africa. Britain had sought to "punish" Igbo people for their *vanguard* role in the campaign to terminate the British conquest and occupation of this region of Africa during the 1930s-October 1960. Britain and Nigeria murdered 3.1 million Igbo or 25 per cent of this nation's population during 44 subsequent months of the most devastating savagery not seen in Africa since Germany

---

[9]Herbert Ekwe-Ekwe, "Ban arms sales to Africa – nothing else required", *openDemocracy*, London, 14 June 2005.
[10]Anthony Barnett, "UK arms sales to Africa reach £1 million mark", *The Guardian*, London, 12 June 2005.
[11]*BBC News*, "UK arming African countries", London, 3 April 2000.

carried out the genocide of the Herero, Nama and Berg Damara peoples in southwest Africa at the first decade of the 20th century. At the apogee of phases I-III of the Igbo genocide, 1968/1969, Harold Wilson, then British prime minister who coordinated the genocide from London, was fulsomely adamant about the objective of the slaughtering: "[I] would accept a half million dead Biafrans if that was what it took" Nigeria to destroy the Igbo resistance to the genocide.[12] Such is the grotesquely expressed diminution of African life, made by a supposedly leading politician of the world of the 1960s – barely 20 years after the deplorable perpetration of the Jewish genocide in Europe.

In May 1999, in pursuant of his *own* contribution to the prosecution of the Igbo genocide, Tony Blair reached out to Olusegun Obasanjo, who had recently become head of regime in Nigeria, to establish close ties in which sales of British arms to Nigeria was going to play a dominant role. Obasanjo is a fiendish genocidist operative who led a brigade in south Biafra in mid-1968-January 1970 slaughtering tens of thousands of Igbo people. In June 1969, Obasanjo ordered his air force to *shoot down* a 3-person crew international Red Cross aircraft bringing urgent relief to the encircled, blockaded, and bombarded Igbo, and he later boasted remorselessly of this crime in his memoirs, aptly entitled *My Command*.[13] True to type, Obasanjo resumed his murder campaign against the Igbo soon after taking office in regions across occupied Biafra. Other state and quasi-state agents especially in north Nigeria also joined in an expansive trail of organised waves of pogroms against diaspora Igbo populations at the time. According to a US justice department report, a total of 50,000 people were murdered in these campaigns between 1999 and 2004,[14] Obasanjo regime's first term, the overwhelming majority of them Igbo.

In March 2015, in yet another ritual bout of a British prime minister reaching out or employing the services of a "recycled" genocidist Nigerian trooper from the earlier phases of the genocide to continue the Igbo slaughter, the mantle now fell on David Cameron. Cameron imposed Muhammadu Buhari, one of the vilest Nigerian genocidist operatives throughout these 50 years of the Igbo genocide, as head of Nigeria regime. Buhari got involved in the genocide right from its launch on 29 May 1966 (four months before David Cameron himself was born in England) and during the Nigerian expansive trail of the mass slaughter of Igbo military and civilians alike in north and west Nigeria regions from 29 July 1966-5 July 1967. The latter dates encapsulate phases I-II of the genocide timeframe. During phase-III of the genocide,

---

[12]Morris, *Uncertain Greatness*, p. 122.
[13]Obasanjo, *My Command*, pp.78-79.
[14]US Department of Justice, "Armed Conflicts Report – Nigeria", Washington, DC, 25 February 2014, p. 1.

the invasion of Biafra, 6 July 1967-12 January 1970, Buhari was commander of a genocidist corps in north and northcentral Biafra, slaughtering to the hilt. Just as the earlier Obasanjo regime mentioned, Buhari has carried out his own spate of murders of Igbo people across Biafra since taking power. His regime has murdered a total of 2000 Igbo between November 2015 and January 2017. Former US President Barack Obama, working collaboratively with Cameron, imposed Buhari as head of this regime. **Obama is the first African-descent president of the US republic in 233 years of existence and his unflinching support for an African-led genocidist regime in Africa, waging a genocide against an African people, is surely an unconscionable, monumental tragedy of his presidential legacy.**[15]

Theresa May's opportunity, the Richard Gozney effect

Cameron resigned his prime minister's position precipitously on 13 July 2016 after losing the "Brexit" referendum on British membership of the European Union. Theresa May has since become prime minister and is presented with an historic opportunity to confront and terminate the British central role in the ongoing Igbo genocide in Biafra. This genocide has gone on for 50 years. May must now reject that baton of the relay race-to-murder-Igbo people that has been passed down the track from Harold Wilson's 10 Downing Street tenure.

Thankfully, there is indeed a British official antecedent that May would find helpful if she plans to bring this gruesome catastrophe to an end. In December 2005, soon after the Olusegun Obasanjo regime forces had just carried out a stretch of murders of Igbo peaceful pro-Biafra restoration-of-independence demonstrators in Owere, Umuahia and Aba (eastcentral Biafra), Richard Gozney, then chief British representative in Nigeria, came out openly and condemned the slaughtering unreservedly.[16] This was and remains unprecedented from such a high profile British state official *since* 29 May 1966.

Four salient features of the genocide must have weighed heavily on Gozney's mind that prompted such a public demonstration: (1) 3.1 million Igbo people had been murdered earlier on in the genocide and tens of thousands in the subsequent decades (2) Harold Wilson's recorded, blatant support for the genocide, "[I] would accept a half million dead Biafrans if that was what it took" *is* harrowing (3) Harold Wilson's own admission in his memoirs that the Nigerian military, equipped zealously by Britain, expended more small arms ammunition in its campaign to achieve its annihilative mission in Biafra than the amount used by the British armed

---

[15]See chap. 12 below.
[16]*The Vanguard*, Lagos, 17 December 2005.

forces "*during the whole*" of the 1939-1945 war[17] *is* harrowing (4) Britain's Lagos (Nigeria) diplomatic mission military advisor Robert Scott's own acknowledgement (at the height of the genocide, mid 1968-January 1970) that, as the Nigerian genocidists unleashed their campaigns across Igbo cities, towns and villages, they were the "best defoliant agent known"[18] *is* harrowing. Grozney would also have observed the stunning Igbo resilience of the Biafra freedom movement and drew the unmistakeable conclusions of its indestructibility...

Maybe Britain and the rest of the world have waited all this while for this very introspective only daughter of a respected vicar in a rural parish in southeast England to become prime minister to end the Igbo genocide, this longest and most gruesome genocide of the contemporary world. All Theresa May requires is to announce to the world that Britain has terminated *all* support – military, political, diplomatic – for the prosecution of this genocide, apologise to Igbo people, pay reparations on behalf of the 3.1 million Igbo murdered during phases I-III of the genocide (29 may 1966-12 January 1970) and the tens of thousands murdered subsequently during its phase-IV (13 January 1970-present day), pay reparations to the survivors, and pay reparations to reconstruct the shattered Biafra economy, Africa's most enterprising economy prior to the genocide.[19]

A May declaration terminating the genocide will bring this crime against humanity to an immediate end. Unquestionably.

* * *

---

[17]Wilson, *Labour Government, 1964-1970*, p. 630.
[18]*Sunday Telegraph*, London, 11 January 1970.
[19]Ekwe-Ekwe, *Biafra Revisited*.

11 BBC: "NATIONALISTS" OR "SECESSIONISTS"[1]

The *British Broadcasting Corporation*, the British state broadcaster, describes Scottish people in pursuit of independence from Britain or the United Kingdom as "Scottish nationalists".[2]

Any researcher can find this characterisation by examining the *BBC*'s well-stacked library of broadcasts and publications on the subject. This is why Alex Salmond, for instance, would be designated as "Scottish nationalist" or "former Scottish nationalist leader" and Nicola Sturgeon is described as "Scottish nationalist" or "Scottish nationalist leader".

Scots are 5 million in population and had in 1707 joined England out of *their own* choice (democratically) to form United Kingdom/British state. As the latter subsequently conquered most of the world to construct a "British empire", Scots played a *critical role* in the enterprise that belied their much smaller population background.[3] This ensured that they, now a constituent nation of the UK, became crucial beneficiaries of the stupendous harvest returns of global conquests and occupations. As a result, Scots indeed became the most unlikely candidates in 2014 who would wish to declare their independence from this 300-year-old immensely fruitful union.[4]

---

[1]This chapter was earlier published in *Rethinking Africa*, 8 December 2015 and *Pambazuka News: Voices for Freedom and Justice*, 15 December 2015.

[2]*BBC*, https://www.bbc.co.uk/news/topics/c0361dy3kv5t/scottish-nationalism, accessed 9 December 2018.

[3]See, for instance, John M. Mackenzie and T.M. Devine, *Scotland and the British Empire* (Oxford: Oxford University Press, 2011) and Andrew Thompson, "Empire and the British State" in Sarah E. Stockwell (ed), *The British Empire: Themes and Perspectives* (Oxford: Wiley-Blackwell, 2008), pp. 39-62.

[4]See Chap. 20 below.

The BBC, on the other hand, categorises the 50 million people of Biafra, southwestcentral Africa, who, since the 29 May 1966 launch date of the Igbo genocide by Nigeria have sought their independence from Nigeria, as "secessionists".[5]

In tune, the BBC describes Chukwuemeka Odumegwu Ojukwu, the founding leader of the Biafran independence movement, "secessionist leader" – a tag it wouldn't dare use to refer to either Alex Salmond or Nicola Sturgeon, not even the "controversial" Douglas Young![6] Similarly, whilst the BBC utilises "secessionist" to refer to hundreds of thousands of Biafran demonstrators across Biafra and elsewhere in the world currently involved in historic peaceful marches for independence, it wouldn't conceivably employ such a term in describing those Scots who voted "Yes" during the September 2014 referendum on Scottish independence. The latter are cited as "nationalists" or "supporters of Scottish independence".

Choice: "primary" vs "privilege"

Some would probably wonder what difference or differences, if any, the BBC's *choice* of terminologies makes: aren't these terms broadly synonymous – indicating the desire of two peoples, Biafrans and Scots, to declare their rights for self-determination or independence from Nigeria and Britain, respectively? No, not totally, except to the cursory observer. In the Scottish example, the BBC is almost straining itself to the hilt to emphasise that the Scots are the *primary*, actuating agency in deciding to exercise this right for freedom from Britain. If one is unaware that the United Nations regards this right for *all* peoples as inalienable, the thrust of BBC's coverage on the Scots has surely demonstrated this as such to its listeners, viewers, readers.

In contrast to the Scots, the BBC's approach to Biafran independence or self-determination couldn't be starker. Here, by harping on its worn "secessionist" signature, and the latter's evidently overarching territorial "decoupling" overtones, the BBC privileges the Nigeria state, this state that conqueror Britain *imposed arbitrarily* on scores of subjugated African nations and peoples in the aftermath of the pan-European leaders' infamous 1884-1885 Berlin-conquest conference on Africa.

Nigeria is arguably the most notorious of Africa's "Berlin states". This is the state, in full alliance with Britain, its creator, that carried out the Igbo genocide, 29 May 1966- 12 January 1970, the foundational genocide of post-(European)conquest state, murdering 3.1 million Igbo or one-quarter of this nation's population and

---

[5]*BBC*, https://twitter.com/bbcafrica/status/737584818926424064, accessed 9 December 2018.

[6]Scottish poet and academic and leader of the nationalist party in the 1940s who was opposed to serving in the British military *as a Scot* during the 1939-1945 war with Germany and was imprisoned consequently.

inaugurating Africa's current *age of pestilence* during which 12 million additional Africans have been murdered in further genocide in Rwanda (1994), Zaïre/Democratic Republic of the Congo (variously, since the late 1990s) and Darfur/Nuba Mountains/South Kordofan (all in Sudan since 2003), and in other wars in Africa. Besides being a scary kakistocratic lair, the Nigeria state also harbours two of the five most ruthless terrorist organisations in the world presently.[7]

Role(s)

So, why is the *British Broadcasting Corporation*, a state broadcaster largely funded by the British taxpayer, trenchantly hostile to the independence of Biafran people in a homeland in southwestcentral Africa, 3140 miles away from Britain in Europe?

Britain played an instrumental role in the Igbo genocide – politically, diplomatically, militarily. Britain's role covered the entire stretch of the genocide, phases I-III, 29 May 1966-12 January 1970, namely, from its conceptualisation in Lagos and Ibadan (west Nigeria) and Kaduna and Zaria and Sokoto (north Nigeria) to its catastrophic outcome. Without Britain, the Igbo genocide probably wouldn't have occurred. It was therefore not surprising that, as the slaughter of the Igbo intensified, particularly in those horrendous months of 1968-1969, Harold Wilson, British prime minister, as we have stated severally in this study, was totally unperturbed as he informed Clyde Ferguson, the United States state department special coordinator for relief to Biafra, that he, Harold Wilson, "would accept a half million dead Biafrans if that was what it took" Nigeria to destroy the Igbo resistance to the genocide.[8]

As for the *BBC*, the role of its *World Service* channel during the Igbo genocide was nothing short of being the external radio station for the prosecuting Nigerian genocidist junta in Lagos. This service was much more robust in its "rationalisation" of the genocide ("one Nigeria", "territorial integrity", "inviolability of colonial-set frontiers", "indissolubility of colonial-set borders", "rebels", "unacceptable precedence for rest of Africa", "secessionist!", "secessionist!", "secessionist!"...) than the rambling, ramshackle *Voice of Nigeria*.

Fifty years on, the *BBC* is still at it – supporting genocide against Igbo people by Nigeria in its broadcasts, as this crime against humanity continues unrelentingly to play out in phase-IV, launched on 13 January 1970. It should be noted that it is this very key *BBC* favourite "secessionist" tag on Biafran independence that the Nigerian regime invoked just last Wednesday, 2 December 2015, news item aptly carried by the

---

[7]Melissa Clarke, "Globally, terrorism is on the rise – but little of it occurs in Western countries", *ABC News*, 17 November 2015, https://www.abc.net.au/news/2015-11-17/global-terrorism-index-increase/6947200, accessed 17 November 2015.
[8]Morris, *Uncertain Greatness*, p. 122.

BBC on its website[9], *before* ordering its forces to attack peaceful Biafran freedom demonstrators in Onicha, the river port of Biafra's Oshimili Delta.

While the BBC has still not found it fit to broadcast the predictable outcome of this Onicha attack to the world, in other words *inform the world of the aftermath* of the Nigerian regime's blatant militarist threat on the peaceful demonstrators which the BBC itself announced hitherto, the following excerpts from the detailed report on what has since turned out as the Onicha massacre from the respected Lagos-based Civil Liberties Organisation is of utmost urgency:[10]

> A contingent of the heavily armed joint task force, consisting of personnel from the Army, Navy, police and Nigeria Security and Civil Defense Corps, last Wednesday [2 December 2015] attacked thousands of unarmed members of the Indigenous People of Biafra (IPOB), a group seeking a separate republic to be called Biafra ... The joint task force stormed the head bridge at 1:30 a.m. last Wednesday and began shooting sporadically into the crowd, killing 11 protesters and injuring numerous more ... This is a case of gross violation of human rights, use of excessive force and a crime against humanity ... This barbaric act has no place in a modern society as it also gravely undermines all UN, AU and other international, regional and national human rights mechanisms. Nothing, whatsoever, can justify this flagrant infraction on the rights of the citizens.

Once again, if anyone needs reminding that Nigeria has been for the Igbo a haematophagous quagmire throughout its history, the saliency of this latest massacre cannot be overstressed. In June 1945 and May 1953, right there under the very watch of the British occupation, the Fulani north region islamist/jihadist allies of the conquest, opposed to the Igbo-led African restoration-of-independence campaign, carried out carefully planned pogroms against Igbo migrant populations in Jos and Kano, respectively. Hundreds of Igbo were murdered in these outrages. The occupation charged no one for these crimes and the pogroms became dress-rehearsals for the May 1966-January 1970 genocide. Since the beginning of phase-IV of the genocide, 13 January 1970, tens of thousands of Igbo have been murdered across Nigeria but especially in the north region including those slaughtered by the Boko Haram terrorists.

Wednesday 2 December 2015 has now become a graphically unnerving day of tragedy across two continents. In north America, an islamist terrorist couple, husband and wife, embarked on the premeditated massacre of 14 peaceful citizens in San

---

[9]*BBC News*, "Nigeria warns Biafran secessionists", 2 December 2015, https://www.bbc.co.uk/news/live/world-africa-34949936, accessed 2 December 2015.
[10]"Pro-Biafra protests: Group accuses military of killing 11, wounding more", *Saharareporters*, New York, 5 December 2015, http://saharareporters.com/2015/12/05/pro-biafra-protests-group-accuses-military-killing-11-wounding-more, accessed 7 December 2015.

Bernardino, California, United States. In Africa, a terrorist Nigerian military brigade, assembled from specialised detachments of navy, army, police, secret police, other undisclosed units, embarked on the premeditated massacre of 11 peaceful citizens in Onicha, Biafra, a number of them college students. In response to these tragedies, the *BBC* has carried out expansive and continuing coverage of the San Bernardino massacre; the *BBC* has yet to cover the Onicha massacre in its broadcasts. Few now doubt the *BBC*'s doggedly entrenched position as a *principal motivational ally* in Nigeria's prosecution of the Igbo genocide, presently humanity's longest stretched genocide.

Babies and children's survivor-leadership

Biafrans will surely free their land. It is high time *BBC* editors got used to this eventuality. Since Friday 6 November 2015, 33 days, hundreds of thousands of peaceful Biafrans have turned their cities and towns and villages into panoramic freedom park marches, unprecedented in Africa, demanding the restoration of the sovereignty of their beloved Biafra and insisting on the release of freedom broadcaster Nnamdi Kanu, illegally detained by the Nigeria regime. Biafrans are redefining the dynamics of the march for freedom in Africa. Biafra will be free. Nigeria, this essentially anti-African imperium created to programmatically enrich British strategic interests in perpetuity is, in fact, in freefall with its epitaph already signposting its dreadful history: Haematophagous Monster.

Lest we forget: Those who lead this current phase of resistance to the Igbo genocide were the babies/children-survivors of the July 1967-January 1970 refugee death camps of Biafra, effectively survivors of that Harold Wilson gruesome death sentence. These great survivors, who have now come of age, will free Biafra.

The crime of genocide, thankfully, has no statute of limitations in international law. No other African peoples have suffered such an extensive and gruesome genocide and incalculable impoverishment in a century as the Igbo. All individuals and institutions involved in committing this crime, wherever they are or emplaced, will one day account for their role in court. In the meantime, the *British Broadcasting Corporation* will much sooner than later begin to come to terms with the fact that "what's good" in the universal right of self-determination for those who live between latitudes 55 and 65°N of the globe, for instance the Scots, "is good" for those who live between latitudes 4 and 14°N, for instance Biafrans.

* * *

12 "AFRICAN AMERICAN SON", US FOREIGN POLICY AND AFRICA: A STATEMENT[1]

In 2001, I called on the leaders of the world's principal arms-manufacturing states to *ban* all arms sales/transfers to Africa.[2] This was in response to the rampaging post-(European)conquest genocide and other wars in Africa, begun catastrophically by Nigeria and its British ally when they both perpetrated the Igbo genocide in May 1966-Janaury 1970 with the murder of 3.1 million Igbo people or one-quarter of this nation's population. Since the Igbo genocide, 12 million additional Africans have been murdered in follow-up genocides in Rwanda, Darfur and in other regions in the Sudan, and the Democratic Republic of the Congo, and in multiple wars across virtually all regions of the continent. Besides being co-perpetrator of the Igbo genocide, Britain has also emerged as the lead arms supplier to Africa including its genocide-states, especially Nigeria.[3]

In June 2009, six months after the inauguration of Barack Obama as the 44th president of the US, I updated the appeal to the globe's lead arms-manufacturing countries and noted, as follows:[4]

> US President Obama, his country's first African-descent head of state, can be assured of a lasting legacy of his presidency by imposing a comprehensive US arms embargo on this continent of

---

[1] An earlier version of this chapter was published in *Rethinking Africa*, 30 March 2016, and in *Pambazuka News: Voices for Freedom and Justice*, 7 April 2016.
[2] Ekwe-Ekwe, *African Literature in Defence of History*, pp. 134-138.
[3] Ekwe-Ekwe, *Readings from Reading*, pp. 129-131.
[4] Ibid., 193.

his fathers at the cusp of constructing new states of organic sensibilities – away from the terror of the genocide state. Obama should expand this initiative to involve other arms-exporters-to-Africa especially on such forums as the UN security council and the G-8. Arms ban to Africa should be internationally mandatory and enforceable.

Seven years and three months into his 2-term presidency which ended nine months later in January 2017, Obama gave an important interview to *The Atlantic* Magazine.[5] It is on his foreign policy during the period. This is a wide-ranging survey but one that hardly focuses on any subject on Africa except the 2011 US-British-French invasion of Libya, itself discussed, instead, within the overarching parameters of Middle East/Arab/islamic affairs. Muammar Gaddafi's regime is overthrown during the course of the invasion, Gaddafi is murdered as well as some members of his family in addition to some influential officials of his regime, most Libyan cities and infrastructure (irrefutable landmark achievements of the Gaddafi years in office) are spectacularly smashed up, and Libya is subsequently an "ISIS haven" (as *The Atlantic* interviewer Jeffery Goldberg terms it),[6] largely controlled by groupings within the islamist jihadist international conglomeration – part of who Gaddafi was at war with prior to the West Trio invasion and murder.

In the interview, Obama describes the aftermath of the Libya invasion as a "mess", a "s*** show"[7], blames the British and French leaders (David Cameron and Nicolas Sarkozy respectively) who he co-led the invasion for this resultant "ISIS haven – that he [Obama] has [latterly] targeted with air strikes"[8] but, curiously, absolves himself from the débâcle. For Obama, Cameron's and Sarkozy's roles in the campaign are those of "free riders"[9] who obviously cherish the perceived political capital that such invasions bring from enthusiastic sectors of domestic political opinion but are often less thoughtful of the consequences that such devastating acts of violence have on the ground or region of the world of perpetration, as they await eagerly for the invasion next time!

So, on Libya, after the troika-invasion, Obama recalls with barely disguised criticism, Cameron and Sarkozy just moved on... Cameron loses interest on this phase of the crisis/emergency, the "follow-up", as he is "distracted by other things" whilst Sarkozy appears more interested to "trumpet the flights he [is] taking in the [invasion's] air campaign" even though, Obama is keen to emphasise, "we [the US]

---

[5]Jeffery Goldberg, "The Obama Doctrine", *The Atlantic*, April 2016. Issue, http://www.theatlantic.com/magazine/archive/2016/04/the-obama-doctrine/471525 , accessed 11 March 2016.
[6]Ibid.
[7]Ibid.
[8]Ibid.
[9]Ibid.

had wiped out all [Libyan] air defenses and essentially set up the entire infrastructure [for the invasion]".[10]

Raft of ironies

What is at the crux of the politics of this post-Libya invasion apparent dilemma is the operationalisation of Obama's so-called leading-from-behind strategy[11] in the pursuit and promulgation of foreign policy projects with his allies, especially those in Europe, on the crucial task of role assignment/rationalisation. On this accord, ironically, Sarkozy's exaggerated claims of France's role in the invasion is a boon to Obama's "leading-from-behind" positioning as it enabled the US to "purchase France's involvement in a way that made it less expensive for us and less risky for us".[12] The key phrase is of course "less risky" and the Africa continent, in focus, where the French already had the notorious record of having carried out forty nine (49) invasions of most of the 22 "francophonie" countries here in the previous 51 years with hardly any international repercussions,[13] couldn't be better placed than anywhere else in the world, particularly the South World, as the geographical site to mount such an aggression involving the US with minimal risks. It should also be noted that "leading-from-behind" is a cardinal feature of the overall presumed "retrenchment"[14] thrust or dynamics of Obama's foreign policy based on his readings of US's international relations in the past: "We have history ... We have history with Iran, we have history with Indonesia and Central America. So we have to understand our history when we start talking about intervening, and understand the source of other people's suspicions".[15] Yet the 2011 US co-led invasion of Libya fits in more appropriately with this "we have history"-heritage than a candidacy for some envisaged "retrenchment" of interventionist/expansionist programmes overseas.

In yet another startling irony, not covered in *The Atlantic* interview, Obama had, in 2010, one year in office, reinstated the trail of France's invasion history in Africa (mentioned above) which President Bush, his predecessor, had frozen for seven years as "punishment" for the French 2003 refusal to join the US-led coalition invasion of Iraq. Soon after the embargo was lifted, Sarkozy ordered the French military, true to

---

[10]Ibid.
[11]James Jay Corafano, "Obama's 'lead from behind' strategy has US in full retreat", *The Heritage Foundation*, 6 February 2015, https://www.heritage.org/global-politics/commentary/obamas-lead-behind-strategy-has-us-full-retreat, accessed 12 March 2015.
[12]Goldberg, "The Obama Doctrine".
[13]Ekwe-Ekwe, *Readings from Reading*, p. 31.
[14]Goldberg, "The Obama Doctrine".
[15]Ibid.

type, to attack Abidjan, Côte d'Ivoire (French invasion no. 49 of an African state since 1960), a *presage* to the following year's Sarkozy-Cameron-Obama Libya invasion (again for the French, Africa invasion no. 50 since 1960), overthrew state president Laurent Gbagbo, arrested him and his wife and dragged them to an international court in The Hague for "trial" on trumped-up charges, installed a local puppet as a Gbagbo replacement, murdered 2300 Africans during the course of the assault, and significantly destroyed several business and residential districts of Abidjan. In 2012, following his loss in the French presidential elections, Sarkozy passes his country's invasion-baton-for-Africa to successor François Hollande, who, in turn, has since dispatched the French military to invade Mali (2013) and Central African Republic (2013).

Not-"retrenchment" and ongoing Igbo genocide in Biafra

It should now be evident that Africa *does not* figure distinctly in the frame of Obama's assumed policy of "retrenchment" of spheres of US interventionism abroad. On the contrary, Africa very much represents the territorial zone of US's not-"retrenchment". Despite Obama's criticism of the British and French leaderships on post-Libya invasion intra-coalition relations, he has in fact privileged the role of these dual lead-conqueror states of Africa in the pursuit of other goals of US interventionism on the continent more under the contemptuous tactical rubric of "Africa is direct responsibility of London and Paris",[16] a throwback particularly to the 1950s-1970 era of the Dwight Eisenhower-Lynden Johnson presidencies, which also manifests itself in that working slogan already cited, "leading-from-behind". We will refer to one other goal as an example and this has profound consequences across the African World and history. Considering this importance, it requires a bit of background for elucidation.

In March 2015, the US, in close collaboration with Britain, imposed Muhammadu Buhari as head of Nigeria regime (echoes of "we have a history with Iran"?/"we have a history with Indonesia"?[17]). Buhari has been known to the British for 50 years – since the outbreak of the 29 May 1966 Igbo genocide, the foundational genocide of post-(European)conquest Africa, co-launched with its client state Nigeria. As already noted, 3.1 million Igbo or 25 per cent of the Igbo population were murdered during the genocide. Britain, which until six years earlier was the conqueror-occupying power in Nigeria for sixty-years, was centrally involved in the prosecution of the genocide politically, diplomatically and militarily – right from its launch date, Sunday 29 May

---

[16]See, especially, Herbert Ekwe-Ekwe and Lakeson Okwuonicha, *Why #DonaldTrump is #great for #Africa* (Dakar and Reading: African Renaissance, 2018), chap. 3.
[17]Goldberg, "The Obama Doctrine".

1966, and throughout its gruesome and devastating three phases during the course of 44 months, ending 12 January 1970.[18] Nigeria launched phase-IV of the genocide on 13 January 1970. This has continued unabated with tens of thousands of Igbo murdered and their Biafra homeland effectively occupied by Nigeria. Britain has actively maintained support for the genocide wholeheartedly and steadfastly during this latter phase.[19]

Muhammadu Buhari himself has been a genocidist operative in the Nigeria military – straight ahead from the launch date of the Igbo genocide and during the Nigerian expansive trail of the mass slaughter of Igbo military and civilians alike in north and west Nigeria regions from 29 July 1966-July 1967 to encapsulate phases I-II of the genocide timeframe. During phase-III of the genocide, the invasion of Biafra, July 1967-January 1970, Buhari was commander of a genocidist corps in north and northcentral Biafra, slaughtering to the hilt. As from 13 January 1970, beginning of phase-IV of the genocide, Buhari has adhered rigidly to or overseen the Nigeria regime's blanket policy of non-development of occupied Biafra, the regime's aggressive degradation of socioeconomic life in Biafra, and the regime's exponential expropriation of the rich oil reserves of Biafra.[20] Biafran assets looted by the occupation stand at US$1000 billion. Over time, since 13 January 1970, Buhari has exhibited a calculated, deafening silence over the course of the murder of those tens of thousands of Igbo people across Nigeria but especially in his north Nigeria homeland by regime forces/allied forces including those massacred by the islamist Boko Haram terrorist organisation[21] in the past six years.

The Igbo Studies Association had in a conference held at Howard University in April 2012 on "Nigeria and Boko Haram terrorism and its impact on the Igbo population in north Nigeria" noted the overall silence by the Obama administration over this emergency. Obama remained unrelentingly adamant, throughout this phase of his presidency, of *not* designating Boko Haram a terrorist organisation despite the latter's murder of thousands of African peoples, overwhelmingly Igbo, at the time (it wouldn't be until November 2013 that the US declared Boko Haram "terrorist" because Washington judged the group was "[now] develop[ing] links with other [islamists] such as al-Qaeda ... to wage a global jihad"[22]). This was despite the evidence, from

---

[18] Ekwe-Ekwe, *Biafra* Revisited.
[19] Ekwe-Ekwe, *Biafra Revisited* and Ekwe-Ekwe, *Readings from Reading*, especially chaps. 1, 15, 22 and 31.
[20] Ekwe-Ekwe, *Readings from Reading*, especially chap. 29.
[21] One of the world's five deadliest terrorist organisations – Melissa Clarke, "Globally terrorism is on the rise – but little of it occurs in Western countries", ABC News, 17 November 2015, https://www.abc.net.au/news/2015-11-17/global-terrorism-index-increase/6947200, accessed 17 November 2015.
[22] *The Telegraph*, London, 13 November 2013.

the grounds in Nigeria, that those who supported Boko Haram, *including* Muhammadu Buhari who Barack Hussein Obama would in March 2015 impose on Nigeria as head of the state's regime, were well known to then Goodluck Jonathan regime in power. Jonathan himself personally acknowledged publicly the extent of Boko Haram infiltration of his regime: "Boko Haram is everywhere in the executive arm of [my] government, in the legislative arm of [my] government and even in the judiciary. Some are also in the armed forces, the police and other security [services] ... Some continue to dip their hands and eat with you and you won't even know the person who will point a gun at you or plant a bomb behind your house".[23] Despite this Boko Haram terrorist insurgency on Jonathan, Barack Obama had no sympathies for the plight of this regime whatever. Olusegun Adeniyi in his *Against the Run of Play* (2017), quotes Jonathan: "Obama made it clear [right from the outset] that he wanted a change of government in Nigeria".[24] Jonathan, an Ijo zoologist, is the first personage in the assemblage of Nigerian public officials *without* any connections or roles in the Igbo genocide to occupy the position of head of regime in Nigeria since 29 May 1966.

So since Buhari came to power in May 2015 as a result of that US-British intervention and imposition, hundreds of Igbo people demanding the restoration of their independence and the release of several members of the freedom leadership including Nnamdi Kanu, head of the Indigenous People of Biafra and broadcaster at Biafra freedom radio, have been murdered – usually shot at sight during peaceful freedom marches by the Nigerian genocidist military and police equipped mostly with British weapons. Beginning at the Oshimili River twin city of Onicha on 2 December 2015, this orgy of massacres by the Nigerian military has spread to other Biafran cities including Asaba (the Onicha twin), Enuugwu, Igwe Ocha, Umuahia and Aba through the remaining of December and into January-March 2016. The massacres have been meticulously documented by several news organisations and individuals and human rights groups.[25] The Nigerian military's perpetrated massacre of 22 Biafrans attending a morning prayer session in a local high school in Aba (east Biafra) on 9 February 2016[26] was particularly gruesome and shocking and very disturbing images from the scene soon went viral on the internet. In a sentence, genocidist Nigeria military contingents were literally at loose in Biafra massacring and maiming defenceless people who expressed their inalienable right to freedom and beginning in early

---

[23]*Reuters*, 9 January 2012.
[24]*allafrica.com*, 26 April 2017.
[25]See, for instance, International Society for Civil Liberties & the Rule of Law, "Corpses of murdered IPOB members in Aba burrow pits set ablaze and burnt to ashes by suspected agents of the government of Nigeria", Onicha, 4 March 2016.
[26]International Society for Civil Liberties & the Rule of Law, Onicha, 21 February 2016.

February (2016), they were joined by Fulani militia terrorists[27] rampaging swathes of villages in north, northcentral and southwest of Biafra. On a comparative note, the Nigerian genocidist troopers have attacked chosen or pre-targeted Biafran population centres with the same spontaneity, precision and virulence that a Boko Haram terrorist cell would employ in attacking fishing communities in Baga, north Nigeria,[28] or a church in Yola (north Nigeria) or an ISIS terrorist unit would effect whilst attacking the *Charlie Hebdo* editorial board meeting in Paris, France,[29] or attacking a Jewish supermarket in Paris[30] or a rock concert in Paris[31] or attacking an airport terminal in Brussels, Belgium,[32] or attacking a metro train in Brussels...[33]

Noticeably, there was no condemnation of any of the manifestations of Nigerian genocidist military attacks on the Biafran public during the 3-month period (launched 2 December 2015) from David Cameron's British government. The same haunting silence pervaded from the Obama administration. Not a word. In sharp contrast, when on 12 December 2015 a Nigeria military brigade operating in Zaria, northcentral Nigeria, attacked and murdered several shiite muslim protesters in a procession, there was a robust response from the US government: "The United States calls on the government of Nigeria to quickly, credibly, and transparently investigate these events in Zaria and hold to account any individuals found to have committed crimes".[34] This *same* US government wouldn't, didn't follow up with similar or any other statements of concern in the following acts of Nigerian genocidist attacks on Igbo population in Biafra: Onicha (17 December 2015), where eight Biafrans were murdered and scores wounded; Aba (19 January 2016), where 10 Biafrans were murdered and scores wounded; Aba (9 February 2016), where 22 were murdered and scores wounded.

No US president, since the outbreak of the Igbo genocide in May 1966 during the Lynden Johnson presidency, has unambiguously supported the mission of genocidist Nigeria as Barack Obama. Obama has in fact disrupted the fulsome goodwill for the people of Biafra begun by the Richard Nixon presidency (Republican president, "right wing"!) soon after the end of phase-III of the genocide (12 January 1970) and continued by subsequent presidencies to date, Republican or Democrat, of an

---

[27]Cousin of Boko Haram's which also belongs to the league of the globe's five deadliest terrorist organisations – *See also Clarke*, "Globally terrorism is on the rise – but little of it occurs in Western countries".
[28]See chap. 9 above.
[29]Ibid.
[30]Ibid.
[31]*The Guardian*, London, 14 November 2015.
[32]*The Guardian*, London, 22 March 2016.
[33]Ibid.
[34]*Daily Mail*, London, 16 December 2015.

enhanced Igbo emigration programme to the US. This accounts for the hundreds of thousands of Igbo Americans presently, 50 years on, many of them in very influential positions in academia, the corporate world, media and information and the state, and their children and grandchildren thriving appreciably...

It is surely an unconscionable tragedy of incalculable historical consequences that Barack Obama, the first African-descent president of the US republic in 233 years of existence was elected in office in November 2008 to end up with an abominable presidential legacy supporting the Igbo genocide – executed on the ground by Nigeria, a Fulani islamist/jihadist-led state, and its suzerain state Britain. The duo genocidist states have murdered 3.1 million Igbo and tens of thousands more since the launch of the genocide on Sunday 29 May 1966.

"African American son"

Finally, in introducing the section of *The Atlantic* interview with Obama that focuses on Israel, Jeffery Goldberg recalls a conversation between Obama and Israeli prime minister Benjamin Netanyahu which perhaps captures the "frosty" characterisation that many an observer has used in describing the relationship between the two officials at the time. "Obama felt that Netanyahu was behaving in a condescending fashion," Goldberg writes, as the Israeli leader had "launched into something of a lecture about the brutal region in which he lives..."[35] Obama retorts: "Bibi, you have to understand something ... I'm the African American son of a single mother, and I live here, in this house. I live in the White House. I managed to get elected president of the United States. You think I don't understand what you're talking about, but I do."[36]

As I indicated at the beginning of these reflections, Africa, the African World, hardly features anywhere as a subject of focus or discussion in this interview covering Obama's foreign policy during seven years in office as US president. The reader may therefore wonder what relevance Obama's reference to "African American son" or indeed his "White House" home address during the exchange with Netanyahu has to the entire thrust of the interview beyond the record reminder, *an important one that must be stressed*, given the pivotal role played by the African humanity in this history, of the first person of African descent to occupy the position of president of the United States 233 years after the founding of the republic. But the focus, surely, cannot begin and just end with an African "entry" in the "White House"! What does the occupier do whilst there in residence? How do they embody and respond to the weight of the

---

[35] Goldberg, "The Obama Doctrine".
[36] Ibid.

The longest genocide

African history antecedent? What is this African history? What has the occupier done whilst there in residence?

African Atlantic discourses

Soon after Obama's inauguration as US president in January 2009, one envisaged the reactivation, in some formats, of those democratic forums and spaces where African Atlantic discourses involving a range of outstanding intellectuals (such as those listed below) were so instrumental in launching and implementing transformative initiatives that have been of profound benefits across the African World especially in the past 300 years. Unfortunately, this reactivation hasn't occurred and, interestingly ironical, that Netanyahu's "lecture"-designation Goldberg referred to in *The Atlantic* interview hasn't been totally dissimilar to what some African continental heads of regime feel has been the trademark of Obama's *own* approach to them, in their relations, during the entire 8-year stretch of the latter's time in office.

Still on the African Atlantic discourses, it is extraordinary to wish to contemplate how the intellectuals engaged in that circle of three centuries of demonstrable cerebral activity would deliberate over the haunting tragedy of *this* African-descent occupier in the "White House" residence who has zealously supported the ruthless mission of Muhammadu Buhari, the head of the islamist/jihadist genocidist regime in Nigeria, southwestcentral Africa, whom he, Obama, had earlier on installed in office in collaboration with the British prime minister: Buhari murders peaceful and defenceless Africans in Biafra so ghastly for a reason not any more complicated than that 7-letter word which has come to define the strategic quest of peoples across the African World for 400 years – *freedom*.

So, what would the following, from some of the brightest minds of the African World, think of this tragedy?: Olaudah Equiano, Sojourner Truth, Harriet Tubman, Edward Wilmot Blyden, Frederick Douglass, WEB Du Bois, James Baldwin, Léopold Sédar Senghor, CLR James, Eric Williams, Martin Luther King, Malcolm X, Chinua Achebe, Cheikh Anta Diop, John Henrik Clarke, Fela Anikulapo-Kuti, George Lamming, John Coltrane, Julius Nyerere, Alain Locke, Nelson Mandela, Steve Biko, Ivan Van Sertima, Aimé Césaire, Nicolás Guillén, Chukwuemeka Odumegwu-Ojukwu, Mariam Makeba, Ossie Davis, Marcus Garvey, Ruby Dee, Louis Armstrong, George James, Walter Rodney, Jacob Carruthers, Toni Morrison, Théophile Obenga, King Jaja of Opobo, Duke Ellington, Samuel Coleridge-Taylor, Christopher Okigbo, Kwame Nkrumah, Martin Delaney, Adu Boahen, Nwafor Orizu, Mbonu Ojike, Bethuel Ogot, Amilcar Cabral, Max Roach, Bob Marley, Robert Sobukwe, George Russell, Okot p'Bitek, W Arthur Lewis, Chancellor Williams, Patrice Lumumba, Kenneth Onwuka Dike, David Diop, Adiele Afigbo, Peter Tosh, Kofi Awoonor, Molefi Kete Asante, Charles Mingus, Uche Okeke, Wangari Maathai, Ifeanyi Menkiti, Esiaba Irobi,

Maurice Bishop, Dedan Kimathi, Theophilus Enwezor Nzegwu Michael Echeruo, Maulana Karenga, Alioune Diop, Flora Nwapa, Eni Njoku, Ama Ata Aidoo, Ngũgĩ wa Thiong'o, Eric Dolphy, Ousmane Sembéne, Mariama Bâ, Léon-Gontram Damas, Agwuncha Arthur Nwankwo, Sydney Poitier, Abbey Lincoln, Uzo Egonu, Langston Hughes, Emmanuel Obiechina, Mariamba Ani, Thomas Sankara, Bessie Head, Hilary Beckles.

* * *

13 WHO WAGES GENOCIDE? WHO PLANS TO INVADE SOMEONE ELSE'S STATE?

Reflections on this emerging orthodoxy of nonsense: Hillary Clinton, "white men", "[not] white men" and Africa[1]

Hillary Clinton has continued her unrelentingly tortured tale of why she lost the November 2016 US presidential election to Donald Trump, her anti-establishment opponent. In the latest episode, narrated to an audience in Mumbai, India, where she was on a visit, Clinton now blames "white men" for her poll defeat: "We [did] not do well with white men and [did] not do well with married, white women. And part of that is ... a sort of ongoing pressure [for the latter] to vote the way [their] husband, [their] boss, [their] son, whoever, believes [they] should...".[2]

The reflections here will not assess the veracity or otherwise of Clinton's claims on the role of "white men" in that election but would focus more pointedly to what impact this demographic constituency, which Clinton undoubtedly feels is crucially important to her political ambitions and destiny, had on her performance and policy

---

[1] An earlier version of this chapter was published as a commentary in *Rethinking Africa*, 23 March 2018.
[2] Jack Crowe, "Hillary: white women were 'pressurised' to vote for Trump by their husbands", *National Review*, 13 March 2018, https://www.nationalreview.com/2018/03/hillary-clinton-white-women-pressured-husbands-vote-trump/, accessed 13 March 2018.

outcomes on Africa specifically, whilst she was US secretary of state in January 2009-February 2013.

Contradictory

The background to Clinton becoming US secretary of state in 2009 would, in the overall, appear to lend some element of credibility to the premise of her presumed problematic relationship with the country's "white men" electorate, albeit contradictorily. In the previous year, 2008, Clinton had had a bitterly fought presidential election contest with Barack Obama, an African American, in which she was beaten. On winning, Obama actively sought Clinton's goodwill by offering her the position of secretary of state in his incoming administration and paying off her huge outstanding campaign debts with surplus funds from the former's campaign organisation. Clinton's acceptance of Obama's cabinet position offer helped in the process of "healing" in the Democratic party after the evidently rancorous poll and her tacit agreement not to challenge the latter in the 2012 election cycle, if he were to seek another term's presidential run, also included an "understanding" that a 2-term President Obama would deploy the incalculable resources of such an incumbency to support his former rival to run again for the presidency in 2016.

So, thanks to Barack Obama, the African American, i.e., "[*not*]white man", indeed the first African-descent elected president after 233 years of the founding of the US republic, Hilary Clinton becomes secretary of state in January 2009 and is duly emplaced on the path of contesting for the presidency, yet again, this time with the expected robust backing of her new "ally" and employer.

Imposition and invasion

On Africa, right from the outset, two distinct policy areas defined the Obama administration's focus: imposition and invasion – not too distinct from generally the case in previous US administrations. And both (new) president and secretary of state were in tandem in the formulation and implementation of this mission. A year in office, Obama reinstated the notorious trail of France's invasion history in Africa which his predecessor, George W Bush ("white man", "right-wing"!), had blocked for seven years as "punishment" for the 2003 French refusal to join the US-led coalition invasion of Iraq. Prior to Bush's ban, the French had carried out 48 military invasions of most of the so-called 22 so-called *francophonie* states in Africa between 1960 and 2003 which every US president of the era each supported.

Elated by the Obama approval, French President Sarkozy at once resumed his country's 50 years of flagrant military campaigns in Africa. Sarkozy ordered his military to invade Côte d'Ivoire (French invasion no. 49 of an African state since 1960) which overthrew the government of President Laurent Gbagbo in the process and installed a new regime headed by an Ivorian puppet who would oversee the vast French economic and strategic interests in the country and region. During the assault, 2300 Africans were murdered and several business and residential districts of the commercial city of Abidjan, the principal focus of the invasion, were significantly destroyed.

Emboldened by the French "success" in Côte d'Ivoire in southwestcentral Africa, Obama mapped out further to the north of the continent, to Libya, a year later, 2011, to implement his next invasion target in Africa which would be executed by the US *and* the French, and Britain, the other lead EuropeanConqueror-state of Africa. This time round, the US would be a far more active, *direct participant* in the operation. Indeed, Hillary Clinton took up the composite range of most uncompromising advocacy for the US involvement in the Libya invasion that its politics and aftermath became the central plank of her record as secretary of state.

Just as in Côte d'Ivoire, the invasion of Libya was catastrophic. The West tripartite force overthrew the Muammar Gaddafi regime during the attack, Gaddafi himself was murdered as well as some members of his family in addition to some influential officials of his regime, hundreds of other Libyans were murdered, and most Libyan cities and principal communication network (outstanding achievements of the Gaddafi years in office) were spectacularly smashed up. Obama could not restrain himself in emphasising the crucial role of the US in this operation: "we [the US] had wiped out all [Libyan] air defenses and essentially set up the entire infrastructure [for the invasion]".[3]

Besides these military invasions of stipulated states, the other method that the Obama administration pursued its aggressive policy of "leadership" imposition in Africa was to interfere or meddle in elections/"elections" in countries elsewhere on the continent as shown in Egypt (2012), Kenya (2013) and Nigeria (2015). Both interferences in the polls in Egypt and Kenya failed spectacularly but in Nigeria Obama *succeeded* in imposing Muhammadu Buhari, one of the vilest Nigerian genocidist islamist/jihadist operatives during these 52 years of the Igbo genocide (1966-present day) as head of Nigeria regime. For Obama, given the historical background noted earlier as the first African-descent president of the US republic in 233 years of existence, his unflinching support for an African-led genocidist regime in Africa waging genocide, a crime against humanity, against an African people is the abhorrent legacy of his presidency. In that last 18 months' duration of the presidency after the Buhari imposition (May 2015-November 2016), the genocidist Buhari military and its Boko Haram and Fulani militia adjunct terrorist forces (two of the world's five deadliest terrorist organisations – Melissa Clarke, "Globally, terrorism is

---

[3]Goldberg, "The Obama Doctrine".

on the rise – but little of it occurs in Western countries", *ABC News*, 17 November 2017) murdered 2000 Igbo across Biafran cities, towns and villages. Neither Obama's White House nor his state department nor his embassy in Nigeria ever condemned any of these stretches of murders.

It should be added that Obama's imposition of Buhari was carried out with David Cameron, then British prime minister, and had been preceded by the Obama-Clinton insistence, *whilst Clinton was secretary of state*, of not designating Boko Haram *terrorist* despite the latter's murder of thousands of African peoples, overwhelmingly Igbo, during the period. It was therefore not surprising to quite a few observers when a US-based social group claimed in November 2016 that the Buhari regime had donated "[US]$500 million to the [Hillary] Clinton [election] campaign".[4] It was no secret that the Buhari regime was confident that Clinton would win the election and continue Obama's support for its genocide against Igbo people.

The score: "white men" vs "[not]white men"

As far as the Obama presidency (January 2009 - January 2017) was concerned, it was in fact business as usual on Africa as its policy programme developed and implemented on the continent explicitly demonstrated. Following Hillary Clinton's choice of that lexical configuration, "white men", other likely expressions in the same semantic field should now be invoked to elaborate on this policy programme in the concluding notes here.

It would undoubtedly be the case that the former secretary of state wouldn't state that she worked for an administration headed by a "white man" *but* a "[*not*]white man". During two terms of presidency, this "[not]white man"-headed government deployed a dual track policy on Africa marked by invasions of states and impositions of "leaders" as we have indicated. Prior to January 2009, in US administrations since the 1960s, *all headed* by "white men", invasions and impositions of leaders, directly or indirectly (especially in approval or in complicity with allies particularly France, Britain, Portugal, South Africa, Rhodesia[5] also featured highly as foreign policy goals in Africa. Indeed, given the overriding importance of Libya to Clinton's work in the Obama administration, we should recall that on 14 April 1986 the "white man"/"right-wing"-led Ronald Reagan government ordered the US air force to bomb Libya, pointedly for a raid that was over in just an hour; 25 years later,

---

[4]*247ureports.com*, "Buhari donated $500 million to Clinton campaign: US group", 16 November 2016, http://247ureports.com/2016/11/buhari-donated-500m-to-clintons-campaign-us-group/, accessed 17 November 2016.

[5]See, for instance, Mohamed A El Khawas and Barry Cohen, ed., *The Kissinger Study of Southern Africa: National Security Memorandum 39 [SECRET]* (Wesport: Lawrence Hill, 1976).

in 2011, another US president, this time a "[not]white man", ordered the same US air force to bomb Libya – but for a much longer duration and the consequences duly recorded. Additionally, it should be noted that Hillary Clinton was closely supported in her hardline "invade-Libya" position by none other than Susan Rice, an African American woman, *another* "[not]white man", Obama's advisor on national security who was assistant secretary of state on Africa in the Bill Clinton presidency back in 1994 during the Rwanda genocide, executed by "[not]white men", and had covered up this crime at the time because the administration she worked for decided not to intervene to stop the slaughter.[6]

It should now be obvious that:

1a. "white man"-president can invade, overthrow, impose; "[not]white man"-president can invade, overthrow, impose

1b. "white man"-state functionaries can pursue policies to invade, overthrow, impose; "[not]white man"-state functionaries can pursue policies to invade, overthrow, impose

2. "white man"-president/"white man"-king/ "white man"-chancellor/"white man"-prime minister/"white man"-general/"white man"-journalist/"white man"-academic/"white man"-cleric/"white man"-farmer... has planned, executed, supported genocide(s) against a people or peoples over the course of recent history

3. "[not]white man"-president/"[not] white man"-king/"[not]white man" attorney/"[not]white man"-journalist/"[not]white man-academic/"[not] white man"-cleric/"[not] white man"-sergeant/"[not]white man"-corporal/"[not]white man"-general... has planned, executed, supported genocide(s) against a people or peoples over the course of recent history.

Surely, a serious, fruitful examination of any feature of human society requires the development, articulation and deployment of critical tools of analysis to help or enhance interpretation and understanding. As we have shown, Hillary Clinton's "white man" lexicon and its variations have surely not been helpful tools to enable us understand what, in fact, presents as the unchanging thrust and tenor in the trajectory

---

[6]Cf. Alice Gatebuke, "On this anniversary of Rwandan genocide, Bill Clinton's words ring hollow", *Huffpost*, 14 April 2017, https://www.huffingtonpost.com/alice-gatebuke/on-22nd-anniversary-rwandan-genocide-bill-clinton_b_9677440.html, accessed 1 June 2018.

of US foreign policy in Africa for the greater part of the past 50 years irrespective of whether or not the president and/or other state officials in office are "white men" or "[not]white men".

Just as in Africa, Clinton's "white man" mantra would hardly be fit for purpose as an explanation for why she lost the United States November 2016 presidential poll.

* * *

The longest genocide

(**sparks of Biafra creativity I**: left-right from the top left: **Flora Nwapa** [first African woman {continental} published novelist], **Michael Okpara** [physician and premier of the then east Nigeria region; visionary who oversaw Africa's most resourceful and dynamic economy assessed at the time as being enroute to emerging as a major manufacturing and industrial power], **Kenneth Onwuka Dike** [historian and doyen of the reconsructory school of African historical studies and the author of the classic *Trade and Politics in the Niger Delta, 1830-1885*; first African vice chancellor of the University of Ibadan], **Chinua Achebe** [Father of African Literature and author of the classic, *Things Fall Apart*], **Chukwuemeka Odumegwu Ojukwu** [historian and general and leader of the Biafra resistance government during the Igbo genocide, phases I-III, 29 May 1966 to 12 January 1970], Igbo women on freedom march in Owere (east Biafra), 17 August 2018, **Theophilus Enwezor Nzegwu** [distinguished electrical engineer, academic Airforce pilot (Royal Air Force) and Airforce commander, Nigerian Air Force], **Christopher Okigbo** [Africa's most celebrated and influential poet], **John Lennon** (of the Beatles) who returns his MBE medal to Queen Elizabeth II of England on 25 November 1969 in protest against British perpetration of Igbo genocide)

III Biafra freedom

Flag of Republic of Biafra

(**sparks of Biafra creativity II:** left to right from the top: **Nnamdi Kanu** [intrepid head of Indigenous People of Biafra {IPOB} and broadcaster of Radio Freedom Biafra], **Ezinne Uko** [winner of $100K first prize at the Econet goGettaz all Africa entrepreneurship contest, Nairobi, January 2018], **Uzo Egonu** [one of the African world's most distinguished painters], **Felicia Ejezie** [dynamic and irrepressible community-based leader of the Biafra resistance, popularly known as "mama Biafra"], Biafra women on freedom march in Owere [east Biafra, 17 August 2018], **Save-a-Soul Quintet of Biafran school girls from Regina Pacis Secondary School Onicha** [southwest Biafra] wins global technovation contest, San Jose, United States [9 August 2018], cover of **Chinua Achebe**'s *There was a Country*, Indigenous People of Biafra officials **Oby Mboma**, **Uche Mefor** and **Carol Munday**)

14 YEAR 50 – BIAFRA BEFORE BREXIT[1]

Denial is the final stage that lasts throughout and always follows a genocide. It is among the surest indicators of further genocidal massacres. The perpetrators of genocide ... try to cover up the evidence ... They deny that they committed any crimes, and often blame what happened on the victims. They block investigations of the crimes, and continue to govern ... with impunity ... unless they are captured and a tribunal is established to try them. The response to denial is punishment by an international tribunal or national courts...

(**Gregory Stanton**, president, Genocide Watch; professor in genocide studies and prevention, George Mason University, Virginia)

On 6 July 1967, Nigeria expands the territorial range of its execution of the Igbo genocide, the foundational genocide of post-(European)conquest Africa, which it launched 14 months earlier, 29 May 1966, murdering 100,000 Igbo people. Now, it embarks on a land, air and sea-borne invasion of Biafra, with the British government, under the leadership of Harold Wilson, playing a key if not *central* role in the campaign[2]. Indeed without British support, pointedly if not ironically 50 years *before* Brexit, the Igbo genocide, this crime against humanity, would probably not have occurred. This phase-III of the genocide stretches for 30 months during which 3 million Igbo are murdered.

---

[1] This chapter was first published in *Rethinking Africa*, 6 July 2016 and *Pambazuka News: Voices for Freedom and Justice*, 21 July 2016.
[2] See chap. 7 above.

The longest genocide

Definitive mission

Nigeria is supported militarily, diplomatically and politically in its invasion by a string of allies, notably Britain, as already stated, Egypt, the Sudan, Saudi Arabia and the Soviet Union. Right from the outset, genocidist Nigeria establishes on the ground and employs rape and abduction of Igbo girls and women and the public execution of Igbo boys and men as pivotal instruments in waging the campaign. Its ghoulish anthem of the genocide, broadcast uninterruptedly on state-owned Kaduna radio (shortwave transmission) and television and with editorial comments on the theme, regularly published in both state-owned *New Nigerian* (daily) newspaper and (Hausa) weekly *Gaskiya Ta fi Kwabo* during the period, has these lyrics in Hausa:

Mu je mu kashe nyamiri
Mu kashe maza su da yan maza su
Mu chi mata su da yan mata su
Mu kwashe kaya su

(English translation: Let's go murder the damned Igbo/Murder their men and boys/Rape their wives and daughters/Cart off their property)

This genocidist intent, particularly its empirically earmarked specifics, is unequivocally explicit and its overarching method sets the precedent of the savagery and barbarity that are the hallmarks of the genocide and subsequent genocides in Africa as Rwanda (1994), Darfur/Nuba Mountains/Blue Nile/South Kordofan (the Sudan, variously since 2004), and Democratic Republic of the Congo (since the late 1990s) attest.

At the apogee of the Igbo genocide, beginning from the second-half of 1968 when thousands of Igbo children and older citizens die daily from starvation (one of the genocidist's publicly-stated "weapons" in the prosecution of the crime as articulated by chief "theorist" and propagator Obafemi Awolowo himself[3]), British Prime Minister Wilson insists, most unconscionably, when he informs Clyde Ferguson (United States state department special coordinator for relief to Biafra) that he, *Harold Wilson*, "would accept half a million dead Biafrans if that was what it took" the Nigerian génocidaires to destroy the Igbo resistance to the genocide.[4] Nigeria in fact ends up murdering 3 million Igbo – 2 and one-half million more than Wilson's grim 500,000 Igbo-death wish. Furthermore, it is indeed a telling irony, given British support for Nigeria and the génocidaires' strategy of rape and abduction of Igbo

---

[3]Chinua Achebe, *There was a Country* (New York: Penguin, 2012), p. 233.
[4]Morris, *Uncertain Greatness*, p. 122.

womanhood in Biafra, that it is in London, in June 2014, forty-seven years later, that the first international conference on "rape and sexual violence" in war, *with emphasis on Africa* (and particular focus on the Democratic Republic of the Congo), is hosted by none other than the British government in which foreign secretary of state William Hague describes rape as "'one of the great mass crimes' of modern times".[5]

In Biafra, beginning 6 July 1967, every Igbo town or village overrun by the Nigerian génocidaires becomes a gruesome milestone in an inexorable march of rape, death, and destruction:

> Obollo Afo ... Obollo Eke ... Enuugwu-Ezike ... Opi ... Ukehe ... Nkalagu ... Owgwu ... Abakaleke ... Eha Amuufu ... Nsukka ... Enuugwu ... Agbaani ... Asaba ... Ogwashi-Ukwu ... Isele-Ukwu ... Onicha-Ugbo ...Agbo ...Umunede ... Onicha ... Nkpo ...Oka ... Aba ... Udi ... Ehuugbo ... Ehuugbo Road ... Okigwe ... Umuahia ... Owere ...Abagana ... Igwe Ocha ... Ahaoda ... Obiigbo ... Azumini ... Umu Ubani/Bonny ... Igwe Nga/Opobo ... Ugwuta ... Amasiri ... Akaeze ... Uzuakoli ...

Clearly invoking Nazi-style "search through population-round off-isolate-and-destroy"-tactics in overrun non-Igbo towns and cities such as Calabar, Oron, Ikot Ekpene, Uyo, Ogoja, Obubara, Obudu, Nkarasi and Eket, the genocidists meticulously profile Igbo nationals. Thousands of such profiled Igbo are shot at sight or marched off and later executed at city limits, forest firing-range sites, river banks, or at specifically dedicated genocidist-occupied barrack venues...

Incubation & manifestation

As contemporary Nigeria demonstrates, most graphically, as these lines are written, grounded genocidist advocates/"theorists"/operatives especially Obafemi Awolowo, Tony Enaharo, Hassan Katsina, Alison Ayida, Olusegun Obasanjo, Gbadomosi King, Umaru Dikko, Benjamin Adekunle, Muhammadu Buhari, Yakubu Gowon, Murtala Mohammed, Yakubu Danjuma, Ibrahim Haruna and Ibrahim Taiwo are perhaps just coming to terms with the realisation that their thoughts and deeds have incubated within *their very own* and become hauntingly cyclical across generations – DNA signature. This is precisely why survivors from these purveyors of state-directed mass slaughter, such as the Igbo, for example, must keep well away from the latter's tent. Boko Haram insurgents now ravaging swathes of territory across the north, northeast and northcentral and elsewhere in Nigeria are *remarching* along the paths

---

[5] *BBC News*, 10 June 2014.

first trodden by their parents/grandparents/greatgrandparents/Nigeriãna-génocidaires, beginning 29 May 1966, 50 years ago to the day.

As for Nigeria's genocide-prosecuting ally Britain, again 50 years to the day, it has, alas, caught up with Biafra, *via* Brexit, to engage, critically, with exercising its right to self-determination – in this instance, to determine whether or not it wishes to be part of the supranational state called the European Union. Unlike the Biafrans, who, 50 years ago, exercised this *same* right but in staggeringly existential circumstances, Britain hasn't sought Brexit from the European Union because it has been threatened or subjected to the crime of genocide by the latter. On the contrary. Similarly, the 5 million constituent Scottish people in Britain do not, 50 years after Biafra, currently seek to exercise their right to self-determination from Britain because they have been threatened or subjected to the crime of genocide by Britain. Not at all.

Just as the Biafrans, 50 years ago, the underlying awareness by the British, as a whole, collectively, or the Scots, separately, is that this right to self-determination is *inalienable* and its exercise by any people across the world is not dependent on prevailing circumstance(s).

※ ※ ※

15 BIAFRA FREEDOM MOVEMENT HAS DINNER PARTY DIMENSIONS IN ITS DYNAMICS[1]

Mao Tse-Tung once proclaimed that a revolution is not a "dinner party" but an "insurrection, an act of violence", in which a group of subjugated people in a power relation overthrows the other that controls this power of subjugation.[2]

In its own reading of prevailing history, 90 years after this declaration, the Biafra freedom movement has projected and is operationalising a liberation strategy with resounding effect that is dramatically antithetical to Mao's: non-violence. And this, surely, could chart a course for the rest of Africa.

It is possible that some may find the Biafra freedom strategy surprising, if not intriguing, as the Igbo have had to resist a genocidist Nigeria, during the course of these past 51 years, an evidently more ruthless murder machine than either the Kuomintang Chinese regime or the (external) Japanese forces that the Maoists confronted nearly a century ago. Neither the Kuomintang nor the Japanese was genocidist – so, any such incredulous observers of Biafran current strategy could feel that the Igbo, given their history, would have been obvious candidates deeply engaged in a Maoist "insurrection, an act of violence", *not* its distinct opposite.

Referendum

Two interlocking factors account for Biafrans' non-violence drive. First, they have channelled the "long march" wealth of experience of one-half century of resistance to genocide to an evocative stream of conscientisation on Biafra freedom and restoration-of-independence across the length and breadth of the Biafran homeland where an essentially alternate Biafra state has begun to flourish, despite the brutish

---

[1]This chapter was first published in *Rethinking Africa*, 23 August 2017 and *Pambazuka News: Voices for Freedom and Justice*, 31 August 2017.

[2]Mao Tse-Tung, "Report on an investigation of the peasant movement in Hunan, March 1927", *Selected Works Vol I*, https://www.marxists.org/reference/archive/mao/selected-works/volume-1/mswv1_2.htm, accessed 22 August 2017.

Nigeria genocidist occupation. The Igbo now dictate the terms of their freedom from Nigeria. They have acquired this pivotal status, in the past 24 months, it should be stressed, without firing a shot – *either* in defence *or* offence. They insist on a referendum to secure the next crucial phase of the process. They have turned Biafran towns and villages into freedom parks for open, participatory creative debates on Biafra, often involving a range of family members, that would have been deemed impossible just a few years ago. The quest for Biafra freedom is at once an occasion for celebration involving all generations of the people. Huge crowds of people across the country, varying from hundreds of thousands to two and three million estimates in the July 2017 Igwe Ocha and Owere assemblies, south and eastcentral Biafra, respectively, and in mid-August (2017) in Ekwuluobia (west Biafra) have attended rallies organised by the Indigenous People of Biafra. In these assemblies, movement leader Nnamdi Kanu has fervently articulated the salient features that map out the current phase of the freedom movement with emphasis, particularly, on a referendum for the people for restoration-of-independence.

Guillotine

Secondly, 51 years after the launch of the Igbo genocide which coincides with the dramatic, ironical upheaval of the historic demands and consequences of Scotland's quest for independence (or, more historically appropriate, restoration-of-independence) from Britain itself, a *co-genocidist state* in this genocide, and Britain's *own* decision (through a referendum) to exit from the European Union (Brexit) that it had been a member for 44 years, Biafrans now regard Britain, not the *on the ground* genocidist Nigeria, as the primary agency that not only funds the genocide but is prepared to maintain its continuing execution as a means of controlling *its* Nigeria-creation in perpetuity. Clearly, Britain is the owner and director of the genocidist guillotine that has murdered Igbo people so gruesomely for five decades. The Nigerians are nothing more than the executioner in this project. For Britain, thanks to Prime Minister Harold Wilson's notorious stance taken right soon after the outset of the genocide on 29 May 1966 ("I would accept a half million dead Biafrans if that was what it took" Nigeria to destroy the Igbo resistance to the genocide[3]), just 18 years after the end of the deplorable perpetration of the Jewish genocide by Germany during which 6 million Jews were murdered, its central role in the Igbo genocide represents an incredibly low-risk strategy for it because the genocide's Africa-based executioner force, headed by Britain's close ally in the region for over 100 years, the Fulani islamists/jihadists, are right there in Biafra to murder the Igbo as ever as they will with no expected condemnation from Britain

---

[3]Morris, *Uncertain Greatness*, p. 122.

– a corresponding position invariably adopted particularly by its West allies as the history of this crime attests.

Beacon

Despite the sheer savagery of this British-led genocide in which 3.1 million Igbo were murdered in the first three phases (29 May 1966-12 January 1970) and tens of thousands murdered subsequently in phase-IV (i.e., since 13 January 1970 to this day), the Igbo have not only survived but have emerged more focused, steadfast, and resilient to free themselves from Nigeria and restore Biafran sovereignty.

Britain must now know that it cannot stop this process of Igbo freedom. No one else can stop Igbo freedom from *Britain*'s genocidist Nigeria. Surely, Britain has no other choice but terminate its role at once in waging this crime against humanity in Biafra, 3130 miles away in southwestcentral Africa, accept full responsibility, apologise to Igbo people, and pay them comprehensive reparations.

As most observers know, Biafra is the beacon of the long-sought African peoples' renaissance of the current epoch.

✳ ✳ ✳

16 SURELY, THERE IS NO HIERARCHISATION OF EVIL

**Unconscionably contrasting responses
to Nigeria genocidist military outrage in Biafra and the Myanmar
Rakhine region[1]**

There has been a commendable worldwide criticism of the Myanmar military for its operation in the country's southwest Rakhine region where the Rohingya people, predominantly muslim, live. Nearly 400,000 Rohingya have fled to neighbouring Bangladesh to escape the increasing violence.

In contrast, the world has remained unconscionably silent over the Nigeria genocidist military campaign in (occupied) Biafra where it has murdered 2000 Biafrans since October 2015. The Nigeria state, created by Britain, is headed by Fulani islamist/jihadists and its military engaged in the genocide in Biafra is led by a phalanx of senior islamist operatives. In the past week alone, hundreds of Biafrans have been murdered in scorched-earth operations mounted by the Nigerians who have laid siege on all Biafran cities and towns (including especially Enuugwu, Onicha, Asaba, Oka, Aba, Orlu, Okigwe, Owere, Igwe Ocha, Abakeleke, Umuahia, Owere, Afaraukwu-Ibeku) in response to the Biafra freedom, restoration-of-independence movement. The Biafra freedom movement is totally peaceful, the most peaceful of its kind in Africa and one of the very few anywhere in the South World.

World stop Igbo genocide now

The world must now wake up from its inexcusable slumber over the Igbo genocide and condemn genocidist Nigeria unreservedly. This condemnation must also extend to Britain, the co-genocidist state in this crime right from its original launch date on

---

[1]First published in *Rethinking Rethinking* Africa, 15 September 2017 and *Pambazuka News: Voices of Freedom and Justice*, 28 September 2017.

29 May 1966, which is the principal exporter of the array of weapons the Nigerian enforcers employ in their slaughter of the Igbo. In this case, it is indeed not without significance that the current phase of the genocide (beginning Sunday 10 September 2017) was mounted shortly after the July/August 2017 visits to Nigeria by Tony Blair (a former British prime minister) and Boris Johnson (current British foreign secretary).

The world must at once stop the Igbo genocide and the occupation of Biafra and support the Biafra freedom movement's programmed process of a referendum to determine the democratic choice of 50 million Biafrans. All those involved in this crime against humanity, the foundational genocide of post-(European) conquest Africa, must be arraigned and prosecuted forthwith in designated international courts. The genocidists murdered 3.1 million Igbo people, 25 per cent of the population during phases I-III of the crime, 29 May 1966-12 January 1970, and tens of thousands of additional Igbo during phase-IV which has been ongoing since its launch date on 13 January 1970. The whereabouts of Nnamdi Kanu, the leader of the Indigenous People of Biafra, and his parents, are presently unknown since the genocidists stormed his Afaraukwu-Ibeku (east Biafra) family home yesterday (Thursday 14 September 2017), murdering a yet undisclosed number of relatives and others therein.

17 ONCE AGAIN, DISMISSING THIS GIMMICK THAT CALLS ITSELF "IGBO PRESIDENCY"[1]

Architects and operatives in Nigeria

Given the critical links between the salient features of the politics of genocidist Fulani-led islamist jihadist Nigeria's occupation of Biafra since 13 January 1970 and the overarching architecture of these 50 years of a genocidal campaign, begun on 29 May 1966, few now doubt that the Igbo termination of the occupation is at once the resumption of their disrupted historic freedom march from Nigeria and the implementation of an expansive socioeconomic programme of reconstruction unprecedented in this southwestcenral region of Africa.

If this is the case, one does not need an "Igbo presidency" in Nigeria to achieve this freedom goal as some Igbo commentators as well as a few others have, at times, contended, but quite uncritically. Just recently, according to reports in the media in Nigeria, even raging génocidaire trooper Olusegun Obasanjo has waded into this perverse advocacy, "supporting [sic] Igbo presidency in 2019".[2] This very development is tellingly dreadful. Obasanjo is one of the most notorious operatives of the Igbo genocide during phases I-III, 29 May 1966-12 January 1970. At its apogee, 1968/1969, an Obasanjo-led brigade, operating in the outstretched south Biafra, had converted this panhandle into a veritable killing field in which it slaughtered tens of thousands of Igbo people – "... everything that moves ... we shoot at everything, even

---

[1]This chapter was first published in *Rethinking Africa*, 27 January 2017.
[2]*Vanguard*, Lagos, 25 January 2017.

at things that don't move", as this brigade's previous commander, the equally notorious Benjamin Adekunle, had so grimly proffered.[3] The skies of Biafra were neither spared from this "shoot-at-everything" **monstrosity by the Obasanjo death squad**. In June 1969, Obasanjo ordered his air force to *shoot down* a 3-person crew international Red Cross aircraft bringing urgent relief to the encircled, blockaded, and bombarded Igbo, and he later boasted fiendishly of this crime in his memoirs, aptly entitled *My Command*.[4]

It is anyone's guess, 50 years on, what indeed a *surviving* Igbo-descent president in a Nigeria is supposed to be working on in their role as "president of Nigeria" as prescribed by precisely none other than one of the most loathsome of the architects and operatives of this genocide.

Inexorable logic

It cannot be overstressed that no "Igbo presidency" in Nigeria, not even one reinforced with an *all*-Igbo personnel in the key cabinet military/police/"security"-positions can halt this ongoing genocide by Nigeria and its British suzerain state. This campaign has now acquired an inexorable logic to its being. The Nigeria military and its adjunct forces, especially Boko Haram and the Fulani militia, now strategise and coordinate the prosecution of the genocide as the world has seen particularly since Muhammadu Buhari, yet another génocidaire, was imposed head of regime in March 2015 by ex-British Prime Minister David Cameron and ex-US President Barack Hussein Obama, the first African-descent president of the United States, 233 years after the founding of the republic. Buhari has murdered 2000 Igbo people since this imposition. Obama's support for the Igbo genocide is the abhorrent legacy of his presidency which formally ended a week ago.

What the emergence of Boko Haram and its Fulani militia cousin (part of the five most deadly terrorist organisations in the world presently, according to the Sydney-based Institute for Economics and Peace,[5] has demonstrated in **Nigeria** is that each of the (now) tripartite-prosecuting agency of the Igbo genocide has become very much *decentred*, very much *motivated*, very much engagingly *virulent*.

The typical Boko Haram suicide-operating cell is a handful-strength, in single digits, and none in the group knows any of the others until they meet at the designated, targeted site of operation – in which they, invariably, are not expected to survive! If any survives, the person, of course, becomes a member of a new cell of

---

[3]*The Economist*, London 24 August 1968.
[4]Obasanjo, *My command*, pp. 78-79.
[5]Clarke, "Globally, terrorism is on the rise – but little of it occurs in Western countries"..

hitherto unknown members and the cycle goes on... A Fulani militia cell, employing this decentred operational flexibility, carries out its terror outrage accompanied by a herd of cattle as cover... An army, air force, navy, so-called DSS ("department of state services")/other terror service units based anywhere in occupied Biafra can organise a murder onslaught anytime on the occupied population without waiting for "direct authorisation" from the genocidist high command back in Abuja, Nigeria...

Inalienable

Prior to this amalgamation of genocidist forces in Nigeria, still on the "Igbo presidency", we mustn't forget that Nigeria was under the leadership of an Igbo general when the genocide began on 29 May 1966. Thus, "Igbo presidency" offers no route to the Igbo halting the genocide, one of the strategic goals of the freedom movement. None whatsoever. The route remains Igbo freedom from Nigeria. This is an inalienable Igbo right *with or without* the genocide as I have argued severally. If the Scots, for instance, one-tenth of the Igbo population and without a genocide antecedent would wish to leave a *union* they have largely been exponential beneficiaries for 300 years,[6] the Igbo, surely, don't require any agonisingly turgid historical nor sociological treatise to wish to leave Nigeria.

Resolution

Genocidist Nigeria does know that the Igbo are not Nigerian. The Igbo are from Biafra. The Igbo are Biafran. Whilst the Igbo worked extraordinarily hard by playing the *vanguard* role in the liberation of Nigeria from the British conquest (beginning from the mid-1930s to October 1960), the Igbo ceased to be Nigerian on Sunday 29 May 1966. This is the day Nigeria launched the Igbo genocide. Consequently, Nigeria became a raging tragedy – one of the five deadliest human-made tragedies in African World history.

The Igbo renouncement of their Nigerian citizenship is the irrevocable Igbo indictment on a state that embarked on the destruction of 3.1 million Igbo people, 25 per cent of this nation's population at the time. Tens of thousands of additional Igbo have subsequently been murdered during phase-IV of the genocide which the Nigerians launched on 13 January 1970. The genocide continues unabated.

The only future a genocide-state has is that those murdered by it or others apprehensive that it could extend its murderous heritage on them abandon it – nothing else. In the specific Nigeria case, that epitome of its savagery, *presidency nigeriāna*, is at once repudiated for what it is worth. It is this

---

[6]See chap. 20 below.

possibility of a transformative future of Africa that the Obasanjos and others in the genocidist lair and war outposts on the continent responsible for the murder of 15 million African peoples in the past 50 years dread most profoundly.

Biafrans have since *abandoned* genocidist Nigeria and are on their way to restore their sovereignty in their Biafran homeland as their resilient and confident freedom movement breathtakingly demonstrates currently. Its outcome on the African scene is of immense epochal consequence, the likes of which we haven't seen. The Biafra flag is on the ascent. There can never be a reversal. This will be one of the most outstanding breakthroughs of the freedom movement of the age.

18 BRITAIN, BREXIT, IGBO GENOCIDE, BIAFRA FREEDOM

Brexit: 29th March 2017

Today, Wednesday 29 March 2017,[1] at 1230 Hours British Summer Time, British Prime Minister Theresa May triggered off the so-called article 50 of the treaty of Lisbon, formally announcing British termination of its membership of the European Union following the country's 23 June 2016 historic referendum decision. In this letter of termination to Donald Tusk, the EU president, May is adamant that Britain is leaving the union to "restore ... our self determination".[2]

For Britain, a country that has spent the greater part of its 300 years of global conquest and occupation of states and peoples, constructing bogus and particularly ahistorical entities called "federations" to enhance its subjugation and expropriation drives,[3] its decision to desperately quit the EU agglomeration of states and peoples, *just* after 44 years, cannot be lost on the individual or collective sensibilities of students and scholars and other keen observers of this subject of history.

Biafra is before Brexit: 29 May 1966

Definitely, this is not lost on the Igbo people of Biafra of southwestcentral Africa who Britain *and* its amalgam of willing and ruthless *pan*-African constituent nations in the British-constructed Nigeria "federation" (including, particularly, the Fulani, Kanuri,

---

[1]This chapter was first published in *Rethinking Africa*, 29 March 2017 and *Pambazuka: Voices of Freedom and Justice*, 6 April 2017.

[2]"Prime Minister's letter to Donald Tusk triggering article 50", *gov.uk*, 29 March 2017, https://www.gov.uk/government/publications/prime-ministers-letter-to-donald-tusk-triggering-article-50/prime-ministers-letter-to-donald-tusk-triggering-article-50, accessed 29 March 2017.

[3]Ekwe-Ekwe, *Readings from Reading*, especially pp. 1-6.

Hausa, Jawara, Nupe, Bachama, Tiv, and Jukun of the north region and the Yoruba, Itsekiri and Edo of its west provinces) have been subjected to the longest, most expansive and monstrous genocide in contemporary history – since Sunday 29 May 1966.

Britain and its pan-African allies in the Nigeria "federation" murdered 3.1 million Igbo people or 25 per cent of Igbo population during 44 months of phases I-III of the genocide (29 May 1966-12 January 1970) to preserve *this* Nigeria "federation"; Britain and its pan-African allies in the Nigeria "federation" have murdered tens of thousands of additional Igbo people since 13 January 1970, phase-IV, to preserve *this* Nigeria "federation"; Britain and its pan-African allies in the Nigeria "federation" are murdering more Igbo people to preserve *this* Nigeria "federation" ... 2000 Igbo have been murdered between October 2015 and presently by the Nigeria regime, currently headed by Muhammadu Buhari (imposed in power in March 2015 by former British Prime Minister Cameron and ex-US President Obama, himself an African American, the first African-descent president after 233 years of the US republic), a notoriously fiendish genocidist operative who has been centrally involved in the genocide since 1966 **to preserve *this* Nigeria "federation"**

The Igbo genocide is the longest and one of the bloodiest genocides of contemporary history. On the record, no single nation or people in Africa has suffered this extent of a catastrophic state-premeditated and organised genocide in history as the Igbo.

Post-Brexit, Biafra freedom

Prime Minster May knows that she must terminate, at once, this horrendous British-led genocide against Igbo people, 3130 miles away. Igbo people expect that a post-Brexit Britain will have no choice but sit down with a free Biafran government and discuss, fully, the entire history of the Igbo genocide, the 400 years enslavement of the people of Biafra, and the subsequent conquest and occupation of Biafra – forced into the genocidist Nigeria "federation".

Britain will surely accept full responsibility for these crimes against humanity, apologise to Biafrans, and pay full reparations.[4]

Now is the time.

---

[4]See chap. 7 above.

19 ANTI-BIAFRA COLUMNIST ACKNOWLEDGES RESTORATION OF BIAFRA DESPITE THEMSELF[1]

An anti-Biafra freedom columnist, writing recently in *saharareporters.com*, notes:

If a referendum were held today, there is no doubt that over 70% of people in the five south-east states would vote YES for separation. A little over 50% in Rivers State would also vote YES. Between 40% and 50% would vote YES in other south-south states: Bayelsa, Delta, Cross River, Akwa Ibom and Edo. A similar result might be reproduced if the people of the south-west were to be subjected to a referendum to determine whether Oduduwa republic should come into being. Therefore, the Federal Government should not agree to a referendum.[2]

Extraordinary! In a swoop, just in four sentences, this columnist is informing the world precisely as follows: "[i]f a referendum were held today", not only would the people in occupied Biafra (since 13 January 1970) vote for the restoration of their country's sovereignty but the majority of the peoples in south Nigeria, including the Yoruba and Edo nations, would also vote for independence from Nigeria.

Peoples in south Nigeria constitute the majority of peoples in Nigeria. Going by the reading of this columnist, *a majority of the population in Nigeria* would vote for independence from *this* state that calls itself Nigeria if given the democratic

---

[1]An earlier version of this chapter was published as a commentary in *Rethinking Africa*, 22 November 2015.

[2]Upper case designations above as well as snippets of the Nigerian-occupation bogus geopolitical lexicon referencing Biafra are in the original.

opportunity to determine their choice. So, what's the fuss of "one Nigeria"? Whose "one Nigeria" is it? Britain's, its creator, *and* the indolent religio-regional retrograde client overseers, also created by Britain, who infamously opposed the African liberation from the British occupation? Who?

Redefining dynamics

As most observers know, including indeed the hapless columnist, the majority of peoples in Nigeria want an early exit from arguably the most notorious of Africa's "Berlin states" – the state that carried out the Igbo genocide, 29 May 1966-12 January 1970, the foundational genocide of post-(European)conquest state, murdering 3.1 million Igbo or one-quarter of this nation's population and inaugurating Africa's current age of pestilence, and the state that harbours Boko Haram and Fulani militia, **two of the world's five deadliest terrorist organisations presently.**[3]

Surely, the Biafrans will have the opportunity for a referendum very soon and they will vote overwhelmingly to restore their independence. As these lines are written, hundreds of thousands of peaceful Biafrans have turned their cities and towns and villages into panoramic freedom park marches, begun at 12 noon on Friday 6 November 2015, unprecedented in Africa, demanding their beloved Biafra and insisting on the release of freedom broadcaster Nnamdi Kanu, illegally detained by the Nigeria regime.

Biafrans are redefining the dynamics of the march for freedom in Africa. Biafra will be free. The columnist must start getting used to this development. Nigeria, this essentially anti-African imperium is, in fact, in freefall with its epitaph already signposting its dreadful history: Haematophagous Monster.

Indictment

Back to referendum, finally, and a quick comment on that historic vote in Scotland last year. The columnist, who is conceivably domiciled somewhere in Europe or north America, is probably aware of that Scottish exercise. If the Scots had voted the 70 per cent score the columnist had assigned to a possible Biafra referendum-run (see quote above), Scotland would have been independent of Britain today! David Cameron, British prime minister, wouldn't have dared oppose this outcome. This is because David Cameron *is* a democrat and *respects* the rights of 5 million Scots to freedom. This is an *inalienable right* for all peoples.[4]

---

[3]Clarke, "Globally, terrorism is on the rise – but little of it occurs in Western countries"..
[4]See chap. 20 below.

The longest genocide

It is therefore a telling indictment on this columnist's brand of education *and* worldview not to appear to be aware that 50 million Biafrans in southwestcentral Africa as well as *every* people elsewhere on planet earth have this right.

* * *

20 RIGHTS FOR SCOTS, RIGHTS FOR THE IGBO[1]

There is, presently, a hearty debate in Britain on the timetable for a referendum in Scotland on Scottish independence or, more correctly stated, the restoration of Scottish independence. Prime Minister David Cameron prefers an early vote, presumably in the next 18 months, with two "straightforward" questions on whether the Scots want independence or wish to continue to be part of Britain as it has been in the past 300 years. Cameron also wishes that the outcome of the referendum is "legally binding"[2], quite an unprecedented position to take as referendums in Britain, in the past, have had "advisory" or "consultative" status. Finally, he wants the minimum age of 18 for participants.

In contrast, Alex Salmond, the leader of the pro-independence Scottish Nationalist Party and Scotland's first minister, insists that, thanks to SNP's majority victory in last May's elections to the Edinburgh Holyrood assembly, his party has the "mandate for the Scottish parliament to organise the referendum [on its own]... It must be a referendum built in Scotland and decided by Scottish people..."[3] Salmond adds that he will schedule the poll in the autumn of 2014 and besides the "yes"/"no" choices

---

[1] This chapter was first published in *Rethinking Africa*, 17 January 2012 and in *Pambazuka News: Voices for Freedom and Justice*, 26 January 2012.

[2] "Does David Cameron have the power to decide when Scotland votes on independence?", *The Guardian*, London, 9 January 2012, https://www.theguardian.com/politics/reality-check-with-polly-curtis/2012/jan/09/scottish-independence-legality, accessed 9 January 2012.

[3] "Scottish independence: Alex Salmond sets poll date – and defies London", *The Guardian*, 10 January 2012 https://www.theguardian.com/politics/2012/jan/10/scottish-independence-salmond-poll-date, accessed 10 January 2012.

favoured by Cameron, he wouldn't rule out a third, more nuanced proto-independence choice for voters (the so-called dev-max or "devolution-maximum") which calls for enhanced financial powers for Scotland, derived from existing devolved provisions – i.e., just short of total sovereignty as these new powers won't affect defence and foreign affairs! For poll participation, Salmond prefers an age limit of 16 rather than Cameron's 18.

Quite clearly, the differences between both leaders on this important subject are merely procedural and not on the substantive issue of the rights of Scots, as a people, to decide their future. Despite the oft-quoted, if irreverent lines from Robert Burns, the Scottish national poet, alluding to the deteriorating Scottish economic situation at the time (caused by the so-called Darién scheme[4]) which contributed to its parliamentarians voting for union with England, formally inaugurated in 1707 ("We're bought and sold for English gold-/Such a parcel of rogues in a nation!"[5]), Scotland has not been "worse off" in the United Kingdom enterprise.

On the contrary, Scots and their country were enriched *exponentially* by this union. Some scholars have dubbed the vast lands of the world that Britain conquered during its 350 years march across the globe the "Scottish empire"[6], rather than "British empire", to underscore this Scottish unprecedented triumph.[7] And they are not so far off the mark in that characterisation! Scottish financiers and merchants, enslavers, enslaved-plantation owners, tobacco, sugar and cotton growers and the like (in the Americas), along with their English counterparts, were already immersed in reaping the gargantuan fortune wreaked from the hegemonic control of African enslavement they now shared with England. This was occasioned by the two states' previous century's dramatic displacement of the central role played hitherto in this Euro-pillaging campaign by Portugal and Spain. Huge profits from African enslavement were ploughed back into Scottish sociocultural and financial institutions and cities to power the gestating industrial revolution (especially in the Glasgow conurbation) and the Scottish age of enlightenment, that very much revered heritage in the country's national narrative. Such was the staggering outcome of this Scottish (and English) transformation that Christopher Hill, the distinguished specialist on this epoch of British history, has observed that, prior to the mid-17th century, these states were

---

[4]John Prebble, *The Darien Disaster* (London: Pimlico, 2002).
[5]Robert Burns, "Such a parcel of rogues in a nation" 1791,
http://www.robertburns.org/works/344.shtml, accessed 30 December 2011.
[6]See, for instance, Michael Fry, *The Scottish Empire* (Phantassie: Tuckwell, 2001).
[7]See also the various contributions in Mackenzie and Devine eds., *Scotland and the British Empire*.

still "cultural and scientific backwater" but soon, into the following century, they had become "centre of world science".[8]

Buoyed

Buoyed by these phenomenal strides in societal fortunes and outlook, the one million Scots, a sixth of the population of the new merger-state relation, pounced on the opportunities thrown up by union with England with much aplomb: Scottish military forces with their specialised fighting units, who in the past fought for English global expansionism, henceforth had a greater stake to defend and conquer ever new seas and lands in continent after continent for the union; Scottish emigration, especially to north America, soared; Scottish conquest administrators prominently policed the union's "empire" – from the east's Asian frontiers through Africa to the west's outstretches of the Americas, and, lastly, its leading intellectuals (philosophers, scientists, political-economists, writers) simultaneously valorised the thrust and goals of union and conquest. Not a few of the latter would join counterparts in England and elsewhere to particularly offer the "requisite" cultural/scientific/literary rationalisation for African enslavement/holocaust and map out the presumed hermeneutical canvass of the cardinal codifiers of European World racism as an ideology.[9] When pro-independence "colonists" in north America in the later part of the 18th century revolted against the union crown, significant sectors of Scottish émigrés (including their Ulster-Scot cousins) and institutions strongly supported freedom for the United States – a position that would obviously have appeared paradoxical for obvious reasons. One-third of delegates who signed the US independence document were of Scottish descent and 75 per cent of all US presidents since the founding of the republic are of Scottish ancestry.

State is transient; people endures

Given the trajectory of what many would feel is an illustrious history sketched above, it could appear that Scots are perhaps the most unlikely people to wish to break from Britain. Interestingly, most opinion polls conducted in Scotland show that majority of Scots do not, currently, want a restoration of their country's independence. Ironically, a most recent of these polls shows that more English respondents (from one of the

---

[8]Hill, "Lies about crimes".
[9]Ekwe-Ekwe, *African Literature in Defence of History*, pp. 1-54.

four constituent nations in the union) than the Scots themselves want the Scots to "go"![10] So, a principal reason that Alex Salmond is working towards a "delayed" referendum date (last quarter of 2014) is to have more time to campaign to garner a majority vote outcome from across a Scottish population still sceptical of the restoration-of-independence for their country. Salmond wants to appeal to younger Scots (hence his intention to lower the minimum deciding voting age to 16), where disposition for independence is much greater than the older population. 2014 also presents Salmond with three "opportunity chords" to play for in the independence drive: commemorating the 700th anniversary of the battle of Bannockburn in which the Scots defeated England, Scottish hosting of the Commonwealth games, and Scottish hosting of the Ryder Cup (golf).

Prime Minister Cameron is very much aware of the Scottish success story in the UK-union and also that a majority of Scots would vote for continuing stay in the union if a referendum on the subject were held presently. The latter particularly explains Cameron's desire for an early poll. Yet despite being first minister of the union who undoubtedly wishes to preserve the union, Cameron accepts the rights of Scots to decide freely on this subject. It is their right.[11] But this right is not only restricted to the Scots or to the English or to the Welsh or to only peoples in Europe... It is, in fact, a universal right that every people enjoys. Every people.

This right to self-determination for *every* people is inalienable and is guaranteed by the United Nations.[12] No people is exempt from exercising this right. As everyone expects, Cameron has not come out demonising Scots for "daring" to wish to leave the union; no, Cameron wouldn't do this because he respects the rights of Scots to exercise their right to self-determination. As everyone expects, surely, Cameron has not come out with the dreadful thoughts of wishing any harm to Scots for wanting to exercise their inalienable rights to self-determination as one James Harold Wilson, who once lived and worked from the same London address that Cameron inhabits today, declared when the Igbo of southwestcentral Africa exercised this right between 29 May 1966 and 12 January 1970.

The Igbo had exercised their right to independence from the Nigeria-union (created by UK-union in 1914!) when this Nigeria-union unleashed the genocide against them with the active participation of key constituent nations (in the union)

---

[10]Patrick Hennessey, "Britain divided over Scottish independence", *Telegraph*, 14 January 2012, https://www.telegraph.co.uk/news/uknews/scotland/9015374/Britain-divided-over-Scottish-independence.html, accessed 14 January 2012.

[11]"Scotland referendum: David Cameron throws down the gauntlet to Salmond", *The Guardian*, 9 January 2012, https://www.theguardian.com/uk/2012/jan/09/scotland-referendum-david-cameron-salmond, accessed 12 January 2012.

[12]"The United Nations and Decolonization", http://www.un.org/en/decolonization/declaration.shtml, accessed 9 January 2012.

such as the Fulani and Kanuri in the north region and Yoruba and Edo of the west provinces. 3.1 million Igbo or a quarter of their population were murdered by Britain and these close pan-African allies.

UK-union supported the genocide politically, diplomatically and militarily – London's calculated "punishment" for the Igbo-lead role (in the mid 1930s-October 1960) to terminate the UK-union-occupation of its Nigeria-union lucre. As the slaughtering of the Igbo intensified especially in those catastrophic months of 1968/1969, James Harold Wilson was totally unfazed when he informed Clyde Ferguson (United States State Department special coordinator for relief to Biafra) that he, James Harold Wilson, "would accept half a million dead Biafrans if that was what it took"[13] the Nigeria-union to destroy the Igbo resistance to the genocide. Such is the grotesquely expressed diminution of African life made by a supposedly leading politician of the world of the 1960s – barely 20 years after the deplorable perpetration of the Jewish genocide. As the final tally of the murder of the Igbo demonstrates, James Harold Wilson probably had the perverted satisfaction of having his Nigeria-union genocidists perform far in excess of his grim target.

Unlike the Igbo, the Scots, pointedly, never faced any pogrom or genocide by the UK-union or organised by any of the other constituent nations of the union (English, Welsh, Irish) during these past 300 years. Finally, as everyone expects, unfailingly, Cameron has not dabbled into some nonsense of the assumed "inviolability" or "indivisibility" of the UK-union in respect to the rights of Scots to self-determination, two oft-repeated vulgarities with reference to the Nigeria-union that the same James Harold Wilson trumpeted with much relish as the Nigeria-union genocidists slaughtered and slaughtered the Igbo during those 44 months of certain death.

What the debate on the 5 million Scots and Scotland has clearly demonstrated is that the people, the nation, is deemed superior to the state. This is the case of any people in the world vis-à-vis the state. This position is correct for all peoples and nations irrespective of race, continent, region, religion/belief system, etc., etc. The people, the nation is enduring; the state is transient. The state is therefore not some "gift" from someone else; definitely not from any conquerors, nor even from gods, but relationships painstakingly formulated and constructed by a discernible group of human beings that inhabit an ascertainable geo-historical territorial expanse on earth to pursue worldviews and interests envisioned and formulated by these same human beings. In Africa, where the contemporary state was created and imposed by the European conquest over decades/centuries as *instruments to expropriate and despoil* Africa in perpetuity, the goal of organically articulated African-created and owned states to radically transform depressing African fortunes is imperative. In the aggressively genocidist-states such as the Nigeria-union, the Sudan-union and

---

[13]Morris, *Uncertain Greatness*, p. 122.

The longest genocide

Democratic Republic of the Congo-union, this task is even more pressing.

Even 1000 states...

The Igbo, with a population of 50 million and whose homeland has been under occupation by the Nigeria-union since 13 January 1970, are arguably the world's most brutally targeted and most viciously murdered of peoples presently. Nigeria is now firmly the obligatory haematophagous monster in Africa whose *raison d'être* appears to be to murder the Igbo most routinely and ritualistically. Since losing 3.1 million during the genocide, tens of thousands of Igbo have been murdered by this monster during the course of the following years, signposted here by the eerie columns that chart the contours of the killing fields: 1980 ... 1982 ... 1985 ... 1991 ... 1993 ... 1994 ... 1999 ... 2000 ... 2001 ... 2002 ... 2004 ... 2005 ... 2006 ... 2007 ... 2008 ... 2009 ... 2010 ... 2011 ... 2012. According to the recently published research (December 2011) by the International Society for Civil Liberties & the Rule Of Law, a human rights organisation based in Onicha, 54,000 people have been murdered in Nigeria-union by the state/quasi-state operatives and agents since 1999.[14] Ninety per cent of these are Igbo. Since last Christmas Day, the Boko Haram islamist insurgent group spearheads these murders. At least 90 per cent of people murdered by the Boko Haram across swathes of lands in north/northcentral Nigeria in the past 23 days are Igbo.

The Boko Haram now issues its threats to murder Igbo people almost habitually, on a daily basis, and, true to its words, executes its mission most ruthlessly, most remorselessly. After each of its outrages, Boko Haram acknowledges responsibility and does this most dispassionately... The regime in Abuja appears cruelly powerless to protect Igbo people emplaced within the jurisdiction of the supposedly sovereign state it controls with the well-known consequences in international law that this shocking relegation of responsibility entails. Regime-head Goodluck Jonathan says as much in a recent astonishing radio and television broadcast to his country and the world: "Boko Haram is everywhere in the executive arm of [my] government, in the legislative arm of [my] government and even in the judiciary. Some are also in the armed forces, the police and other security [and] in the judiciary. Some continue to dip their hands and eat with you and you won't even know the person who will point a gun at you or plant a bomb behind your house".[15] The Nigeria-union has, since 1945, gained considerable notoriety for consistently evolving new levers and institutions

---

[14]Innocent Anaba, "How rights abuse led to killings in Nigeria", Vanguard, 5 January 2012. https://www.vanguardngr.com/2012/01/how-rights-abuse-led-to-killings-in-nigeria/, accessed 10 January 2012.

[15]"Worse than we thought", *Vanguard*, Lagos, 12 January 2012, https://www.vanguardngr.com/2012/01/worse-than-we-thought/, accessed 12 January 2012.

and processes within itself to murder the Igbo. Following from Jonathan's proclamation, it is conceivable that right there closeted in his regime, there are operatives deeply complicit in the ongoing murder of the Igbo. No doubt, Jonathan cannot but elaborate further on this broadcast to a restless, eagerly awaiting world. Not since 29 May 1966-12 January 1970 (phase-I and phase-II of the Igbo genocide) has Igbo life in the Nigeria-union Malebogle acquired such a *gripping existential emergency...*

The right of peoples of Africa to form their own state, away from the extant, murderous European-created state, is the central focus of my *The Biafra War, Nigeria and the Aftermath*, the second of the two books on the Igbo genocide I published in 1990. In the concluding pages of this book I note the following:[16]

> Either in peace, or war, the existence of the European post-colonial state is inimical to the interests of African peoples. It is a state that cannot provide the fundamental needs of Africans ... The African humanity is presently gripped in a grave crisis for survival. It is now time that it abandoned the contrived post-colonial state in order to survive ... African nations, [namely] Igbo, Wolof, Yoruba, Asante, Baganda, Bakongo, Bambara, etc., etc ... remain the basis for the regeneration of Africa's development ... [and] the sites of the continent's intellectual and other cultural creativity ... What is being stressed here is that African peoples, themselves, must decide on the ... issue of sovereignty ... even if the outcome were to lead to 1000 states ... For the future survival of the African humanity, let no more Africans have to die for the defence of, or for upholding the territorial frontier of any post-colonial state. No precious life should be wasted for its preservation.

Twenty-eight years on, these words remain crucially pivotal in focusing our minds on the very survival of the Igbo and all other African peoples. The Igbo and all others who have lived through the terror of the post-(European)conquest state must abandon it at once to survive and advance towards the construction of higher levels of civilisation. They have no other choice. Each and every constituent African people or nation can build this civilisation outside the existing genocide state of enthralled and degenerative union. Let Africa's constituent peoples or nations unleash a dazzling contest of creativity and progress, a continuing mutual bombardment and sharing of ideas and streams of possibilities, akin to what the world has seen in Asia, Latin America and elsewhere in the past 40 years – not mass murdering ... mass murdering ... mass murdering ... pillaging ... pillaging ... pillaging ... nihilism ... nihilism ... nihilism ... Most surely, now is the time to embark on this beginning.

---

[16]Herbert Ekwe-Ekwe, *The Biafra War, Nigeria and the Aftermath* (New York, Lewinston/Queenston/Lampeter: Mellen, 1990), pp. 124-125.

21 ON THAT "HANDSHAKE-ACROSS-THE-NIGER" SUMMIT IN ENUUGWU, BIAFRA[1]

Undoubtedly, the underlying problem of this Enuugwu conference[2] is that Igbo-Yoruba relation is predicated, essentially, on these two nations in this state that calls itself Nigeria. But Nigeria is a genocide state that has focused on the slaughter of Igbo people, one of Africa's leading entrepreneurial and academically endowed nations, as an enduring programme of *state policy* in the past 52 years – since 29 May 1966, in which the Yoruba have been a key participatory perpetrator among other constituent nations of Nigeria.

3.1 million Igbo, 25 per cent of the Igbo population then, were murdered in phases I-III of the genocide (29 May 1966-12 January 1970) and tens of thousands more Igbo have been murdered during the course of phase-IV of the genocide which began on 13 January 1970. The genocide goes on as these lines are written... History shows that a genocide state is abandoned, dismantled. There can be no other solution to this outcome. For the Igbo, Biafra brings this tragedy to a screeching halt.

"Successor" state(s)

Those who commit genocide on a people, as Germans have demonstrated since 1945, particularly their intellectuals,[3] must carry out a thorough introspective interrogation subsequently as the beginning of a journey to achieve some form of absolution for having committed this horrific crime against humanity. As it should

---

[1] This chapter was first published as a commentary in *Rethinking Africa*, 12 January 2018.
[2] "Handshake across the Niger summit", *Vanguard*, Lagos, 9 January 2018.
[3] See, for instance, A Dirk Moses, *German Intellectuals and the Nazi Past* (Cambridge: Cambridge University, 2007).

now be obvious, this crucial process cannot occur within the space of the genocide state but in "successor" state(s). Consequently, Igbo-Yoruba relations would have acquired the possibility of a conducive platform for a more dispassionate discourse.

The longest genocide

Flag of Republic of Biafra

INDEX

Aba, 115, 116, 136
Abacha, Sani, 4
Abagana, 131
Abakaleke, 131, 136
ABC News, 123
Abidjan, 113
Abubakar, Abdulsalem, 4, 96, 97
Aburi (Ghana), Aburi accords, 39-45, 58-59
    "cleverest", "compulsive-logic", 41-43
Achebe, Chinua, xi, 20, 20n18, 21, 23, 23n9, 24, 24nn12, 13, 14, 15, 25, 25nn18, 19, 22, 26nn23, 24, 26, 27, 28, 27, 27n29, 28, 28n32, 29, 68n78, 75, 76, 78, 78n15, 18, 89, 91, 118, 126, 128, 130n3
    Father of African Literature, xi, 22
    "prophet"?, 22
    oeuvre, Achebean oeuvre, 23-25
    predictive insights of, 22, 28
Achebe, ECN, 88
Achukwu, William, 91
Ada, ix
Adebayo, Robert, 42, 43
Adekunle, Benjamin, ix, 38, 63, 131, 138-139
    Igbo genocide definitive goal: "we shoot at everything, even at things that don't move", xii, 63, 138-139
Adeniyi, Olusegun, 115
Afaraukwu-Ibeku, 136
Afghanistan, 95, 99

Afigbo, Adiele, 89, 91, 118
AFP, 30
Africa, African peoples, ix, 1-20 *Passim*
    "African American son", *see* Barack Obama
    African-Atlantic discourses", 118-119
    African-centred scholarship, 33 34
    age of pestilence of, xi, 11, 72, 107
    ban all arms to, 12-13, 110-111
    Barack Obama supports Igbo genocide: monumental tragedy of presidential legacy, 103, 117
    "Berlin-state" of subjugation in, 12, 14, 34, 35
    contemporary Africa works!, 6-7
    enslavement of Africans by EuroConqueror league-states, 148-149
    EuroConqueror league-states of, 7
    fatality, 1914-1918 war: 1 million, 15
    fifteen million Africans murdered in genocides and wars in, 12
    "francophonie Africa", 7
    gargantuan wealth Britain expropriates from, 99-100
    genocide-states of, 7
    gibberish names of conquest of, 11
    "illicit financial outflows" to West

World, 1970s-2018: US$854
billion/US$1,8 trillion, 5
"loss of national sovereignty", 25
net-exporter of capital to West
World during 1980s-2018:
US$400
billion, 5, 33
"over population" fallacy, 8-11
"pan-African-'Goodcountry'-
assemblages"-of-terror on, 27
population, food, future of, 8-11
principal exporters of capital back
to Africa, 33
racist, humiliating and unprintable
epithets on Africans, 13-14
range of African emigration,
1980s-2018, 7
state in, 1-14
"sub-Sahara Africa", racist
epithet,
7, 7n20, 30-34
"testing ground" for presumed
global community's resolve to
fight genocide, post 1939-1945,
71
vast food production capacity of,
9-11
vast strategic minerals' capacity,
10
What would some of African
World's brightest minds think of
Barack Obama's support of the
Igbo genocide?, 118-119
"African-Atlantic discourses", *see*
Africa, Barack Obama
Against the Run of Play (Adeniyi),
115
Agbaani, 131
Agbo, 131
age of pestilence, 11 *See also* Africa
aggressive British arms-sales
programme to Africa, *see* Britain,
Tony Blair

Aggrey, JEK, 89
Aguyi-Ironsi, Johnson, 41
Ahaoda, 131
Ahidjo, Ahmadou, 4, 68
Ahmadu Bello University, 40
epicentre of planning and
execution of Igbo genocide, 40
Aidoo, Ama Ata, 90, 119
Akaeze, 131
Akaezuwa, Emeka, 10n26
Akan, 13
Akpan, NU, 91
al-Bashir, Omar, 4
al-Qaeda, 114
al-Qaeda in the Arabian Peninsular,
95
al-Qaeda in the Islamic Maghreb, 95
al-Shabaab, 95
Algeria, 30, 31, 62
"All The Things You Could Be By
Now If Sigmund Freud's Wife
Was Your Mother" (Mingus), 82
Allison, Simon, 97, 97n8
Amadi, Elechi, 75, 76
Amaechi, ix
Amaka, ix
Amasiri, 131
Americas, 7, 12, 33, 51, 62, 99, 100,
112, 148, 149
central, 12
south, south of Amazon: "sub-
Amazon South America", 33
"sub-Arctic Americas", 33
Anaba, Innocent, 152n14
Angola, 9, 10, 62
Ani, Mariamba, 90, 119
Aniebo, Ijeoma, xii
Aniebo, INC, 75
Anikulapo-Kuti, Fela, 90, 118
Ankrah, Joseph, 40, 59
Anozie-Young, Gloria, xii
Anyidoho, Kofi, 90
AP, 30

Arab, Arab World, 30, 31, 111
arap Moi, Daniel, 4
Argentina, 8, 34
Armstrong, Louis, 90, 118
Arrow of God (Achebe), 21, 29
Asaba, 38, 115, 131, 136
   Igbo genocide memorial at, 38
Asante, Molefi Kete, 89, 118
Asia, 7, 60, 61
Atlantic, The, 111, 112
"Atlantic Charter", 18 *See also*
   Winston Churchill
Attenborough, David, 8, 8n21
   comprehensively disingenuous, 8
Australia, 32
   "sub-Great Sandy Australia, 32
Austro-Hungary, 16, 17, 19
Awolowo, Obafemi, ix, 38, 68, 87,
   130, 131
   chief genocidist "theorist", vice-
   chair of genocide-prosecuting
   junta and head of finance
   ministry, 68, 87
Awoonor, Kofi, 90, 118
Ayida, Allison, ix, 131
Ayler, Albert, 90
Azikiwe, Nnamdi, 55
Azumini, 131
Azuonye, Chukwuma, 74n1, 91

Bâ, Mariama, 90, 119
Babangida, Ibrahim, 4, 96, 97
babies and children's survivor-
   leadership, 109 *See also* Biafra
Bachama, 143
Baga, Baga massacre, 95-97, 116,
   116n27
Boko Haram terrorist attacks, 95-
   97, 116
Bakongo, 13
Baldwin, James, 89, 118
Balewa, Abubakar Tafawa, 22
Bamileke, 13

ban all arms to Africa, *see* Africa
Banda, Kamuzu, 4
Bangladesh, 9, 32
   "sub-Himalaya Asia", 32
Barnett, Anthony, 101n10
Bass, Gary, 70nn84, 85, 86
Beckles, Hilary, 119
Beetles, The, 126 *See also* John
   Lennon
Beier, Ulli, 76
Belgium, ix, 16, 17-18, 58, 62, 87, 99
   perpetrator of genocide against
   constellation of African peoples in
   Congo basin of central Africa,
   1878-1908, 16-17, 58
Bello, Ahmadu, sardauna of Sokoto,
   ix
   threatens Igbo with
   "bloodshed",
   effectuated 29 May 1966 as Igbo
   genocide is launched, ix
Benin Republic, 69
Benjamin, Walter, 19, 19n15, 20
   "On the concept of history", 19-20
Berg Damara, Berg Damara genocide,
   ix, 11, 16, 58, 102
Berlin, 13, 69
"Berlin-state" of subjugation in
   Africa, 12, 14, 34, 35, 105, 106-
   107 *See also* Africa
Bhutan, 32
   "sub-Himalaya Asia", 32
Biafra, ix, x, 11, 37-38, 39-40 *passim*
   babies and children's survivor-
   leadership, 109
   Bakassi peninsular, 68
   Barack Obama supports Igbo
   genocide: monumental tragedy of
   presidential legacy, 103, 117
   Biafra before Brexit, 142-143
   Bight of Biafra, 40
   contrasts of historical
   backgrounds

in Igbo and Scottish freedom movements from Britain, 150-153
"dinner party dimensions" in freedom movement, 133-135
Indigenous People of Biafra (IPOB), 108, 115
Land of the Rising Sun, x
referendum reflections, 144-146
What would some of African World's brightest minds think of Barack Obama's support of the Igbo genocide?, 118-119
will surely be freed, 73, 109, 135
Biko, Steve, 90, 118
Bishop, Maurice, 90, 118
Biya, Paul, 4
Black Orpheus, 76
Blackwell, Ed, 90
Blair, Tony, 100-101, 137
   aggressive British arms-sales programme to Africa, 100
   "ethical foreign policy", 100-101
Blyden, Edward, 27, 89, 118
Boahen, Adu, 118
Bokassa, Jean-Bédel, 4
Boko Haram, 95-97, 114-116, 122-123, 131-132, 139-140, 145
   terrorist attack on Baga by, 95-97
   See also Baga
Botswana, 9, 10, 16, 51
Brathwaite, Edward Kamau, 90
Brazil, 8
Brexit, *see* Britain
Britain, ix, xi, 5, 6, 7, 8, 9, 11-12, 15, 16, 17-18, 22, 25, 26-27, 39, 44-45 *passim*
   "Abameisation" of Igboland, 26
   aggressive arms-sales programme to Africa by, 101
   "Atlantic Charter", 18, 60
   Biafra before Brexit, 142-143
   Brexit, 129, 132, 142-143
   "centre of world science", 100 *See also* Christopher Hill
   co-perpetrator (with Nigeria) of genocide against Igbo people of southwestcentral Africa, 11-12 *passim*
   Conservative party, 65
   contrasts in historical backgrounds of Igbo and Scottish freedom movements from Britain, 150-153
   "cultural and scientific backwater", 100 *See also* Christopher Hill
   "empire", 105
   enslavement and conquest of Africa by, 100-101, 148-149
   ex-British conquest administrators, 44
   expansive range of control and expropriation of rich multisectoral economy in occupied Nigeria by, 51-54
   gargantuan wealth from Africa expropriated by, 99-100
   genocidist guillotine director: five decades of Igbo genocide, 134-135
   Labour party, 64
   "letting the little buggers starve out", as foreign office official acknowledges British government's definitive goal in Igbo genocide, 69
   "punish" Igbo for daring to spearhead termination of occupation by, 51
   Scottish freedom, restoration-of-independence, 147-151
   stretch of predatory commercial enterprises in occupied Nigeria from, 53-54
   wide range of weapons to Nigeria to prosecute Igbo genocide, 49-50
Brown, James, 89
British Broadcasting Corporation, 17, 30, 105-109

external service of radio Nigeria, 107-109
  high time editors got used to eventuality of Biafran freedom, 109
  "nationalist" vs "secessionist"?, 105-108
  principal motivational ally in Nigeria's prosecution of Igbo genocide, 109
  state broadcaster, 105
  tags of "rationalisation" of Igbo genocide, 107
  telling contrasts in news coverage of San Bernardino and Onicha massacres, 108-109
  "Voice of Nigeria", 107-109
Buhari, Muhammadu, ix, 4, 38, 96, 97, 102-103, 113, 114-115, 118, 122-123, 131, 143
  imposed on Nigeria as head of regime by ex-US President Barack Obama and ex-British Prime Minister David Cameron, 38, 103, 115, 118, 122-123, 143
Burns, Robert, 148n5
Burundi, 17, 28, 32, 72, 101
Busch, Gary, 7n18
Bush, George W, 112, 121
Byard, Jaki, 90

Cabral, Amilcar, 90, 118
Calabar, 131
Calder, Angus, 81n38
Cambodia, 32, 62
  "sub-Himalaya Asia", 32
Cambridge University Press, 76
Cameron, David, 102, 103, 111-113, 116, 139, 143, 145, 147, 148, 150
  Anglo-US-French invasion of Libya, 111-113
  supports right of Scots to self-determination unambiguously, 150
  working collaboratively with then US President Barack Obama, imposes vile genocidist Muhammadu Buhari on Nigeria as head of regime, February 2015, 103, 139, 143
Cameroon, 10, 16, 17, 68, 69
Carey, George, 19
Caribbean, The, 33, 51, 99
  "sub-Appalachian Americas", 33
Carruthers, Jacob, 90, 118
Carter, Ron, 90
Carver, George Washington, 89
Central African Republic, 11, 72, 89, 113
Centre for African Studies/Igbo Conference (SOAS), University of London, 21n1
"centre for world science", 100 *See also* Britain, Christopher Hill
Césaire, Aimé, 13, 90, 118
Chad, 6, 11, 31, 32, 72
Charles Mingus Presents Charles Mingus (Mingus), 82
Charles, Ray, 89
Charlie Hebdo (Paris), 95, 116
Cherry, Don, 90
Chibundu, ix
Chibuzo, ix
Chidi, ix
Chido, ix
Chikwendu, ix
Chile, 33
  "sub-Atacama South America", 33
China, 8, 12, 32, 34, 60, 61, 62, 133
  Kuomintang party, regime, 133
  "sub-Gobi Asia", 32
Chinelo, ix
Chinweizu, Onwuchekwa Jemie and Ihechukwu Madubuike, 78nn17, 19, 88n74

Chinyere, ix
Chioma, ix
Chomsky, Noam, 60nn55, 56, 57
Chukwuemeka, ix
Chukwumerije, Uche, 91
Chukwuka, ix
Chukwuma, ix
Churchill, Winston, 18, 60
   "Atlantic Charter", 18, 60
   opposes African peoples' restoration-of-independence, 18, 60
Civil Liberties Organisation (Lagos): report on massacre of Biafra freedom marchers by phalanx of Nigeria genocidist forces, 108
"civil war", 35-36
Clapham, Christopher, 3, 3n1, 4, 4n7
Clarke, John Henrik, 90, 118
Clarke, Melissa, 107n7, 114n21, 116n27, 122-123, 139n5, 145n3
Clarke-Bekederemo, John Pepper, 22, 76
"clash of civilisations", 25 *See also* Igbo
Clay, James, 90
Clifford, Hugh, ix
Clinton, Hillary, 120-125 *See also* Barack Obama
   aggressive track on foreign policy to Africa, particularly, whilst secretary of state (2009-2013), including invasions of states – especially **Côte d'Ivoire** and Libya, 121-125
   trendy "white men" politicking trope and critique, 120-125
   US Democratic party presidential candidate, 2016, 120
   US Democratic party presidential contender against Barack Obama, 2008, 121
   US secretary of state in Barack Obama's first term presidency, 2009-2013, 121-125
CNN, 30
Cobb, Jimmy, 90
Cohen, Barry, 123n5
Cohen, Warren, 68n71
Coleman, George, 90
Coleman, James, 54n36, 55, 55n37
Coleman, Ornette, 90
Coleman, Steve, 90
Coleridge-Taylor, Samuel, 118
Coles, Johnny, 90
Coltrane, Alice, 90
Coltrane, John, 89, 118
Congo, Democratic Republic of, ix, 6n17, 8-9, 12, 17, 18, 28, 32, 62, 71, 72, 89, 101, 107, 110, 130, 131, 152
   ongoing genocide in, 6n17, 8-9, 28, 71, 72, 89, 107, 110, 130, 152
Congo, Republic of (Congo Brazzaville), 18, 28, 32, 60, 89
contrasts in historical backgrounds of Igbo and Scottish freedom movements from Britain, 150-153 *See also* Biafra, Britain, Igbo People and Scots
Cookey, SJ, 91
Corafano, James Jay, 112n11
Costa Rica, 33
   "sub-Rocky North America", 33
Côte d'Ivoire, 10, 28, 72, 99, 113, 122-123
Croatia, 32
   "sub-Alps Europe", 32
Crocker, Chester, 5, 5n12
Cronje, Suzanne, 57n46
Crowe, Jack, 10n2
Crummey, Donal, 53n32
Cuba, 62
Cullen, Countee, 90
"cultural and scientific backwater",

see Britain, Christopher Hill
Cumming-Bruce, Francis, 37
   British chief representative in Nigeria at outbreak of genocide, pro-consul, lead go-between conferencing with prominent Fulani genocidists on the ground, 57-58
Curson, Ted, 82
Curtis, Mark, 49n15

Dahomey, *see* Benin Republic
Daily Comet, 55 *See also* Nigeria vanguard liberation press, restoration-of-independence, Nigeria, 55
Daily Maverick, 97
Damas, Léon-Gontran, 90, 119
Danjuma, Yakubu, ix, 40, 131
Danquah, JB, 89
Darfur, Darfuri, 12, 28, 13, 71, 107, 110, 130
   genocide in Darfur, 12, 28, 71, 107, 110, 130 *See also* the Sudan
Davidson, Basil, 4, 4n8
Davies, Carole Boyce, 83n45
Davis, Miles, 90
Davis, Ossie, 90, 118
Davis, Richard, 90
de Gaulle, Charles, 7, 18, 60
   opposes African peoples' restoration-of-independence, 18
Debussy, Claude-Achille, 81
Dee, Ruby, 90, 118
Delaney, Martin, 90, 118
Deschambs, Hubert, 18n13, 60n60
Destruction of Black Civilization, The (Williams), 27
Devine, TM, 105n3, 148n7
Dike, Kenneth Onwuka, 89, 91, 118, 126
Dikko, Umaru, 131
Diop, Alioune, 88, 90,
(ed., *Présence Africaine*), 88
Diop, Cheikh Anta, 21, 24-25, 89, 118
   "loss of national sovereignty", 25
   See also Africa
Diop, David, 90, 118
Distances (Okigbo), 83
Doe, Samuel, 4
Dolphy, Eric, 82, 82n41, 90, 119
Douglass, Frederick, 89, 118
Dowden, Richard, 4-5, 5n9
Drechsler, Horst, 58n49
Du Bois. WEB, 27, 90, 118
Duiganan, Peter, 18n13, 60n60
Duvivier, George, 89

East bloc-West bloc politics, rivalry, post 1939-1945 war, 61-62
Ebbe, Obi, 56n40, 57n43
   "Without the Igbo, there is no Nigeria. They ... have the skilled [hu]man power that held Nigeria together...", 57
Echeruo, Kevin, 91, 94
   "Lament of the Artist", 94
Echeruo, Michael, 90, 91, 119
Edinburgh, 147
Edo, 49, 143, 144, 151
eerie columns that chart contours of Igbo killing fields – Igbo genocide phase-IV, 1980-2012: 152 *See also* Igbo people
Efiong, Philip,
Efuru (Nwapa), 78
Egbunike, Louisa Uchum, 21n1
Egonu, Uzo, 119, 128
Egypt, 30, 31, 121, 130
Eha Amuufu, 131
Ehuugbo, 131
Ehuugbo Road, 131
Eisenhower, Dwight, 113
Ejezie, Felicia, 128
Ejoor, David, 42, 43

Eke, Ifeagwu, 91
Eket, 131
Ekundare, R Olufemi, 52nn22, 23, 26, 27
Ekwe-Ekwe, Herbert, 6n13, 6n15, 11n27, 16nn5, 6, 17n9, 22n4, 26n25, 28n31, 30n1, 35n1, 47nn5, 8, 9, 48nn12, 14, 51nn19, 20, 56n39, 57n47, 58n51, 59n52, 92nn78, 79, 100nn3, 5, 7, 101n9, 104n19, 110nn2, 3, 4, 112n13, 113n16, 114nn18, 19, 20, 142n3, 149n9, 153n16
Ekwensi, Cyprian, 91
Ekwuluobia, 134
El-Khawas, Mohamed A, 123n5
Ellington, Duke, 81, 90, 118
Empire: What Ruling the World Did to the British (Paxman), 46-49
Enaharo, Tony, ix, 131
Enders, John, 10n25
England, 33, 105, 148-150
  "sub-Pennines Europe", 33
Enuugwu, xii, 28, 39, 115, 131, 136, 154
  shooting of miners at Iva valley colliery (1949) by British occupation police, xii, 28
Enuugwu-Ezike, 131
Enwonwu, Ben, 75
Equiano, Olaudah, 27, 89, 118
Eritrea, 35, 62
Ethiopia, 8, 28, 35, 71
Europe, 7, 8, 15, 16, 25, 27, 32, 34, 39, 57, 64, 84, 98, 99-100, 106, 131, 142
EuroConqueror league-states of Africa, 7
European Union, 132, 142
  "sub-Arctic Europe", 32
  external service of radio Nigeria, *see* BBC
Eyadéma, Gnassingbé,

Eze Nri, 89
Ezekwe, Godian, 91
Ezera, Kalu, 91
Ezira, Inna, xii

Fagunwa, DO, 76
"failed state(s)", 1-5 *See also* Fund for Peace
Fanon, Frantz, 89
Farmer Art, 90
Fawehinmi, Gani, 90
Ferguson, Clyde, x, 50, 64, 66, 98, 107, 130, 151
Ferris, Geoff, 22n7
Fido, Elaine Savory, 82n49, 83n50, 84nn60, 61
Financial Times, 30
Fischer, Hike, 17
Fitzgerald, Ella, 89
Food and Agricultural Organisation, FAO, 10n24
"Four Canzones" (Okigbo), 81
"Fragments out of Deluge" (Okigbo), 83
France, ix, 7, 7n18, 9, 16, 17-18, 33, 58, 60, 61, 62, 95-97, 99, 112-113, 116, 123
  east/southeast France: "sub-Alps Europe", 33
  "francophonie Africa" – expropriation, invasions, occupation: 7, 7n18, 99, 112-113
  "free French forces", 18
  islamist terrorist attacks in Paris, January 2015, 95-97
France24, 30
Franck, César, 81
Franklin, Aretha, 90
Frazier, E Franklin, 90
freedom, 118
Freud, Sigmund, 82
Freund, William, 53n32
Fry, Michael, 148n6

Fulani, ix, xi, 22, 27-28, 47, 48, 49, 51, 55, 56, 57, 62, 116, 117, 118, 122-123, 134, 136, 139, 140, 142, 145, 151
  genocidists, islamists, jihadists, militia terrorists, ix, xi, 22, 27-28, 116, 117, 118, 122-123, 134, 136, 139, 140, 145
  wanted continuing occupation of homeland by Britain, 47 *passim*
Fund for Peace, 1-5, 6
"failed state(s), "failed state(s)-index, 1-5
Furness, Hanna, 8n23

Gaddafi, Muammar, 111, 122
Gambia, 16, 51
Gann, LH, 18, 60n60
Garba, Joe, 43
  gargantuan wealth, *see* Africa, Britain
Garrison, Jimmy, 90
Garvey, Marcus, 27, 90, 118
Gatebuke, Alice, 124n6
Gbagbo, Laurent, 113
Gbulie, Ben, 91
génocidaire quintet, *see* Nigeria
Genocide Watch, 129
genocidist dyarchy, *see* Britain, Nigeria
genocidist guillotine director: five decades of Igbo genocide, 134-135 *See also* Britain
Germany, ix, 9, 11, 15, 16, 51, 58, 71, 99, 101-102
  perpetrator of genocide against Berg Damara, Herero and Nama peoples of southwest Africa, 1904-1911, 11, 16-17, 58, 101-102
Ghana, 3, 9, 16, 39-45, 51, 58-59
  Aburi, Aburi Accords, 39-45, 58-59
Gĩkũyũ, 13, 15, 19, 62

Mau Mau restoration-of-independence movement, 62
Gillespie, Dizzy, 90
Gimbiya, Deola, xii
gimmick of Igbo presidency in Nigeria, *see* Igbo people
Glover, Danny, 90
Goldberg, Jeffery, 111, 111nn5, 6, 7, 8, 9, 112nn10, 12, 14, 15, 112n17, 113n17, 117nn35, 36, 122n3
Goldie, Taubman, 53
  British conqueror entrepreneur, occupied Nigeria, 53
Gould, Michael, 57nn42, 44
Gowon, Yakubu, ix, 4, 40, 41, 43, 49, 96, 97, 131
Gozney, Richard, 103
Graves, Anne Adams, 83
Grenada, 62
Guatemala, 33
  "sub-Rocky North America", 33
Guillén, Nicolás, 90, 118
Guinea-Bissau, 28, 62, 72
Guinea (Conakry), 28, 72

Habré, Hissène, 4
Hague, William, 131
Hancock, Herbie, 90
handshake across "successor"-states, 154-155 *See also* Igbo, Yoruba
Haruna, Ibrahim, ix, 131
Harvard University, 75n5, 89n75
Hassan, Baba Abba, 96
Hausa, 47, 143
Hayford, Casely, 90
Haynes, Roy, 90
Head, Bessie, 119
Heavensgate (Okigbo), 74-75, 76, 79, 80
Henderson, Joe, 89
Hennessey, Patrick, 150n10
Herero, Herero genocide, ix, 11, 16, 58, 102

Higgins, Billy, 90
Hill, Andrew, 90
Hill, Christopher, 100, 100nn4, 6, 148-149, 149n8
  "centre for world science", 100 *See also* Britain
  "cultural and scientific backwater", 100 *See also* Britain
Holiday, Billie, 90
Hollande, François, 7, 113
Homecoming Singer, The (Wright), 74
  African-American affirmation, 74
Honduras, 33
  "sub-Rocky North America", 33
Horn, 76
Horton, James Africanus Beale, 89
Hughes, Langston, 90, 119
Hurston, Zora Neale, 89
Hutu, 71

Iberia, 100
Ibiam, Akanu, 91
Ibibio, 13
Idi Amin, 4
Idoto, goddess, river, 75, 80
Ifekandu, ix
Ifeoma, ix
Ifeyinwa, ix
Igbo people, Igbo genocide (phases I-IV), ix-x, xi, 1-12, 13, 19, 22, 23-24, 25, 26-29, 35, 36, 37-38, 39-40 *passim See also* Biafra
  Aru, 27
  Barack Obama supports Igbo genocide: monumental tragedy of presidential legacy, 103, 117
  Britain: genocidist guillotine director, five decades of Igbo genocide, 134-135
  "clash of civilisations", 25
  construct civilisation in Biafra where African life, human life, fundamentally, is sacrosanct, 72-73
  contrasts in historical backgrounds of Igbo and Scottish freedom movements from Britain, 150-153
  eerie columns that chart contours of Igbo killing fields – Igbo genocide phase-IV, 1980-2012: 152
  "final solution" of "Igbo question", 45
  foundational genocide of post-(European)conquest Africa, 11
  genocide: indescribable barbarity and carnage not seen in Africa since early 1900s, 11-12
  gimmick of "Igbo presidency" in Nigeria, 138-141
  Igbo Americans, 117
  Igbo Studies Association, 114
  Igbo-Yoruba relations, 154-155
  no "Igbo presidency" in Nigeria can halt Igbo genocide: 139-140
  ogu umu nwanyi Igbo or Igbo women-organised and led resistance against the British conquest and occupation of, xii
  survival anthem, 91
  tablet that proclaims Igbo survival of genocide, ix
  "talented people", 48, 49, 56
  testament of resistance, 90-91
  What would some of African World's brightest minds think of Barack Obama's support of the Igbo genocide?, 118-119
  will surely free Biafra, 73, 135
Igwe Ocha, 115, 131, 134, 136
Igwe Nga/Opobo, 131
Ike, Chukwuemeka, 75, 76, 91
Ikechukwu, ix
Ikejiani, Okechukwu, 91
Ikenga, ix

Ikoku, Alvan, 91
Ikot Ekpene, 131
Imagistes,
IMF, 30, 61
India, 8, 32, 34, 99
  "sub-Himalaya Asia", 32
Indigenous People of Biafra (IPOB),
  see Biafra
Indo-China, 60, 62
Indonesia, 32, 112, 113
  "sub-Gobi Asia", 32
"Initiations" (Okigbo), 76, 79
Innes, CL, 5, 5n10
intellectuals in defence of Igbo people
  during genocide, 91
International Court of Justice, 61
International Institute for
  Environment Development, IIED,
  10n24
International Society for Civil
  Liberties & the Rule of Law,
  115nn25, 26, 152
Iran, 9, 112, 113
Iraq, 99
Ireland, 85
Irobi, Esiaba, 118
Isele-Ukwu, 131
Isidore Ndaywel è Nziem, 17, 58
islam, islamist, ix, 111, 118
Islamic State, 95, 111
Italy, 15, 33, 99
  "sub-Alps Europe", 33
Itsekiri, 49, 143

Jackson, Mahaila, 90
Jahn, Janheinz, 76
James, CLR, 90, 118
James, George, 90, 118
Jammeh, Yahya, 4
Japan, 18, 19
  "sub-Gobi Asia"
Jawara, 143
Jews, Jewish genocide, 63, 70, 71, 95

Johnson, Boris, 137
Johnson, Lynden, 67-68, 113
  US president's "get those n*****
  babies off my tv set"'s racist slur
  on Igbo children being subjected to
  genocide by Britain and Nigeria, 68
Johnson, Mobolaji, 42, 43
Jola, 13
Jonathan, Goodluck, 4, 115, 152
Jones, Elvin, 89
Jones, James Earl, 90
Jordan, Clifford, 90
Jos, 28, 48, 55, 108
  pogrom of Igbo immigrant
  population, organised by Fulani
  islamist/jihadist north Nigeria
  leadership (June 1945): "dress
  rehearsals", Igbo genocide, 29 May
  1966-present day, 28, 48, 49, 55,
  107,
Jukun, 143

Kaduna, 107
Kalu, ix
Kalu, Ogbogu, 91
Kamene, ix
Kanayo, ix
Kano, 28, 48, 55-56, 108
  pogrom of immigrant Igbo
  population, organised by Fulani
  islamist/jihadist north Nigeria
  leadership (May 1953): "dress
  rehearsals", Igbo genocide, 29
  May 1966-present day, 28, 48, 49,
  55-56, 107
Kanu, Nnamdi, 115, 128, 137, 143
  head of Indigenous People of
  Biafra (IPOB), 115, 137
Kanuri, 142, 151
Karenga, Maulana, 90, 119
Katsina, Hassan, 42, 131
Kelly, Wynton, 90
Kemet ("ancient Egypt"), 81, 84

Kennedy, Edward, 70
Kenya, 15, 16, 51, 62, 122
Khartoum, 30
Kikiyu, *see* Gĩkũyũ
Kimathi, Dedan, 119
King, Gbadomosi, 65, 131
   destroys International Committee of Red Cross plane over south Biafra, 65
King, Martin Luther, 89, 118
King Jaja of Igwe Nga (Opobo), 40, 89, 118
King Leopold II of the Belgians, ix, 18, 58, 87
Kissinger, Henry, 68
   Nixon-Kissinger reflections on Biafra: Rectitude?, 70
Kogbara, Ignatious, 91
Korea (North, South), 60
Ku Klux Klan, 83

Labyrinths with Path of Thunder (Okigbo), 77, 86
Lagos, xi, 39, 43, 46, 47, 49, 54, 55, 58, 107
"Lament of an Artist" (Echeruo), 94
"Lament of the Drums" (Okigbo), 87
"Lament of the Lavender Mist" (Okigbo), 81, 82
"Lament of the Masks" (Okigbo), 81, 85
"Lament of the Silent Sisters" (Okigbo), 87
Lamming, George, 90, 118
Laos, 32
   "sub-Himalaya Asia", 32
latitudes of freedom, self-determination, 109
Le Monde, 30
Leapman, Michael, 65n63
Lee, Spike, 90
Lennon, John, 126
Lesotho, 16, 51

Lewis, W Arthur, 118
Liberia, 28, 72, 89
Libya, 28, 30, 31, 72, 99, 111-113, 122, 123-124
Lincoln, Abbey, 119
Limits (Okigbo), 78, 83
Little, Booker, 90
Locke, Alain, 118
London, x, 18, 113
Lord Shepherd (Malcolm Shepherd), 50
Love, Motherhood and the African Heritage (Nzegwu), 77
Luba, 13
Lugard, Frederick, 53
   first British conquest state administrator, occupied Nigeria, 53
Lumumba, Patrice, 62, 87, 90, 118
Lunn, Joe Harris, 16n4
"Lustra" (Okigbo), 76
Lyons, Terrence, 68n73

Maathai, Wangari, 15, 15n2, 20, 20n19, 118
MacKay, Claude, 90
Mackenzie, John M, 105n3, 148n7
Macmillan, Harold, 46-49
Makarere University, 76n7
Makeba, Mariam, 118
Makonnen, Ras, 27
Malcolm X, 89, 118
Mali, 28, 32, 113
Man of the People, A (Achebe), 21, 22
Mandela, Nelson, 89, 118
Mao Tse-Tung, 133, 133n2
   "insurrection, an act of violence", 133
Marley, Bob, 90, 118
Marsalis, Wynton, 90
Mathews, Elbert, 59
Mau Mau restoration-of-independence movement, *see* Gĩkũyũ
Mauritania, 30, 31, 32

Maxwell, DE and SB Bushuri, 85n63
May, Theresa, 99, 103-104, 142, 143
Mazrui, Ali, 88, 88nn72, 73, 89,
  89n75, 91-92, 92n79
  Igbo genocide supporter, projects
  testament of Nigerian genocidists,
  88-89, 91-92
  Igbo's historic and successful
  challenge of extra-continental
  ideoreligious dogma of, 91-92
Mbakwe, Sam, 91
Mbanefo, ix
Mbanefo, Louis, 90, 91
Mbari Club, 76n6, 87n68
Mbazulike, ix
Mboma, Oby, 128
McLean, Jackie, 90
*Meeting of the Supreme Military
Council – at Aburi, Accra,
Ghana, 4-5 January 1967, The*
(Government Printer, Enugu),
41nn3, 4, 5, 6, 7, 8, 9, 45n17
Mefor, Uche, 128
Melson, Annick Thebia, 13
Melvern, Linda, 58n50
Mende, 13
Mengistu Haile Mariam, 4
Menkiti, Ifeanyi, 1, 1n1, 118
Mexico, 9, 33
  "sub-Rocky North America", 33
Mezu, Okechukwu, 91
Middle East, 88, 95, 111
Mingus, Charles, 81, 82, 82n41, 89, 118
Mobutu Sese Seko, 4, 62, 87
Modebe, Anthony, 91
Mohammed, Murtala, ix, 38, 4, 40, 131
  genocidist commander of brigade
  of slaughter in Asaba, west Biafra, 38
Mojekwu, CC, 91
Mokelu, Janet, 91

Momah, Chike, 75, 76
Mongo, 13
Monk, Thelonious, 81,89
Moore, Carlos, 21, 24-25, 25nn16, 17
Morgan, Lee, 90
Morocco, 30, 31
Morris, Roger, xn1, 50n16, 64n62,
  65n63, 67n69, 69n79, 98n9,
  102n12, 107n8, 130n4, 134n3,
  151n13
Morrison, Toni, 89-90, 118
Moses, A Dirk, 154n3
Mozambique, 62
Mphahlele, Ezekiel, 76
Mugabe, Robert, 4
Munday, Carol, 128
Munonye, John, 76, 91
Murray, David, 90
Murray, Sunny, 90
Museveni, Yoweri, 4
My Command (Obasanjo), 65, 102, 139
Myanmar, 18, 32, 136
  Rohinga region, 136
  "sub-Himalaya Asia", 32

Nama, Nama genocide, ix, 11, 16, 58, 102
Namibia, 9, 11, 16, 17, 51, 62, 101
"nationalist", "nationalism", *see*
  British Broadcasting Corporation
Ndebele, 13
Ndem, Okoko, 91
Ndu, Pol, 91
Ndubuisi, ix
Ndukaeze, ix
Nepal, 32
  "sub-Himalaya Asia", 32
Netanyahu, Benjamin, 117-118
Neto, Agostinho, 90
"Newcomer" (Okigbo), 76, 80
New Nation (London), 100
New Zealand, 33

South Island: "sub-Southern Alps New Zealand", 33
Ngara, Emmanuel, 23, 23nn10, 11, 24, 24n12
Ngozi, xi
Ngũgĩ wa Thiong'o, 90, 119
Nicaragua, 33, 62
"sub-Rocky North America", 33
Nichols, Herbie, 90
Niger, 11, 31, 32
Nigeria, ix, xi, 1, 5, 11-12, 16, 22, 39 *passim*
   arguably most notorious of Africa's "Berlin-states", 106-107
   bogus geopolitical lexicon referencing Biafra occupation, 144
   Barack Obama supports Igbo genocide: monumental tragedy of presidential legacy, 103, 117
   co-perpetrator (with Britain) of genocide against Igbo people od southwestcentral Africa, 11-12 *passim*
   Daily Comet, vanguard liberation press, restoration-of-independence in, 55
   expansive range of British control and expropriation of rich multisectoral economy in occupied Nigeria, 51- 54
   Gaskiya Ta Fi Kwabo, 130
   génocidaire quintet, 97
   genocidist and kakistocratic, 5, 107
   genocidist dyarchy, 97-98
   haematophagous monster, 63
   Igbo genocide anthem, 62, 130
   "illicit financial outflows" to West World, 1970s-2018: US$89.5, 5
   National Council of Nigeria and the Cameroons (NCNC), lead restoration-of-independence party of, 54-55
   New Nigeria, 130
   stretch of British predatory commercial enterprises in occupied Nigeria, 53-54
   What would some of African World's brightest minds think of Barack Obama's support of the Igbo genocide?, 118-119
   West African Pilot, vanguard liberation press, restoration-of-independence in, 55
   wide range of British weapons to Nigeria to prosecute Igbo genocide, 49-50
Nile, River, 68, 130
   Blue Nile, 130
Nixon, Richard, 69-70, 116-117
Nixon-Kissinger reflections on Biafra: Rectitude?, 70
Njoku, Eni, 89, 91, 119
Nkalagu, 131
Nkarasi, 131
Nkechi, ix
Nkeiiru, ix
Nkemakolam, ix
Nkemdilim, ix
Nkpo, 131
Nkrumah, Kwame, 1, 1n1, 27, 118
Nnadozie, ix
Nnamdi, ix
Nneka, ix
Nnoli, Okwudiba, 52n28, 53nn29, 30, 31, 55n38
no hierarchisation of evil, 136-137
North Atlantic Treaty Organisation, 61
Nsukka, 131
Nuba, Nuba Mountains, 12, 28, 71, 107, 130
   genocide in Nuba Mountains, 12, 28, 71, 107, 130 *See also* the Sudan
Nupe, 143

Nwafo, ix
Nwakaego, ix
Nwankwo, Agwuncha Arthur, 119
Nwankwo, Nkem, 76, 91
Nwaoyiri, ix
Nwapa, Flora, 76-77, 89, 91, 119, 126
Nwoga, Donatus, 89, 91
Nwokedi, Alex, 91
Nwoko, Demas, 76
Nwokolo, Chukwuedo, 91
Nyerere, Julius, 90, 118
Nzegwu, Femi, 77, 77n13, 78n14, 89n75
Nzegwu, Theophilus Enwezor, 90, 119, 126
Nzekwu, Onuora, 91
Nzimiro, Ikenna, 53n33

Obama, Barack, 103, 110-119, 120-125, 139, 143
   "African American son", 117-119
   "African-Atlantic discourses", 118-119
   aggressive track on foreign policy to Africa, particularly, including invasions of states, especially Côte d'Ivoire and Libya, beginning with Hillary Clinton's time as secretary of state during first term president, 2009-2013, 121-125
   collaboratively working with then British Prime Minister David Cameron, imposes genocidist Muhammadu Buhari on Nigeria as head of regime, February 2015, 103, 115-117, 139, 143
   supports Igbo genocide: monumental tragedy of presidential legacy, 103, 117, 139, 143
   "this continent of his fathers", 110-111
   US-British-French invasion of Libya, 111-113
Obasanjo, Olusegun, genocidist commander, Igbo genocide, 4, 38, 65, 65nn64, 65, 66, 67, 96, 97, 102, 102n13, 103, 131, 138-139, 139n4, 141
   orders destruction of International Committee of Red Cross plane over south Biafra, 38, 65, 102, 139
Obenga, Théophile, 90, 118
Obi, Chike, 89
Obiageli, ix
Obiechina, Emmanuel, 80, 80n22, 90, 119
   Christopher Okigbo: "poet of destiny", 80
Obiigbo, 131
Obioma, ix
Obollo Afo, 131
Obollo Eke, 131
Obote, Milton, 4
Obubara, 131
Obudu, 131
Obumselu, Bebedict, 91
Ofokaaja, ix
Ogbaro, Ego, xii
Ogoja, 131
Ogonna, ix
Ogot, Bethuel, 118
ogu umu nwanyi Igbo, xii *See also* Igbo people
Ogwashi-Ukwu, 131
Ohadike, Dan, 90
Ojike, Mbonu, 90
Ojoto, 75
Ojukwu, Chukwuemeka Odumegwu, 39, 40, 41, 42-45, 45n16, 59, 89, 91, 106, 118, 126
   "cleverest", compulsive logic", 41-43 *See also* Aburi accords
Oka, 131, 136
Okadigbo, Chuba, 91
Okafo, ix

Okara, Gabriel, 75, 91
Okeke, Uche, 89, 118
Okenwa, ix
Okigbo, Anna Onugwalobi, 75
Okigbo, Christopher Ifekandu, 74-94, 118, 126
 Christopher Okigbo International Conference, Harvard University, 24 September 2007, 74n1, 89n75
 extensive scholarship and influence:
 Kemet ("ancient Egypt"), Nri, Babylon, Judaism, Hinduism, Buddhism, Christianity, Greece and Roman as well as the poetry of Ovid, Virgil, Dante, Milton, Yeats, Mallarmé, Eliot, Pound, Tagore, Lorca, Hopkins, 81
 multiform interests and roles in civil service, teaching, editing, business and Biafran resistance movement, 1956-1967, 76
 Okigboan landmark signature, 74-75 *passim*
 Ok igboan poetics, 79 *passim*
 own "testament", 92-94
 "poet of destiny", 80
 poetry constructed through intensely pursued labour of exposition, 80ff
 spiritual: crucial sphere of resistance and restoration of lost sovereignty, 80
Okigbo, James Okoye, 75
Okigbo, Pius, 73, 89, 91
Okigwe, 131, 136
Okonkwo, ix
Okonta, ix
Okpanku, Agwu, 91
Okpara, Michael, 126
Okuzu, Inyom Victoria, 75n5
 Christopher Okigbo's sister, 75n5
Okwu, Celestine, 91

Okwuonicha, ix
Okwuonicha, Lakeson, 113n16
Oliver, Roland, 4, 4n6, 8n21
Omotoso, Kole, 25, 25nn20, 21
 "mere episode, a catalytic episode only", 25
 "strange Difference, an Other, a Contradiction, an encounter that can only be negative in terms of the effect on Igbo", 25
Onicha, 108, 115, 116, 126, 128, 131, 136, 152
Onicha-Ugbo, 131
Onimode, Bade, 51n21, 52nn24, 25
Onwuatuegwu, ix
Onwuatuegwu, Tim, 91
Onwuejiogwu, Angulu, 89
Onyango-Obbo, Charles, 7n19
Onyeka, ix
Onyekachi, ix
Onyewe, Chioma, xii
 Ranconteur Production, xii
Opi, 131
Oragwu, Felix, 91
Orizu, Nwafor, 118, 118
Orlu, 136
Oron, 131
Osadebe, Dennis, 91
Osadebe, Osita, 91
Osei-Nyame, Kwadwo, 21n1
Oshimili Delta, River 108, 115
Osita, ix
Owere, 126, 128, 131, 134, 136
Owgwu, 131

Pakenham, Thomas, 5, 5n11
Pakistan, 9, 32
 "sub-Himalaya Asia", 32
Panama, 33
 "sub-Rocky North America", 33
Paris, 95-97, 113, 116
 islamist terrorist attacks, January 2015, 95-97, 116

Parker, Charlie, 81, 90
"Passage, The" (Okigbo), 76
Path of Thunder (Okigbo), 78, 79, 86-87, 92-94
Paxman, Jeremy, 46, 46nn1, 2, 3, 47, 47nn4, 10, 48, 48nn11, 13, 49nn4, 10, 48nn11, 13, 57n45
p'Bitek, Okot, 90, 118
Pettiford, Oscar, 89
Philadelphia, 99
Poitier, Sydney, 90, 119
Porter, AN, 19, 60n58
Portugal, ix, 62, 99, 100, 123, 148
 enslavement and conquest of Africans by EuroConqueror league-states, ix, 99, 100, 123, 148
Post, Ken, 22
Powell, Bud, 90
Prebble, John, 148
Présence Africaine (Paris), 88
principal motivational ally in Nigeria's prosecution of Igbo genocide, 109 See also British Broadcasting Corporation

Queen Elizabeth II, 126

racist, humiliating and unprintable epithets on Africans, see Africa
Ransome-Kuti, Funmilayo, 90
Ravel, Joseph-Maurice, 81
Rawlings, Jerry, 4
Rawls, John, 1, 11, 11n28, 12, 12n30
 "liberal people", 11, 12
 "outlaw state"/"rogue state", 11-12
Rawlsian, 1
Regina Pacis Secondary School, Onicha (east Biafra), 128
 Save-a-Soul Quintet, 128
Republican party (US), 99
Reuters, 30
Rhodesia, 123
Rice, Susan, 124

Richmond, Dannie, 82n41, 89
Rivers, Sam, 90
Roach, Max, 90, 118
Roberts, Marcus, 90
Robertson, James, 22, 46-49
Rodney, Walter, 18n10, 89, 118
Rollins, Sonny, 90
Roosevelt, Franklin, 18, 60
 "Atlantic Charter", 18, 60
Rotimi, Oluwole, ix
Rusk, Dean, 67
Russell, George, 89, 118
Russia, 12, 16, 19
 Czarist Russia, 16, 19
 east Russia, east of the Urals: "sub-Siberia Asia", 32
Rwanda, 12, 17, 28, 32, 62, 71, 89, 101, 110, 130

saharareporters.com, 143
Salmond, Alex, 105, 106, 147-148, 150
San Bernardino, California, US, 108-109
San Jose, US, 128
Sanders, Pharoah, 90
Sankara, Thomas, 119
Sarkozy, Nicolas, 111-113, 121-122
 French-US-British invasion of Libya, 111-113
Saro-Wiwa, Ken, 75
Saudi Arabia, 130
Scotland, Scots, Scottish-referendum, 105-106, 109, 132, 145, 147-151
 See also BBC
 battle of Bannockburn, 150
 Commonwealth games in, 150
 contrasts in historical backgrounds of Igbo and Scottish freedom movements from Britain, 150-153
 Darién scheme, 148
 enslavement of Africans by EuroConqueror league-states, 105,

148-149
Ryder Cup competition (golf) in, 150
"Scottish empire", 148-149
support of US freedom movement, 149
Ulster cousins, 149
Scott, Robert, 39, 50-51, 104
"best defoliant agent known", 39, 104
Seacole, Mary, 89
"secession", "secessionist(s), *see British Broadcasting Corporation*
Sembene, Ousmanne, 90, 119
Sénégal, 10
Senghor, Léopold Sédar, 90, 118
Serer, 13
Shagari, Shehu, 96
Shaw, Woody, 89
Shekau, Abubakar, 95-96
Shepp, Archie, 90
Shonekan, Ernest, 96
Shorter, Wayne, 90
Sierra Leone, 16, 28, 51, 72, 89
"Silences" (Okigbo), 86, 87
Silver, Horace, 89
Simone, Nina, 89
"Siren Limits" (Okigbo), 83
Slovenia, 33
  "sub-Alps Europe", 33
Smith, Harold, 22n3, 47, 47nn6, 7
Sobukwe, Robert, 118
Sojourner Truth, 89, 118
Sokei, Chudi, 91
Solanke, Ladipo, 90
Somalia, 6, 9, 15, 28, 72, 95
South Africa, 9, 25, 30, 31, 51, 53, 62, 123
  "frontline states", 31
  "South Africa sub-continent", 31
  "sub-Sahara Africa", 31
  "white South Africa", 31
South Korodofan, 12, 18, 71, 107, 130
  genocide in South Korodofan, 12, 28, 71, 107, 130 *See also* the Sudan
South Sudan, 5, 8, 9, 51
South World, 9, 60, 61-62, 112, 136
Soviet Union, 19, 130 *See also* Russia
Soyinka, Wole, 74, 76
Spain, ix, 99, 100, 148
  enslavement and conquest of Africans by EuroConqueror league-states, ix, 99, 100, 148
Sri Lanka, 32
  "sub-Himalaya Asia", 32
St Vincent, 40
Stanton, Gregory, 129
  president, Genocide Watch, 129
Stewart, Michael, 50, 57
Stockwell, AA, 18n12, 60n58
Stockwell, Sarah E, 105n3
Sturgeon, Nicola, 105, 106
Strayhorn, Billy, 90
Stylistic Criticism and the African Novel (Ngara), 23
"sub-Sahara Africa", racist epithet, 7, 7n20, 30-34 *See also* Africa
"subs of the world"?, 32-33
Sudan, The, 5, 6, 8, 9, 11, 12, 16, 28, 30, 31,32, 51, 101, 107, 110, 130, 151
  genocide in Darfur, Nuba Mountains, South Korodofan, 12, 28, 71, 107, 110, 130
Sun Ra, 89
  supports Igbo genocide: monumental tragedy of presidential legacy, *see* Africa, Barack Obama, Biafra, Igbo, Nigeria, United States
Sutherland, Efua, 90
Swaziland, 16, 51
Sydney, 139
Syria, 99

tablet that proclaims Igbo survival of genocide, *see* Igbo, Igbo genocide
tags of "rationalisation" of Igbo genocide, *see British Broadcasting Corporation*
Taiwo, Ibrahim, ix, 131
Tamil Eelam, 62
Tanganyika, *see* Tanzania
Tangri, Roger, 31n2
Tanzania, 15, 16, 17, 51
Tatum, Art, 90
Taylor, Charles, 4
telling contrasts in news coverage of San Bernardino and Onicha massacres, *see British Broadcasting Corporation*
Terry, Clark, 89
Thailand, 32
  "sub-Himalaya Asia", 32
the future: even if it takes 1000 states to exorcise this evil, 152-153
The Hague, 113
There was a Country (Achebe), 29, 128
Things Fall Apart (Achebe), xi, 23, 28, 78
"this continent of his fathers", *see* Barack Obama
Thompson, Andrew, 105n3
Thomson, George, 49
Togo, 17
Tosh, Peter, 90, 118
Toure, Sekou, 4
Transition, 76, 83, 87n68
Trial of Christopher Okigbo, The (Mazrui), 88-89
  Igbo genocide supporter, 88-89
Tubman, Harriet, 89, 118
Tucha, River, 15
Tucker, Nancy Bernkopf, 68n73
Tunisia, 30, 31
Turkey (Ottomans), 16

Tusk, Donald, 142
Tutuola, Amos, 76
Tutsi, 71
Tyner, McCoy, 89

Uchendu, ix
Udechukwu, Obiora, 91
Uganda, 9, 16, 51, 72, 89, 101
Ugwuta, 131
Ukehe, 131
Uko, Ezinne, 128
Ukpabi, ix
Umu Ubani/Bonny, 131
Umuahia, 115, 131, 136
Unbowed (Wangari Maathai), 15
UNCTAD, 30
UNDP, 30
United Kingdom, *see* Britain
United Nations, 30, 61, 64, 70
United States, x, 8, 49, 59-72, 99, 107, 108-109
  "Atlantic Charter", 18, 60
  Barack Obama supports Igbo genocide: monumental tragedy of presidential legacy, 103, 113
  "grand area" conception, planning, implementation and European-occupied Africa, 59-62
  never condemned Igbo genocide by British ally unambiguously, 71
  US Department of Justice, 102n14
  US Department of State, 59nn53, 54, 67nn70, 71, 72, 68nn74, 76, 77, 69nn80, 81, 71n87
  US National Security Council Interdepartmental Group, 66n68, 68n75, 70nn82, 83
  varied grouping of US citizens and organisations donate to appeals to support survivors of Igbo genocide, 67-68
  What would some of African World's brightest minds think of

Barack Obama's support of the Igbo genocide?, 118-119
Universidade Federal de Pernambuco, Recife, 74n1
Universidade Federal do Rio de Janeiro, Rio de Janeiro, 74n1
University of Leicester (IDeoGRAMS Conference: Contemporary Media, September 2017), 30n1
University of London College, 75
University of London SOAS, 21
University Weekly (ed., Christopher Okigbo), 76
Uphopho, Kenneth, xii
Urhobo, 49
Useni, Jeremiah, ix
Uyo, 131
Uzo, ix
Uzuakoli, 131

Van Sertima, Ivan, 90, 118
varying typologisations: Igbo genocide, 66
Versailles (1919), Treaty of, 17
Vietnam, 32, 62, 68
  "sub-Himalaya Asia", 32
"Voice of Nigeria", *see British Broadcasting Corporation*

Wali, Obiajunwa, 76
war, 1914-1918, 15, 16, 17-20, 21, 51
war, 1939-1945, 7, 16, 17-20, 47, 51, 63, 104, 106
Washington, 1, 5, 61, 114
Washington, Denzel, 90
Washington Post, 30
"Watermaid" (Okigbo), 76
Wellesley College, 1, 1n1
West, West World, 12, 31-32
West African Pilot, 55 *See also* Nigeria

vanguard liberation press, restoration-of-independence, Nigeria, 55
Wey, Joseph, 42, 43
"What Love" (Charles Mingus), 82
What would some of African World's brightest minds think of Barack Obama's support of the Igbo genocide?, 118-119 *See also* Africa, Barack Obama, Biafra, Igbo, Nigeria, United States
What neutrality to crime of genocide?, 66-70 *See also* United States
Whitelaw, Marjory, 76n9. 77nn11, 12
WHO, 30
Widstrand, Carl, 53n33, 54nn34, 35
Williams, Chancellor, 27, 27n30, 90, 98, 98n10, 118
Williams, Eric, 118
Williams, Tony, 90
Wilson, Harold, ix, x, xi, 49, 50, 50n17, 64-65, 66-67, 69, 72, 98, 102, 103-104, 104n17, 107, 109, 130, 134, 151
  catastrophic extent of Biafra annhilative mission restated in memoirs, 50, 103-104
  rubric of the expressed "diminution-of-African life" chorus, 72
  Wilsonian logic of Igbo mass slaughter, x, 109
  "would accept a half million dead Biafrans if that was it took", x, xi, 64, 66-67, 98, 102, 107, 130, 134, 151
Winfrey, Oprah, 90
Wolof, 13
"Women's War" (Uphopho), xii
Wonder, Stevie, 90
World Bank, 8n23, 30, 33, 34n3, 61
World War I, *see* 1914-1918 war

Wren, Robert, 22-23
Wright, Jay, 74, 74n2, 75n4, 90

Yaoundé, 68
Yar'Adua, Umaru Musa, 4
Yeats, WB, 85
Yoruba, 25, 39, 49, 68-69, 143, 144, 151, 154-155
    Igbo-Yoruba relations, 154-155

Young, Douglas, 106

Zaïre, *see* Democratic Republic of the Congo
Zambia, 16, 51
Zaria, 107, 116
Zimbabwe, 16, 51, 62, 101

www.ingramcontent.com/pod-product-compliance
Lightning Source LLC
Chambersburg PA
CBHW021156160426
43194CB00007B/766